The Nazi Dictatorship and the Deutsche Bank

This book examines the role of Deutsche Bank, Germany's largest commercial bank, in the Nazi dictatorship and asks how the bank changed and accommodated during a transition from democracy and a market economy to dictatorship and a planned economy. How did the new Zeitgeist influence the bank? What opportunities for profit did the bank see in the National Socialist route out of the Great Depression? What role did anti-Semitism play in its business relations and its dealing with employees? The book sets out the background of the world Depression and the German banking crisis of 1931 and looks at the restructuring of German banking. It offers new material on the bank's expansion in central and eastern Europe and summarizes recent research on the bank's controversial role in gold transactions and in the financing of the construction of Auschwitz. The book also examines the role played by particular personalities in the bank's development, notably Emil Georg von Stauss and Hermann Abs.

Harold James is Professor of History at Princeton University and chairman of the editorial board of *World Politics*. He is the author of several books on German economy and society, including *The Deutsche Bank and the Nazi Economic War Against the Jews* (Cambridge 2001).

The Nazi Dictatorship and the Deutsche Bank

Harold James
Princeton University

CAMBRIDGE
UNIVERSITY PRESS

PUBLISHED BY THE PRESS SYNDICATE OF THE UNIVERSITY OF CAMBRIDGE
The Pitt Building, Trumpington Street, Cambridge, United Kingdom

CAMBRIDGE UNIVERSITY PRESS
The Edinburgh Building, Cambridge CB2 2RU, UK
40 West 20th Street, New York, NY 10011-4211, USA
477 Williamstown Road, Port Melbourne, VIC 3207, Australia
Ruiz de Alarcón 13, 28014 Madrid, Spain
Dock House, The Waterfront, Cape Town 8001, South Africa

http://www.cambridge.org

First published 2004

Printed in the United States of America

Typefaces Sabon 11/14 pt. and ITC Stone Serif Semi Bold   *System* LATEX 2$_\varepsilon$ [TB]

A catalog record for this book is available from the British Library.

Library of Congress Cataloging in Publication Data
James, Harold, 1956–
    The Nazi dictatorship and the Deutsche Bank / Harold James.
        p.   cm.
    Includes bibliographical references and index.
    ISBN 0-521-83874-6
    1. Deutsche Bank – History.   2. National socialism – Economic aspects.
    3. Germany – Economic policy – 1933–1945.   I. Title.
    HG3058.D4J363   2004
    332.1′2′094309043 – dc22   2003069687

ISBN 0 521 83874 6 hardback

Contents

Figures and Table

Figures

Table

Preface

The basis for this book is a chapter on the history of Deutsche Bank published in 1995 to commemorate the 125th anniversary of the founding of the bank. The bank invited five historians to produce this volume, originally Thomas Nipperdey (whose part was eventually written, after his death, by Lothar Gall), Gerald Feldman, Harold James, Carl-Ludwig Holtfrerich, and Hans Büschgen. We worked on that project in complete independence from the bank, and the book was widely hailed as a milestone in the writing of corporate history.

The chapter on the Nazi period aroused substantial interest at the time. Since the publication in 1995, the further opening of archives in the United States, Russia, and Central Europe has brought to light additional materials that allow the treatment of some aspects of the bank's activities and policies that were neglected in the 1995 history. Most notably this is the case for gold transactions, the documentation of which principally stems from microfilmed copies of the Reichsbank's gold ledgers, which were rediscovered in the National Archives in 1997 in the course of investigations into the affair of Swiss banks and their links with

Nazi Germany. In response to these revelations, the Deutsche Bank invited five historians to form a historical commission to investigate the issues raised by the newly available documentation. This commission included three of the 1995 authors, Feldman, Gall, and James, as well as Avraham Barkai and Jonathan Steinberg. Steinberg prepared a study of the Deutsche Bank's role in the gold transactions, which was published in 1998, and which was based not only on the National Archives microfilm, but also on material found in Frankfurt from the former Istanbul branch of Deutsche Bank. I wrote a further study of so-called "Aryanization," the takeover of Jewish businesses and banks in Germany as well as in the areas occupied by Germany, especially Austria and Czechoslovakia. It was based to a large extent on archives stemming from bank branches all over Germany that had not been assembled and inventoried before but that have now been collected in Frankfurt in response to the intense public discussion of restitution issues and the responsibilities of banks. I also used a substantial amount of material from Czech, Polish, and Russian archives, which had not been available to researchers before, and which shed a great deal of new light on the activities of the bank outside Germany. The study was published in 2001 by Cambridge University Press (*The Deutsche Bank and the Nazi Economic War Against the Jews*).

The results of these findings, as well as other recent discoveries (relating above all to Auschwitz, and to the use of forced labor), are included in the present enlarged version of the 1995 chapter, which is now presented as a study in its own right: a study of the interplay of a modern barbarism and business structure and business logic.

Harold James
Princeton, January 2003

I

The Setting

In the 1930s, as now, Deutsche Bank was the largest German bank, whose economic power was the subject of debate and controversy. At that time, its full name was Deutsche Bank und Disconto–Gesellschaft.[1]

Deutsche Bank was founded in 1870, in anticipation of a new law that permitted the establishment of joint-stock banks in Prussia. This was a few months before the unification of Germany and the creation of the German Empire. The bank's founders had a national–patriotic purpose in mind, which was indicated by the (rather ambitious) title they chose for their bank. It was supposed to challenge the preeminence of the London City in the financing of overseas trade.[2]

In the first years of its existence, it very rapidly emerged as an energetically expanding international bank. It participated first in the establishment of the "German Bank of London" in 1871, and in 1873 it created its own London agency. In 1872 and 1873 it bought into New York and Paris banks, and in 1872 it founded agencies in Shanghai and Yokohama. In 1874 it participated in a South American bank, and in 1886 it created its own institution for South

America, the Deutsche Übersee Bank (later Deutsche Überseeische Bank or Banco Alemán Transatlántico). Besides trade finance, it carried out a number of important operations for the German government including the sale in Asia of much of the Prussian stock of silver, as the Empire prepared for the transition from a silver to a gold-based currency.[3]

One of the first managers of the bank was Georg Siemens, who had previously worked for the electrical firm Siemens & Halske, founded by his father's cousin, Werner von Siemens. This enterprise was a major beneficiary of the creation of the new Empire and its demands for communications technology. Georg's bank rapidly became involved in industrial finance.

Another founder of the new bank was a prominent liberal politician, Ludwig Bamberger. As a young man, he was a participant in the abortive revolution of 1848 in the Palatinate, was sentenced to death, and fled to London, where he worked in a bank owned by relatives of his mother. He later moved in the same business to Rotterdam and Paris and learned about the interconnections between economic and national development and between money and politics. In 1868 he was elected to the Customs Union [*Zollverein*] parliament, the predecessor of a German national parliament, and after unification he became a member of the Reichstag. There his major achievement was as rapporteur to the committee, which created the legislation establishing a new central bank (the Reichsbank).[4]

The early years set a pattern in which the new bank moved in the interstices of international finance, industrial finance, and politics. Before World War I, it played a major role in the growth and consolidation of German industry, especially the electro-technical industry. It promoted the formation of syndicates in which businesses were grouped in cooperative partnerships, as well as a wave of mergers, which left the German electrical industry dominated by just two large firms by the beginning of the twentieth century: Siemens and AEG. Deutsche Bank also played a prominent part in financing the great project of extending German power into the Balkans by the construction of a Berlin to Baghdad railway.[5]

Organization of the Bank

At first it was a Berlin-based bank, with branches only in the two port cities (which were not yet members of the German customs area), Bremen and Hamburg. It was only in 1886 that Deutsche Bank opened a branch in Frankfurt, then in Munich in 1892 and in Dresden and Leipzig in 1901. In the first decade of the century, it owned a substantial amount of stock in corporations in the industrial basin of the Rhine–Ruhr. These were amalgamated with the bank only after 1913. In 1914 the bank took over one of the largest regional industrial banks, the Bergisch Märkische Bank. It was only in the 1920s that the bank became a truly multi-branch bank, with tentacles spreading all over Germany. At the time of the merger in 1914, the Deutsche Bank had only 15 branches, whereas the Bergisch Märkische Bank had 35. By the end of 1926, there were 173 branches.[6] Branches clearly brought the bank into a new sort of business: customer accounts and smaller scale financing of small and medium-sized enterprises. One of the attractions of a larger branch network was that it brought a stable supply of deposits, and the bank tried to develop this business by launching savings accounts. In the 1920s, however, the Deutsche Bank, like the other big joint-stock banks based in Berlin, still dealt mostly with large-scale industrial finance, and with international trade, and was frequently and bitterly criticized for its neglect of small business [*Mittelstand*] customers.[7] This criticism, which was in the later years of the Weimar Republic most radically expressed by the National Socialist Party (NSDAP), may have been one reason some of the managers of Deutsche Bank believed they should become more involved with the financing of small and medium-sized businesses and hence participated in the "Aryanization" of such enterprises, which is a major theme of this book. Most *Mittelstand* finance, however, was conducted by other sorts of financial institutions, small private banks, regional banks, or the many savings and cooperative banks spread all over Germany.

The biggest of the bank mergers took place in 1929, with the Disconto–Gesellschaft, one of the four so-called D-banks (besides

Deutsche, the others were the Dresdner and the Darmstädter-und Nationalbank). The Disconto was more conservatively managed than the Deutsche had become, and its high-level management regarded itself as less tainted by expansion. The complexities of the merger had not been fully digested before the full fury of the world Depression hit Germany.

How was an institution as complex as Deutsche Bank managed, and how did it do business? The immediate executive responsibility lay, as with all German companies, with a management board [*Vorstand*], composed in 1932 of 10 members. Each had responsibilities for a particular region and for some particular function of the bank. This was a body of equals, though one member might be designated as the speaker [*Sprecher*].

A supervisory board [*Aufsichtsrat*] was chaired by convention by a former member of the management board. Its other members were prominent business figures, usually from major companies with which Deutsche Bank had had a longstanding business relationship. In 1932, this board had 102 members, in addition to two representatives from the Works Council. This was clearly a very unwieldy institution, which met infrequently and could not exercise any real control. As with almost all German supervisory boards at that time, its function was as much social as it was operational. A committee of this board, however, met more frequently, and this committee's role was strengthened in the course of institutional redesign during the Depression. It then became known as the credit committee, and its major function was to supervise large credits, which had been one of the problematical areas of bank policy before 1931.

In the course of this redesign during the Depression, the number of members of the supervisory board was reduced dramatically to fourteen plus the two members of the works council by the beginning of 1933. But later, as it was important to accommodate politically influential figures in the new regime, such as the tobacco magnate Philipp Reemtsma, the number increased again, so that there were twenty-nine members of the supervisory board by 1936.

Another way for the bank to expand its business contacts was through the institution of a large "main committee" [*Hauptausschuss*], which took over from the larger, pre-1932 supervisory board. This was complemented by a nationwide pattern of regional advisory committees [*Beiräte*].

Members of the management board were members of the supervisory boards of industrial enterprises and derived a substantial amount of their income from their remuneration as members of those supervisory boards (these fees were called *Tantiemen*). From this resulted a deep relationship between banks and industry, in which a bank would characteristically first give loans to an enterprise, sometimes secured, sometimes in the form of a current account overdraft [*Kontokorrentkredit*].[8] When there was a favorable moment on the stock market, banks would organize new issues, of shares or bonds, and would use their customer base as a market for the newly issued securities. Many customers kept their securities with the bank, in custody or *Depot* accounts, and the bank would then use these securities to vote in company general meetings. It was the mixture of financial instruments that gave the German "universal" banks their particular power, a power which probably reached its height in the first decade of the century, at the time of the great wave of mergers and the establishment of many large trusts, and which was analyzed by the pre-war Marxist economist Rudolf Hilferding in his classic work *Finanzkapital*.

Such a board system worked well at a time when most of the business was Berlin-based or foreign oriented. It did not really fit well with the organizational structure required by an extensive branching system. There was a central Berlin office that dealt with branches [*Filialbüro*], supervised by one member of the management board. In addition, each member of the management board had general responsibility for a particular region. But some of the large companies had a particular relationship with another managing director.

The branches behaved in many ways as if they were miniature versions of the bank. Between one and three leading managers were called directors and they served on the supervisory boards of companies smaller than those on which the bank's managing directors served.

The existence of a quite dense network of branches meant that the bank had much greater contact with a variety of regional and local sub-economies. This meant too that it had substantial business interests in those areas of Germany where there was a considerable amount of Jewish-owned business: in Saxony, where there were many Jewish-owned textiles, leather, and fur firms; in Silesia, where Jewish owners worked in textiles and also in heavy industry; in southwestern Germany with its craft traditions, where there were also extensive Jewish-owned manufacturing enterprises and where by coincidence the Deutsche Bank had acquired a particularly dense network of branches as a result of mergers with other banks.[9]

At the beginning of the 1930s, then, the Deutsche Bank was not a perfectly centralized institution but rather had an imperfectly articulated hierarchy: it might even be termed "polyarchy." It looked in some ways like a mirror of the republican state, which the legal and political theorist Carl Schmitt described as "polycratic" (a term many historians have used to analyze the amorphous distribution of power in the post-1933 Nazi state).[10]

Depression and Financial Crisis

The enterprise itself, and the business and political culture within which it functioned, were both quite radically transformed in the early 1930s, first by the general economic and financial crisis, and then by the political revolution of National Socialism (which would have been unthinkable without the background of the economic crisis). Because the banking system had historically been a transmission mechanism for market signals, in the 1930s it faced potential redundancy as the enthusiasts of new forms of economic organization took over. Banks were especially vulnerable because of the disaster of 1931.

The reputation and influence of all German banks had been considerably weakened by the great banking crisis of July 1931. The one most affected was the Darmstädter und Nationalbank (Danat or Danatbank), led by the charismatic Jakob Goldschmidt, who had appeared to Germans as well as to foreign observers to be the incarnation of the power and attraction of the German mixed banking model. The report of the British Macmillan Committee, which held Goldschmidt up as a model, was by an odd coincidence published on July 13, 1931, the day the Danat closed its doors. The basic weakness of the Danat lay in a combination of a massive overextension of loans to a single borrower, the apparently very successful and dynamic Bremen firm of Nordwolle, with large-scale purchases of its own shares to support its price in a weakening market. The firm was then swept away by an international wave of panic that followed the collapse in May of the Viennese Creditanstalt. The Danat was merged in the course of a state rescue operation with the almost equally damaged Dresdner Bank, and the old management of both banks was replaced. The fact that the state de facto owned the new Dresdner Bank, and that the replacement of the board was not complete by January 30, 1933, almost inevitably later gave the Nazi party a substantial influence on the bank.

Danat was the weakest German bank, but it was not the only bank affected. There was in fact a general weakness of German universal banking, which had originated in the aftermath of war and inflation. Banks had lost most of their capital and were reestablished in 1924 on a precariously narrow capital basis. Competitive pressures, in large measure the result of Goldschmidt's aggressive management of Danat, forced them to borrow (largely abroad) and extend loans on a small capitalization, and with liquidity ratios substantially below the prewar levels. In addition, they were exposed to a substantial currency risk, as their liabilities (the foreign loans) were in dollars or pounds or Swiss francs, whereas their assets were largely German and denominated in Reichsmark (RM). So any doubt about the currency, such as developed in the aftermath of the protracted reparations negotiations of 1929–30 and then as a consequence of the political crisis of the Weimar Republic, would quickly translate into a lack of confidence in banks. Banking weakness and doubts about the currency were in fact intertwined in a way that presaged some of the currency crises of the 1990s, in particular the Asian crisis of 1997, and which are now discussed in the economics literature as "twin crises."[11] If investors were worried about banks (as they were after the Austrian Creditanstalt crisis), they might make withdrawals of short-term deposits from banks, but they would also withdraw Reichsmark deposits and convert them into foreign exchange; and if investors were worried about the currency, they would withdraw Reichsmark deposits, which would weaken the banks. So currency doubts as well as specific bank problems meant that all the major banks, which were involved in international business, lost deposits (smaller banks were less internationally exposed and thus more secure).

The Deutsche Bank was not as badly affected by the crisis, but it also depended on government money to continue in business and had to deposit 72 m. RM of its shares with the Deutsche Golddiskontbank, a subsidiary of the central bank, the Reichsbank, in return for a government loan. The speaker of the management board, Oscar Wassermann (Figure 1), had been responsible for the problematical loans to a bankrupt large brewery, Schultheiss Patzenhofer, and had failed to check the creditworthiness of Schultheiss. There was also a bitter controversy – stimulated by the management of the failed banks – as to whether Deutsche Bank had deliberately worsened the crisis to hurt its competitors. This version, actively propagated at the time by Jakob Goldschmidt, was later repeated by the then-Chancellor Heinrich Brüning, in his posthumously published memoirs. (Brüning apparently found it hard to write the section on the banking crisis. Whereas most of the manuscript was complete in the 1930s, Brüning wrote the banking section in the 1950s, while consulting Goldschmidt, who had fled from the Nazis to New York.)[12]

The essence of the criticism was that Deutsche Bank had frustrated a rescue that might have prevented a generalized banking crisis (and thus the worsening of the business depression). Very late in the development of the bank crisis, on July 8, Goldschmidt had proposed a merger of the Danat with the Deutsche. Wassermann had refused, wisely, as it was impossible to gauge the extent of the Danat's losses (and a similar takeover of a problematical bank,

Figure 1. Oscar Wassermann: Member of management board 1912–33, Speaker 1923–33.

Source: Courtesy of Deutsche Bank AG.

the Bodenkreditanstalt, had been responsible for the losses and then the failure of the greatest Viennese bank, the Creditanstalt). But Wassermann also disparaged individual banks and thus heightened the general climate of nervousness. A few days before July 8, Wassermann spoke repeatedly at a meeting of industrialists and bankers about a specific "Danat problem," whereas in reality all banks were vulnerable because of withdrawals and the unwillingness or inability of the Reichsbank to support the commercial banks by discounting bills. Later, Wassermann told the government that the Danat could not be saved, and on July 10 he informed Chancellor Brüning that the other banks were not threatened. On July 11 the Deutsche Bank's directors refused to provide credit to the Danat; and indeed, Wassermann began to insist that the Dresdner Bank was tottering.[13]

After the banking crisis, in October 1931, Deutsche Bank drew up a lengthy memorandum defending itself against the accusation that its lack of solidarity with the other big banks had brought about a general crisis. The memorandum attributed the responsibility for the banking crisis to the international environment; it also criticized very strongly the Reichsbank's policy of restricting credit (rediscounting) to the commercial banks. Indeed the Reichsbank's actions did not conform to the classic central banking recommendations of Walter Bagehot (who believed that in the face of a panic the central bank should lend freely but at a penalty rate). But the Deutsche Bank's memorandum did not take into account the way in which the Reichsbank had been forced into this course by other central banks, in particular the Federal Reserve Bank of New York and the Bank of England, which had made such credit restrictions a precondition for any international assistance.[14] Throughout the subsequent months, Deutsche Bank remained quite critical of the Reichsbank and its President, Hans Luther. The issue remained sensitive after the war, as in the 1950s former Deutsche Bankers feared that their work would be presented in a hostile light in Brüning's imminent memoirs, and the bank's dossier on the 1931 crisis was kept with Hermann Josef Abs's personal papers.

It is easy to see how such an attack could be mounted. Whoever was responsible for the banking crisis had significantly worsened the German depression; and without that worsening, it is quite conceivable that Brüning might have survived longer and that Hitler and his movement might have faded into "complete oblivion" (as a former British Ambassador to Germany stated rather prematurely in his memoirs published in 1929).[15] In 1953, Brüning had a long conversation about the crisis with the past (and future) star of the Deutsche Bank, Hermann Abs. A note of this talk records that: "Abs has the impression that Brüning believes this crisis to be the root of all subsequent ills, and has from somewhere gained the impression that the events were very influenced by competition between the banks, and that the Deutsche Bank's unwillingness to support the Danatbank aggravated the situation."[16]

Certainly in the eighteen months that followed the banking crisis, Deutsche Bank's senior management remained frightened and vulnerable to attack and denunciation, as well as commercially weakened. The crisis of 1931 seemed to teach the general lesson that a banking system only harmed the rest of the economy. Would it not, the critics argued, be more efficient if the state directly realized its objectives by administrative fiat?

At the end of January 1933, Adolf Hitler became Chancellor of Germany and created a party dictatorship around the monopoly of power of the NSDAP that would last until Germany's defeat by the Allies in 1945. The new regime aimed at complete control of economic as well as social, political, and cultural activities. In economics, it interpreted the Depression as evidence of the failure of the private market economy and of the necessity of state intervention. Although earlier in the Weimar Republic there had already been a great deal of government intervention – for instance in the housing market and in wage policy – the Depression brought a call for new controls and regulation: the German government imposed restrictions on international capital movement and a partial debt moratorium for agriculture.

The Depression, with its enormous human suffering, the almost seven million unemployed, bankrupt farmers, and closed banks, seemed unambiguous evidence that the unplanned individualistic market economy and also "finance capitalism" did not work. Banks had called in many loans to protect their severely endangered liquidity, and they earned the hatred of many small and medium-sized enterprises. At the same time, to remain in business, banks had demanded, received, and become dependent on, state subsidies.

The National Socialist New Order inherited from the Depression governments a network of controls and proceeded to make it ever more extensive. In 1934 a system of managed trade was inaugurated, as well as the allocation of raw materials and the restriction of dividend payments; and after 1936 came a far-reaching regulation of prices. Jewish property was subject to at first apparently spontaneous attacks from local fanatics, then to official discrimination and, in the end, to expropriation.

With the exception of the racially motivated attack on Jewish possessions, the fundamental principle of private ownership was left untouched. The laws defining what ownership involved, the "property rights," however, were utterly transformed. Germany remained a private economy but without the guidance of those signals usually associated with the operation of a market: freely determined (not administered) prices, interest rates, and exchange quotations. It was an economy without a market mechanism, which was supposed to behave as its new masters wished. Prices are essential to the market: their suppression and distortion leads to a command economy.

It is difficult to distinguish clearly in the story of Germany's way out of depression and into the economics of control what followed more or less inevitably from the financial and economic catastrophes of the Depression, and what originated from the political vision of the new masters of Germany. The capital market, for instance, became smaller and less relevant to economic activity. Bank loans recovered much more slowly than did the rest of the economy from the world depression. But both these phenomena were characteristic not only of Germany and dictatorship but also of the development of the whole European economy. As a result, some economists formulated a law of a long-term decline in the demand for loans.[17] The capital market seemed to have been destroyed by the experience of depression and by the organizational measures, such as increased cartelization in financial markets, that accompanied the market failure of the 1920s and early 1930s. It required no National Socialist government opposed to finance capitalism to marginalize the German capital market. In this sense, a large part of the macroeconomics of Germany's 1930s experience would have happened anyway, whatever the form of the government.

At first, little bank financing of new investment was required because of the availability of unused capacity. Later expansion could be paid out of high profit levels, or through government credits in the case of firms producing on public contracts.

The Deutsche Bank und Disconto–Gesellschaft gave substantially more new credits in 1933 (118,000) than in 1932 (17,000), but the total volume of credit fell steadily until 1937. As a proportion of the bank's balance sheet, it declined from 55.4 percent in 1932 to 35.4 percent in 1937. Though there was a brief recovery of bank lending in 1938, during the War, bank loans continued to decline (see Figure 2).

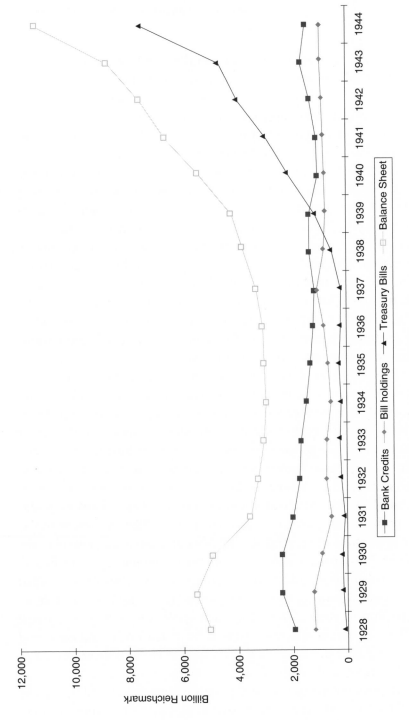

Figure 2. Deutsche Bank Assets 1928–44.

13

In 1933, in response to criticism that the Great Banks had neglected credit to small and medium-sized enterprises (an old line of attack that dated back to before World War I, which Nazi economic experts eagerly took up), Deutsche Bank prepared detailed statistics on the regional, sectoral, and size-specific distribution of its credits. Regionally, by far the largest share (32.04 percent) went to Rhineland–Westphalia; the next largest shares of credits were taken by the Berlin office (8.97 percent) and by Baden (8.92 percent). Manufacturing industry received 32.96 percent of loans, basic industry 15.25 percent, commerce 16.12 percent, and retail trade 4.34 percent. Only 0.58 percent of credits went to artisan manufacturing. The bank provided a breakdown of these figures by the size of credit: 18.83 percent of all the loans to manufacturing industry were "small and medium credits" of under 100,000 RM, whereas only 3.95 percent were over 5,000,000 RM. 35.10 percent of credits to commerce and 87.21 percent of credits to artisanal producers were small or medium credits.[18]

Bank lending contracted in part because firms learned the lesson of the Depression as meaning avoidance of indebtedness. But banks also had their own reasons to be cautious in the aftermath of 1931, when they had been obliged to liquidate many loans in a great hurry and in the process had incurred massive hostility from their clients. Any wise banker would draw lessons from the banking disaster. Time after time in the course of the economic recovery, Deutsche Bank urged restraint on its credit officers. Thus a circular to branch managers in August 1933 read: "We are interested as far as possible in keeping our liquidity at a satisfactory level in the future."[19] Eduard Mosler, the speaker of the management board, in October 1936, told branch managers: "As a result we needed a certain caution in our credit policy. We should not aim at an extension of credit." Karl Kimmich spoke to the board in 1938: "There is the danger that we will be called on by industry, and we must alter our attitude [...] We shall try to convert long and middle term credits into short term loans."[20]

Deposits of all the major German banks also contracted in the initial phases of the recovery period, as major firms started to use

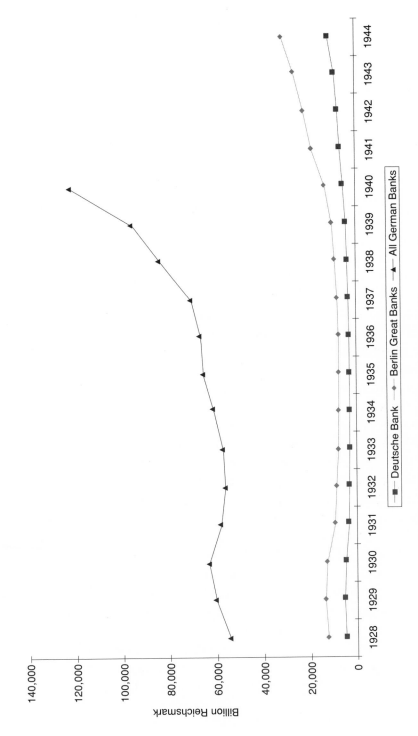

Figure 3. Balance Sheets of German Banks 1928–44.

their deposits for investment.[21] A process of financial disintermediation set in. Foreign deposits dropped particularly sharply, in the case of the Deutsche Bank to 403 m. RM at the end of 1933 (compared with 685 m. RM in 1931). But after the end of 1934, the total of deposits rose steadily. Faced with low demand for loans, banks found they could do little in the later 1930s except channel these new funds into state paper. Starting in 1933, holdings of securities shown in the bank's balance sheet rose. To a substantial extent these were government securities. After 1937, as the government became more dependent on short-term borrowing, the number of treasury bills in the bank's portfolio also rose. This process was described in Germany as the "silent financing" of a government whose expenditures and deficits rose as it took on ever more tasks. In practice the result was the financing through the banking system not simply of the government sector of the economy but also of a rearmament drive.

As the traditional business of the bank in taking business deposits and extending commercial credit contracted, its position within the German economy was diminished. In addition, traditionally a major strength of the German Great Banks, and that of the Deutsche Bank in particular, had lain in overseas financing. The dramatic reduction of world trade in the Depression, the protectionist environment of the 1930s, and Germany's managed foreign trade regime reduced the scope and significance of foreign economic relations. All these considerations combined to ensure that the Deutsche Bank, along with all the other Berlin Great Banks, lost its share of German banking business (see Figure 3).

In the 1930s it was largely the savings banks [*Sparkassen*] that expanded at the expense of the traditional banking giants. Thus from 1932 to 1939 the total assets of the Berlin Great Banks rose by 15 percent and those of the Sparkassen increased by 102 percent. Both in the Depression and in the following recovery, the savings banks regained the position they had lost in the post–World War I hyper-inflation. This development had its parallel in other European countries, where in the course of the 1930s caisses d'épargne (in France) or cantonal banks (in Switzerland) or building societies (in Britain) or postal savings banks grew rapidly. The fact that the competitive erosion of the position of big commercial banks was a Europe-wide phenomenon suggests that the explanation does not lie solely in German legislation or institutional peculiarities or in a National Socialist favoring of more "popular" banks, let alone in the business strategy of a particular bank. In the first place, a more equal distribution of wealth and income in the interwar period favored the savings banks of the "little" people: although after 1927 the German Great Banks had taken savings deposits (and the Deutsche Bank was a pioneer in this regard), traditionally they had made little effort to cultivate lower or lower middle class depositors. Secondly, the quasi–cartel-like arrangements on interest rates, which existed in many countries, restricted the scope for expanding business, because for many firms the lending rates were often higher than the cost of internal accumulation. Germany, which had already developed an interest-rate cartel in 1931, made the cartel's provisions generally binding under the terms of the Banking Law of 1934 (§36). But in Germany in the 1930s, there was an additional factor involved in the relative decline of traditional banking: the rise of large state-owned institutions with a privileged legal status. The Bank für Industrie-Obligationen (Bank for Industrial Bonds) and the newly created Bank der Deutschen Luftfahrt (Aero-Bank) could be much more generous in their credit policy as they had an automatic guarantee of being able to rediscount bills at the Reichsbank [*Rediskontzusage*] and thus could operate a greatly expanded business on a very narrow capital basis.

The Problem of Banks

If banks existed more and more to channel private savings into state debt, was there any justification at all for their continued independent activity? In the directed economy, did banks not belong to the apparently discredited world of the individualistic nineteenth century past? Such was the tenor of the arguments put forward by believers in the new economic doctrines of management and control through party and state. Banking, particularly as it had developed in Germany, is concerned with identifying and assessing risks in a capital market, or (more generally) in evaluating the future. In the 1930s, many politically inspired commentators believed that the state could do all these tasks better – and above all more closely in accordance with the dominant social and political doctrines of the time. And this is where the character of the new regime made a distinct difference.

The new doctrines had been defined unambiguously by Hitler in a series of programmatic writings and speeches. He frequently declared "unalterable" the twenty-five point NSDAP party program of 1920, which included the demand for the "breaking of the servitude of interest" and (Point 13) "the nationalization of all businesses which have been formed into trusts." Again and again he declared that the economy should be subordinated to the good of the people. On the fourth anniversary of the National Socialist "seizure of power," a few months after the inauguration of the Four-Year Plan for the mobilization of the German economy, Hitler insisted on this demand:

> "The will is crucial, by which the economy will be given the role of serving the people and capital of serving the economy. National Socialism is, as we know, the keenest enemy of the liberalistic view in which the economy is there for the sake of capital, and the people is there for the economy. We were thus determined from the first day to break with the false conclusion that the economy could lead an uncontrolled, uncontrollable and unregulated existence in the state. There can no longer today be a free economy, just left to its own devices. Not only would this be politically unacceptable; it would also have impossible economic consequences."[22]

An elaborate propaganda machine helped to reinforce this picture of the limited role of the entrepreneur and of his "social responsibility" before the "higher good" of the national community. In Veit Harlan's film The Ruler [Der Herrscher], the industrial magnate Clausen, played by the great German actor Emil Jannings, eloquently set out the credo of the National Socialist businessman and a new ethos of "responsible" business activity: "The goal of every economic leader who is aware of his own responsibility must be to serve the people's community. This my will (*sic*) is the supreme goal for my work. Everything else must be subordinated to this goal, without contradiction, even if as a result I run the entire enterprise out of existence."[23]

According to this vision Germany's business elite should resemble, nothing so much as Hagen's vassals in the old Teutonic sagas, with bankers assigned a particularly lowly and subordinate position. Throughout the duration of the National Socialist dictatorship, the party launched periodic attacks on banks and bankers. It associated them with the allegedly defunct economy of "liberal individualism" and found them to be at odds with its notions of state-led economic activity.

How should banks respond to dramatic changes in political and moral values? Bankers recognized quite well that the new principles of Germany in the 1930s aimed fundamentally at the destruction of the economic system in which and for which they functioned. Yet at the same time, their historic role in evaluating and judging future trends meant that they could not but take seriously the new doctrines. The history of the Deutsche Bank in the Third Reich is the story of the clash of these two strategies of adaptation: on the one hand, self-defense against the intrusions of party and state; but accommodation and compromise on the other. The management of the Deutsche Bank might well have tried to retreat to purely economic activities; but it lived under a regime that had declared economic actions to be political.

Personnel policy and attitudes towards employees defined by new racial criteria as "non-Aryan," towards Jewish businesses, towards economic activity abroad, and even on the subject of what kind of enterprise was most socially desirable were all inevitably affected by bankers' perceptions of the social and political environment in which they moved. Banks do not make their own destiny. In a rather different context, the great Hamburg banker, Max

Warburg, spoke in the early 1920s about the nature of banking history:

> "I should set great store on demonstrating how large a role chance plays in the development of such a business, and indeed how much more economic development altogether is to be ascribed to chance opportunities and naturally occurring growth than to the so-called working to a goal of some individual. Throughout the work there should be a certain respect for these spontaneous developments; for most people suffer from exaggerated notions of their importance, and bank directors especially, when they write their annual reports three to six months after year-end, ascribe to their acts after the event a foresight that in fact never existed."[24]

The construction of a historical account of the bank in the Nazi period is particularly difficult, because the written material relating to business contacts, overall strategy, and certainly to political behavior is much scarcer than that from the republican and democratic atmosphere of the 1920s. Perhaps the shift to a less written culture was simply a coincidence produced by a move away from nineteenth-century patterns of behavior; but it is more obvious to think of it as emanating from the fear of politics in the dictatorship. The party and the secret police were highly interested in business behavior – especially, as we shall see, during World War II. The result of the paucity of revealing documents on motivation and strategy – which remains despite recent discoveries of substantial documentation – is that interpretations have often been developed on the basis of prior assumptions by the historian.[25]

Modern critics who, motivated by suspicion of and hostility to capitalism, see the bank as forming an integral part of the dictatorship's machinery of exploitation have presented a fundamentally misleading interpretation. The historiography of the German Democratic Republic (GDR), and also those who uncritically based their work on the material provided in the postwar U.S. military government (OMGUS) reports, relied on a narration of the banks' and bankers' business and social contacts.[26] Following the unsubstantiated assumption that such connections inevitably meant political pressure, these analyses went on to imply that political leverage was constantly being exercised by business. They took for granted the conclusion that they claimed to be proving, they forgot about the way in which power functioned in a totalitarian state, and they ignored what was really involved in the business of banking. They read even participation at arm's length in such a body as the South East Europe Association [*Südost-Europa-Gesellschaft*] as the hatching of imperialist and annexationist schemes, or they presented forced contributions to the National Socialist charity "Winter Help" [*Winterhilfswerk*] or to the "Adolf-Hitler-Spende" as the provision of subsidies for fascism. The OMGUS reports reflect the New Deal attitudes of the wartime U.S. Treasury and its officials, who were extremely hostile to banks and big business.

On the other hand those authors who see in every action of a business or a bank resistance to the new political authorities and believe that everything not directly politicized must have constituted an act of defiance are also giving a distorted and one-sided picture. In practice, the financial world offered little direct opposition to the regime. Instead, confronted by a world that no longer appeared to need them, bankers explained their compliant position to themselves by saying that they were doing nothing more than facing realities and then trying, however ineffectually, to mold them as best they could.

2

The Initial Challenge: National
Socialist Ideology

At the beginning of 1933, Germany's bankers came under a number of different attacks: as financial institutions, in the wake of the 1931 collapse; as political agents; and as the embodiment of "Jewish exploitation." These critiques, from different perspectives, mutually reinforced each other. They were reinforced by the simple economic facts of the diminished importance of banking transactions, both within the national economy (as credits to industry shrank) and internationally (as international trade collapsed in the 1930s). The new ideologies of economic control and anti-Semitism emanated from the new German government, from the Nazi party, from a plethora of local pressures, and from bank customers. But these ideologies also took root within banks themselves, where they were adopted with particular enthusiasm by some junior and middle level employees (at least if they were not Jewish), who may have seen the new doctrines as convincing but may also have believed them to be a road to personal advancement within the bureaucratic structure of the institution.

The Bank Inquiry

In September 1933, the most focused challenge to the financial world from the party came during the hearings of an Inquiry (*Bank-Enquête*) called to reform the banking system to avoid a repetition of the catastrophe of 1931. Wilhelm Keppler, on whom Hitler had bestowed the grandiose but ultimately meaningless title of Commissar for Economic Issues [*Beauftragter für Wirtschaftsfragen*], repeated during the Inquiry's sessions a long litany of familiar complaints about banks and their position. "In addition, capital tried to make itself the master of the economy instead of serving. Purchases of blocs of shares, participations and majorities in annual general meetings and supervisory boards were the order of the day, although this should not properly belong to the sphere of banks' activity." The banks had become too centralized in Berlin "in ever larger units [...] with an impersonal and bureaucratic character." They had taken on "tasks which were concerned with speculation rather than with banking in the strict sense." They had neglected credits to small and medium-sized enterprise. Keppler called for a "decentralization of decision-making," an extension of the activities of savings banks ("for political reasons"), and a general reduction in interest rates.[27]

The newly appointed State Secretary in the Reich Economics Ministry, Gottfried Feder, who had previously distinguished himself as the inventor of a scheme for inflating the money supply by means of a rapidly depreciating unit [*Feder-Geld*], and who now viewed himself as the exponent of the best and purest form of Nazi economic ideology, echoed these radical sentiments. "As a result of the rise of the Jewish, purely trading spirit in banking, the Great Banks had failed with the result that billions of Marks needed to be paid by the state for their rescue." The conclusion that the new government should "do something" about the abuses of banking was obvious: "Of course the banks need to be directed by the state [...] One cannot accuse our government of a lack of initiative. Today the greatest initiative belongs to Adolf Hitler."[28]

But these sentiments did not prevail in the deliberations of the Inquiry. Major industrialists testified that they had not felt any "pressure of the Great Banks on their customers." Small businessmen said that they had not been dependent on credit from the Great Banks and had had ready access to other sources. Eduard Mosler from the Deutsche Bank und Disconto–Gesellschaft explained how activity on the supervisory board involved advice and information, helpful suggestions rather than autocratic control by banks. "The banker can give the industrialist important advice about filling crucial positions, he can supply experience derived from other branches, experience which could only otherwise be gained with the greatest of difficulties."[29]

Apparently even the ideologues of state control were convinced by all these arguments from the practical men of business – at least for the moment. Feder admitted rather timidly: "I am completely satisfied. I have won the impression that in general people want to see closer personal contacts between enterprises and banks." The view was now that perhaps banks should not be managed as part of a gigantic apparatus of state planning. Hjalmar Schacht, reappointed by Hitler as Reichsbank President, had, it seemed, carefully stage-managed the whole of the Inquiry's discussion, as he freely boasted in the company of foreign observers: "The whole object of the Inquiry in his view was to let all the people with new theories talk themselves out, and to bring them face to face with competent experts, who would give the real answers to their theories [...]" Dr Schacht believed in fact the party theorists would have no great influence in this affair.[30]

In the end, the party activists knew they had been defeated by "the private Great Banks under the leadership of Reichsbank President Dr. Schacht," but they wanted to renew the attack in a different forum.[31] The National Socialist movement, they thought, should not let itself be outwitted by smooth-tongued financiers. And indeed the ideological offensive against the banks was launched again, and much more effectively, but only after Schacht had departed from the Reichsbank. In the meantime, the ideologues had to be content with inflicting petty humiliations on Schacht and on the bankers he had protected. At the end of 1934, for instance, the party and the government demanded an emergency donation from businesses. Schacht and the three presidents of the stock exchange committee were obliged literally to hold out collecting boxes in which the leading business executives were personally to deposit bank notes (of a prearranged value): the Deutsche Bank was committed to contributing 1,000 marks (otherwise Schacht would have been forced to conduct this begging operation in the street). It was a colossal and public symbolic submission of the business community.[32]

The Inquiry, however, had left the banking structure untouched: there was no breaking up of the system into a network of regional banks, as had been proposed by many critics of banking in the wake of 1931. The legislative result, in the form of the December 5, 1934 Reich Credit Law [*Reichsgesetz über das Kreditwesen*], created instead a new regulatory environment: the recognition of cartel conditions on interest rates, minimum reserve requirements for banks, limitations on the size of large loans, and supervision through a Supervisory Office for Credit. In practice, it institutionalized the ad hoc emergency regulatory system that had developed since the bank collapses of 1931. The new law also placed savings banks on the same footing as other banks.

Credits

Ironically, the new regulations appeared for the moment to be redundant. Bankers now, unlike in the 1920s, needed no persuasion to be hesitant and cautious. The reduced demand for credit during the recovery of the 1930s meant that in the first years of its existence the Supervisory Office "had not been very effective."[33] Credit activities were certainly greatly reduced but not because of legislative or regulatory control.

The profit and loss accounts reveal the contours of the Deutsche Bank's basic business. The immediate legacy of the Depression brought bad debts and losses. From 1931 to 1934, write-offs eliminated the bank's operating profit; in the next year profits were used to pay off the state's share-holding taken in 1932. In February 1934, the bank still needed an emergency credit from the Reichsbank.[34] After 1936, profit was held at a constant level through declared and undeclared contributions to reserve funds. Share dividends and thus in practice declared profits were controlled by the state. The revenue side of the accounts shows falling fee income until 1936, and only then a brief recovery, associated with the short-lived revival of the issue business (see page 28); and revenue from interest only started to recover after 1935. In other words, the decline in banking made itself felt for a long time while the production figures of the German economy were already surging ahead (see Figure 4).

The new credit norms restricted banks' activities much less than did a parallel law, issued on December 4, 1934. Through a ceiling imposed on company dividends, the Dividend and Bond Law [*Anleihestockgesetz*] made less attractive both the ownership and the issue of equities. Share issues throughout the 1930s remained at levels below a quarter of that of the later 1920s, and even below the volume of the crisis year 1931. Only in one year, 1938, was there an apparent burst of new issues, but it was provoked by the activities of semi-state companies, not genuinely private corporations: the Reichswerke "Hermann Göring" and the Hydration Works of Pölitz. Apart from this brief spurt of activity, the market for new share issues stagnated (see Table 2.1).

The intention of the Dividend Law was to make bonds more attractive, and in consequence prepare for a conversion of government debt in 1935. The management of the capital market was consciously aimed at improving the market for state paper and thus enabling a financing of rearmament without a large and unstable short-term debt.[35] The improvement of the fixed interest market in 1935 generated in the short term a great deal of business, as private corporations followed the state in converting debt to lower interest

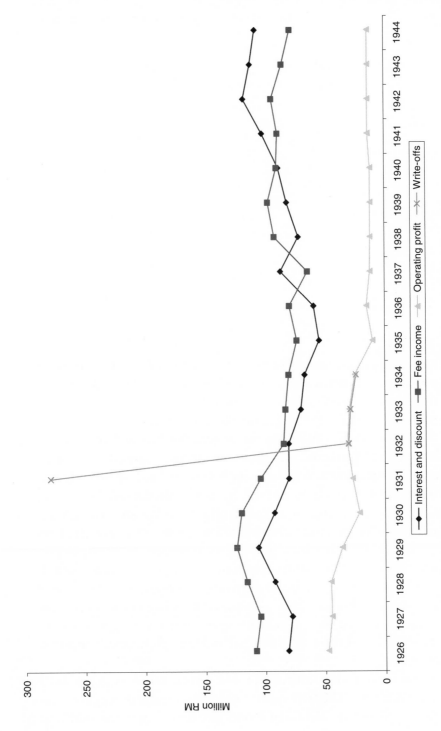

Figure 4. Deutsche Bank und Disconto-Gesellschaft: Profit and Loss, 1926–44.

Table 2.1. New Issues: Bonds and
Equities in Germany 1927-38[a]

	Bonds	Equities
1927	2854	1376
1928	2905	1339
1929	1685	979
1930	2926	555
1931	1338	635
1932	521	150
1933	1031	91
1934	338	143
1935	1646	156
1936	2718	395
1937	3408	333
1938	7851	827

[a] Amounts given in millions of RM.

rates. In 1936 private conversions even exceeded in volume those of
public corporations. The Deutsche Bank managed several of these
transactions: most importantly the February 1937 exchange of 5
percent Daimler–Benz bonds for those at 6 percent.[36]

In the case of public sector bonds, the holder had a choice
between accepting the state's conversion terms, which included a
once-only payment of a 2 percent bonus, or holding onto the old
bond which would, as a result of newly introduced legislation,
not be traded or eligible as collateral for bank loans. The private
sector conversions were somewhat less egregiously in breach of existing law. The loan was called in, as provided for in the issuing
prospectus, and the holder thus had an opportunity to be repaid.
Holders who chose conversion received a bonus, as in the case of
public sector bonds; the sum required to repay bondholders was
raised by issuing new bonds at a new lower rate. Figure 5 shows
the share of debt conversions attributable to government or public
companies.

There were also some major new private bond issues: in 1937
a 24,500,000 RM 5 percent issue for Hoesch through a syndicate led by the Deutsche Bank; and more after the outbreak

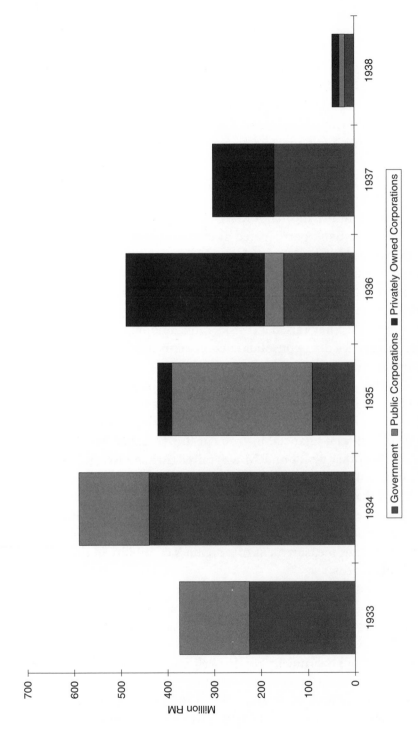

Figure 5. Debt Conversions 1933–8.

of war in 1939: Hoesch, BMW, Daimler, Accumulatoren Fabrik AG (part of the Quandt concern), and Mannesmann.

Some of the old syndicate activities could be revived in a market once again favorable to issues. The Deutsche Bank led jointly with the Dresdner Bank two major credits to finance trade with the USSR: a 200 m. RM order in 1936 and another 200 m. order in 1939 after the conclusion of the German–Soviet Non-Aggression Pact (Molotov–Ribbentrop Pact).[37]

There were also the major Reich Bond issues [*Anleihen*] in which the Deutsche Bank participated as comanager in a revised version of the venerable state bond syndicate. Its quota was 16 percent in all except the first 1935 issue, launched after the introduction of universal conscription and the acceleration of Germany's armaments preparations. There were three issues in both 1936 and 1937 and four in 1938. They raised a considerable amount of money, which was largely used to consolidate short-term public debt and thus indirectly to finance German rearmament.

Of the 3,150 m. RM derived from bond issues in 1937, 2,854.5 m. RM was used to provide long-term funding of the short-term financing of armaments that had been conducted through the issue of a special financial instrument (the so-called Mefo-bills).[38] In 1938 another 7,744 m. RM was raised through issues. But these gigantic issues caused increasing nervousness for authorities who believed that a failure by the public to subscribe to the bond issue could be treated as a vote of no confidence in a regime, which permitted no other kind of voting on its record. Buying public debt is a very obvious measurement of a regime's credibility in the eyes of well-off citizens.

The Deutsche Bank's ability to place Reich bonds with its customers gradually decreased, as weariness and suspicions about the build-up of public expenditure set in. Whereas for the first operation in 1935, the Deutsche Bank had sold 24.17 percent of the total stock of government bonds (well above its quota in the syndicate), it sold only 19.33 percent of the first 1937 issue and 21.0 percent of the first 1938 issue. From the Deutsche Bank's internal figures, however, in which the size of the average purchase and the geographic distribution were carefully tabulated for each issue, it is clear that for some time private subscriptions held up rather better. These purchases reflect the symptoms of an already evident inflationary money overhang, caused by increased incomes combined with reduced purchases following the deterioration of quality because of import restrictions in many consumer goods. On the other hand, the Deutsche Bank's industrial customers began to be less willing to buy state paper, although the Four-Year Plan administrators tried to promote the investment of surplus corporate funds in this manner. Whereas industry had bought 48 percent of the 1935 issue, in the first 1938 bond issue the share had fallen to a disappointing 34.2 percent.[39]

It was in 1938 that the big blows came. In October, the third bond issue of that year had been over-subscribed in the wake of a resurgence of political confidence following the Munich agreement with Italy, France, and Britain, which brought the hope that the establishment of a greater Germany could be achieved peacefully. The government, desperate to force the pace of rearmament, added an additional 250 m. RM bonds to the 950 m. originally offered. After Munich, suddenly, there appeared to be no end to the willingness of Germans to hold public debt, and all the doubts vanished. But this mood was short-lived. Soon after the success of this operation came the spectacular failure of the fourth bond issue of 1938 (of a massive 1,500 m. RM), which prompted a major confrontation between the Reichsbank and the government, in which the large banks were drawn in as members of the Reich issuing syndicate. 275 m. RM were to be sold to the savings banks and credit cooperatives [Genossenschaften], and the remainder was to be channeled through the Reich syndicate.

In December 1938 the Reichsbank wrote to the Finance Minister that: "We too are of the opinion that the capital market can for the moment no longer accommodate bond issues of this kind, and that the tasks entrusted to your responsibility in the areas of economic rearmament and the Four-Year Plan cannot be accomplished on the scale intended." The banks had been able to place most of the bonds (900 m. RM out of 1,138 m. RM), but the failure to place the rest had shown how Germany had reached its financial limit. The market had gone on strike. Discussion of the implications of the bond issues led the Reichsbank to prepare for Hitler the fiercely critical memorandum of January 7, 1939, which included the following text: "The Reich and other public sector enterprises must not take on expenditures, guarantees or commitments that cannot be met out of taxes or out of sums raised through bond issues which do not disturb the capital market." The January 7 memorandum led to the dismissal on January 20 of Schacht, Vice-President Fritz Dreyse, and Director Ernst Hülse. Wilhelm Vocke and Karl Blessing together with Carl Ehrhardt were dismissed later.[40]

The Reichsbank directors also involved the leading German bankers in their examination, and criticism, of government policy. On January 10, 1939 the "narrow" Reich bond issuing syndicate of the major banks held a crisis meeting in the Reichsbank building, with the participation of the Reichsbank directorate and representatives of the Finance Ministry. After a long argument, the participants agreed that the "narrow" syndicate should take up the outstanding bonds but exclude from this operation the twenty-three smaller banks that had a quota of less than 1 percent in the syndicate. Eduard Mosler of the Deutsche Bank opposed the omission of the smaller firms on the grounds that they should not be exempted from making a sacrifice, but he was overruled on the grounds that "one should not expose the failure to excessive publicity." As a result, the Deutsche Bank was obliged to hold a total of 75 m. RM of the Fourth 1938 bond issue in its own portfolio.

The syndicate also held a very extensive debate about the causes of the failure and listed: "Absence of industrial purchases of government bonds, unwillingness of the public to buy, removal of Jewish purchasers, non-participation of purchasers who are spending money on aryanization purchases, concern about the demand of the Reichsbahn [State Railways] for funds, an excessive supply of government bonds without the availability of industrial bonds." The participants reached a general agreement that "only a limitation of public expenditure will bring about a change."[41]

The government's financing had also, as the December memorandum made clear, destroyed the market for industrial bonds. An "Emissionsverbot" (ban on issues) was used to protect the market for state paper, and the secondary market was weakened by the extent of new public issues available. The Reichsbank had pointed to "the lack of confidence" as evidenced "in the continual fall of prices of industrial bonds."[42] The industrial market remained extremely restricted in 1939. In the summer an issue by the Deutsche Bank and the Dresdner Bank of AEG bonds placed only two-fifths of the bonds with the public, and the banks fell back on the insurance companies to raise the missing sum.[43]

But many of Germany's largest companies were desperate to obtain investment resources, and they tried to approach the banks. The case of IG Farben, a business that traditionally had organized itself very independently of banks (and had indeed run its own "house bank" as an alternative to external financing), is a significant example. Most of the investments of IG Farben in the 1930s were financed through some kind of state support, either directly (as in the case of synthetic rubber production), or from the firm's own resources but in response to government orders and contracts. Between 1936 and 1938, about three-fifths of investments in new facilities were managed through the Four-Year Plan.[44] In addition, the costly construction of a synthetic rubber (Buna) works at Hüls near Recklinghausen and at Schkopau near Merseburg was financed through funds provided at 5 percent by the Raw Materials Office and derived, appropriately enough, from revenue from the rubber tariff.[45]

But by 1939, the firm needed extra funds desperately to deal with the costs of absorbing enterprises from Austria and the former Czechoslovakia, and it needed the consent of the Deutsche Bank before it could apply to the Economics Ministry for permission to make a flotation on the stock exchange. The IG Farben bond operation of 1939 was preceded by an intensive discussion with the Deutsche Bank, which managed the issue, and initially suggested 50 m. RM rather than the 100 m. that the IG wanted, and a coupon of 5 percent, rather than the 4.5 percent on which the IG insisted.[46]

In the end, the Deutsche Bank gave in on both matters to its big industrial customer. It was represented on the supervisory board of IG Farben by its most prominent directors, first by Eduard Mosler (the speaker of the management board), and then by the rising star of the bank, Hermann Abs.

Industrial activity by bankers had historically involved the gathering of large quantities of information. One of the most visible activities of bank directors – who had incurred heavy criticism as a result – had been the holding of positions on large numbers of supervisory boards. This time-consuming activity brought gains to the companies on whose boards the bankers sat, as Mosler pointed out in the 1933 Enquête, because it involved casting the banks' information net as widely as possible; but participation on large numbers of boards made any sort of tight control of firms' management impossible. Jakob Goldschmidt, in particular, had been widely criticized in the 1920s for the number of boards on which he sat. One common response to the debacle of 1931 was that banks had been excessively lax in their imposition of financial discipline on their clients because they were too busy on too many boards to really follow a company's affairs. In 1937, any bank director was limited to twenty seats, and at the same time the size of most supervisory boards was reduced. A big reshuffling occurred in which members of the bank's management board were replaced on the supervisory board of many smaller companies by *Direktoren der Bank* (senior vice-presidents). (Even this regulation was soon broken: during World War II, some bankers were allowed to hold larger numbers of seats on supervisory boards of non-German companies.)

Reprivatization

Regulating banking appeared to the regime as a safer and more economically sound alternative to demands from some of the party radicals for direct control of finance through socialization. In fact banks were allowed to reprivatize themselves as their positions

recovered from depression losses and to buy out the state participations built up in the aftermath of the 1931 banking crisis. The
Deutsche Bank was the first bank able to do this, because it had
received by far the smallest extent of state support during the crisis. In November 1933, it was able to exchange the empty bank
building in Berlin of the Disconto–Gesellschaft between the Behrenstrasse and Unter den Linden for government-owned shares.[47] The
bank building could be turned into offices for a government whose
scope and personnel were both constantly on the rise. In 1936, the
Deutsche Bank bought back the remaining shares from the Reichsbank's Golddiskontbank subsidiary and resold them to its private
customers.

The increased activity of the state worried both the bank and
its customers. One of the most important points of contact was
in the semi-private environment of the regional advisory councils
[*Beiräte*], where leading businessmen met to talk about general
economic conditions. These councils presented bankers with an
opportunity to dispense information about the bank's policy, listen
to descriptions of local conditions and problems, and to demon-
strate that the bank was in touch with the priorities of its customers.
These meetings offer a highly revealing barometer of German business opinion.

In the industrial area of Rhineland–Westphalia, Managing Director Karl Kimmich throughout the 1930s presented an account
that was consistently critical of the regime's attempts to plan and
control. In late 1935, he commented: "We are living in a state-led
boom; we are all in the same boat. Industry cannot live without government orders, since exports cannot be increased adequately [...]
The German economy cannot do without individual performance.
It is extraordinarily difficult to find extremely capable people, and
for that reason the 'Führerprinzip' [leadership principle] cannot
be carried out, as there are not enough leaders."[48] In the spring
of 1936, Kimmich criticized the effects of the armaments boom
on the German economy and argued in very forthright terms that
Germany should return as soon as possible to what it was best at –
namely exporting on the world market.

"After we have now become esteemed again in the world through our rearmament, it would be in the interest of a healthy fiscal system to take up again endeavors for a general disarmament. In the long run, it is impossible to keep on consolidating the short-term unfunded debt of the state through the banks and insurance companies [...] As a result, we must restore our links with the world market. It is completely wrong to attempt to expand production for domestic orders."[49]

After 1936, Kimmich complained that Hermann Göring's Four-Year Plan and its redirection of investment was making impossible that connection with the world economy and export orientation that in past eras had been the key to German economic success. "It is regrettable that we are forced to take part in an investment boom at a time when we could be selling on an expanding world market." In 1936 and 1937 many companies experienced acute shortages in the supply of raw materials and needed to limit their output in consequence. Later the criticism of the planned economy became even more explicit: it was like a "grafted tree [...] whose growth is limited and which eventually dies branch by branch [...] The businessman needs room for maneuver otherwise he will become merely an employee."[50] Even after the outbreak of war, when discussion of public policy became harder, the message was clear, and the planned economy was still blamed for Germany's problems. "We entered the war with a much less elastic economy than in 1914; and the effects are visible everywhere."[51]

Such observations had to be kept confidential. To the outside, echoes of the unease over economic policy appeared in the bank's annual general meetings, where shareholders and the press were in attendance, but they were heavily veiled. Eduard Mosler used his opportunity as speaker of the bank after 1933 to defend the private economy against encroachments but never to directly criticize state actions. He believed that it was possible to influence government policy only very marginally and that speeches at the annual general meeting mattered only as statements. Hermann Abs, who replaced Kimmich as the Deutsche Bank's representative on the

Rhineland–Westphalia Advisory Council, kept his wartime comments to a bare minimum (at least as far as the written record is concerned), with many statistics and facts and no interpretation. Handling the politics of banking became a sensitive, time-consuming, and eventually (as we shall see for the wartime period) very dangerous job.

3

Anti-Semitism and the German Banks

In the first months of 1933, politics intruded into banking. No one would deny that the magnitude of the 1931 crisis revealed severe shortcomings in the German banking system and in the behavior of its luminaries. The discussion about bank reorganization in the aftermath of 1931 personally threatened the leading figures involved in that debacle. But by the time of the National Socialist seizure of power, the personnel issues had been by no means completely resolved, and an additional element now entered the calculation. To what extent should the banks reflect the beliefs of what was thought to be the New Germany, beliefs expressed not only by the new political leadership, and in the streets, but also in the press, by many of the banks' customers, and not least by some of the banks' employees? The NSDAP used the opportunity of bank restructuring to attack the position of Jews in German economic life. The fact that the structure of business organization had been so severely shaken by the Great Depression made a purge much easier.

Finance and Anti-Semitism

Banks had come under intense public scrutiny in the aftermath of World War I and especially during the Depression, and many Germans criticized the "Jewish" character of banking. This was an opinion widely shared and by no means restricted simply to the political adherents of the NSDAP. The two men centrally responsible in the last years of the Weimar Republic for dealing with the aftermath of the banking crisis, Chancellor Heinrich Brüning and Finance Minister Hermann Dietrich, both expressed such views in private. At the height of the banking crisis in July 1931, State Secretary Hans Schäffer of the Finance Ministry had a "fantastic row" with his Minister Dietrich when the latter made disparaging remarks about "Jewish bankers." At the end of 1931, when discussing bank reorganization with cabinet members, Dietrich had set out his version of the populist myth that banks strove for economic dominance. "The banks should support the economy. But they wanted to dominate it and formed industrial trusts, which were then too large for them."[52] Pernicious anti-Semitic prejudices may have underlain the fraught relationship of Brüning with Wassermann.

In the Deutsche Bank, Oscar Wassermann had been in charge of the bank's overall policy in the late 1920s, and was widely blamed for the 1931 crisis. He was also subject to attack as a Jew and a Zionist. Chancellor Heinrich Brüning, for instance, remained throughout his life convinced that Wassermann had contributed to the catastrophe by refusing to help prop up the Danat Bank before its closure on July 13, 1931. Two non-Jewish members of the management board bore a heavier responsibility than Wassermann for the mismanagement of the Deutsche Bank's business. Werner Kehl resigned from the board because of the large speculative foreign exchange positions of the Düsseldorf branch in 1931, which fell within his regional domain.[53] Emil Georg von Stauss was held to account for the bank's losses on loans to the fraudulently managed Schultheiss–Patzenhofer brewery, over whose supervisory board he had presided.

The lessons of the 1931 banking crisis were drawn in an internal organizational reform of the Deutsche Bank that originated from an initiative of one of the most dynamic members of the pre-1933 supervisory board, the Rhineland lignite industrialist Paul Silverberg. Silverberg had been bitterly critical of the firm's pre-1931 management and had suggested an overhaul of the management board. In response, in early 1932 the Deutsche Bank Board tried to push Silverberg, whom they saw as irritating, out of the supervisory board, on the grounds that the reformed law on joint-stock companies required a reduction in the size of the supervisory board.[54]

Silverberg replied by suggesting the removal of the existing members of the management board on the bank's credit commission (with one exception, the industrial credit specialist of the bank, Oscar Schlitter) and the creation of a new more general committee of the supervisory board. It would include eight members and have the responsibility "of checking credits and advising the management board and preparing the decision of the supervisory board." This body would no longer be called the credit commission, but simply "Committee of the supervisory board."[55] This body after 1933 became known as the Working Committee. Composed eventually of nine members, it laid down central guidelines for the bank's policy, as well as discussing the largest credit operations (credits up to 1 m. RM could be approved by individual members of the management board).

Silverberg had a particular, and strongly personal, motivation in suggesting this change. He wanted to destroy the power and influence of Emil Georg von Stauss. "The Bank is today no longer in the position of being able to afford to be in conflict with public opinion, and it has every reason to draw the consequences for its personnel from the general development. This is particularly true of Herr von Stauss." Stauss's involvement in irresponsible actions before 1931 had been too obvious for him to remain on the management board, and Kehl had also left. But Silverberg's triumph

Figure 6. Theodor Frank: Member of management board 1929–33.

Source: Courtesy of Deutsche Bank AG.

was incomplete in that Stauss moved to the supervisory board and remained a very powerful figure thanks to his close connections with the National Socialist party (see below, pages 152–5). In general in 1932 there was still a substantial degree of continuity with the pre-1931 management board.

Then in May 1933, a new purge of the board began, carried out for very different reasons. Here the New Germany made itself felt. As part of the political concessions made by the bank to National Socialism, the Jewish directors Theodor Frank (Figure 6) and Oscar Wassermann resigned from the board.[56] Wassermann as the bank speaker had been in a particularly exposed position. The internal bank memorandum on the events leading to his departure argued that Wassermann had failed decisively in the bank crisis. After listing the scandals involving other managing directors, the author asked,

"Where was the man who could not be blind to affairs such as these? Where was the hand that should have intervened decisively before it was too late? Where was the fist banging on the table to bring colleagues back to reason who had lost the understanding for what risks were appropriate? Where was the first among equals, who, less burdened by commitments on supervisory boards, should have kept a supervision over the whole, ensuring continuity, and felt responsible morally to the bank and his colleagues. Where was Herr Wassermann? [...] Whether Herr Wassermann was a Jew or a Christian had nothing to do with all this."

In practice, of course, it had a great deal to do with business politics in the radicalized climate of 1933.[57]

In the absence of Wassermann, Reichsbank President Schacht had spoken (on April 6, 1933) with two leading figures in the bank, Georg Solmssen (Figure 7) and the chairman of the supervisory board, Franz Urbig, and suggested the removal of some of the Jewish members of the management board. Wassermann initially agreed to leave by the end of 1933, but on May 20, his colleagues decided to announce the resignation before the bank's annual general meeting scheduled for 1 June. The bank's speaker was thus pushed out prematurely.[58]

The bank clearly found these changes profoundly embarrassing and emphasized in its public declarations the nonracial and nonbusiness grounds for the departures. The press communiqué pointed out that Wassermann was 64 years old and Frank 62, and it stated an intention of electing them to the bank's supervisory board ("suggested for election to the supervisory board"), though neither of them did in fact move upstairs.[59] They were replaced on the management board by Karl Kimmich, who had been a director of the Disconto-controlled A. Schaaffhausenscher Bankverein until its merger with the Deutsche Bank in 1929, and Fritz Wintermantel from the Deutsche Bank's Berlin city office. Georg Solmssen, who had been bank speaker in 1933, and whose father had been Jewish, also soon moved onto the supervisory board. Three additional new members of the management board in 1933 – Oswald Rösler, Hans Rummel, and Karl Ernst Sippell (who took responsibility for the bank's personnel department) – made for an almost complete change of leadership. The only figures remaining

Figure 7. Georg Solmssen: Member of management board 1929–34, Speaker 1933.

Source: Courtesy of Deutsche Bank AG.

from the pre-1933 world were Eduard Mosler, who succeeded Solmssen as speaker, and the bank's foreign specialist and German delegate on the Standstill Committee (which dealt with the substantial volume of frozen German international debts), Gustaf Schlieper.

The removal of the Deutsche Bank's Jewish directors was an acutely painful process. It was morally and personally repugnant to their colleagues; but even seen from a pragmatic angle, the exercise had dangers. Suppose that the National Socialist revolution was not permanent? When Wassermann and Frank were not made members of the supervisory board, Franz Urbig, the supervisory board chairman, wrote to another board member:

> "I feel – as I am sure you do also – uneasy about the thought of going back on a promise made in this way. Other times can come, and we must avoid the possibility of the reproach being made at any time that the bank's decision-making body or its representatives played

a role in making non-Aryan members of the management board leave."[60]

Georg Solmssen, the speaker in 1933, saw more clearly than anyone else in the bank what was happening. But this was a new illumination. Before 1933, Solmssen, a very conservative German who believed wholeheartedly in the idea of a German national cause, had worried much more about the radical and half-baked economic and political ideas of the Nazis than about their anti-Semitism. He told the agrarian leader von Batocki (who had made the argument of the center-right that Hitler and his party might be educated by being brought into governmental responsibility) that:

> "I would point to the necessity of mobilizing against the dangers contained in the national socialist program. This is so excessive, agitatorial and unrealistic, in economic matters, especially in regard to financial issues, that in my view something must be done to illuminate the contents and ensure that those circles who are attracted by the national ideas of the party, and who believe that the government inadequately represents the national idea, should move away from the extremists and toward a truly conservative party based on the Conservative People's Party."

To one of the leading German economists, Bernhard Harms of the Kiel Institut für Weltwirtschaft, Solmssen wrote of his discussions with Luther, who had, he said, agreed that "the bourgeoisie should engage every effort to combat the spreading of crazy ideas, such as those contained in the program of the NSDAP." What about Nazi anti-Semitism? Solmssen in 1930 treated this issue as less than serious. "I entirely disregard the anti-Semitic statements of the party, because they will come to nothing, and regard it as enough to resist the economic declarations."[61] In early 1932, he continued to regard Nazi economic doctrines as a joke, albeit a poor one. He told the Club von Berlin, an assembly of bankers, that Escherich (a former Freikorps leader, who had organized the infamous "Orgesch") had asked people why they had voted for Hitler and had received the reply: "I have to pay alimony, but Hitler will cancel all debts!"[62]

In 1933 the situation was obviously quite different. A letter Solmssen wrote on April 9, 1933 to Franz Urbig is both moving and chillingly prophetic. It is worth quoting at length:

"Dear Herr Urbig, The exclusion of Jews from state service, which has now been accomplished through legislation, raises the question of what consequences this measure – which was accepted as self-evident by the educated classes – will bring for the private sector. I fear that we are only at the beginning of a conscious and planned development, which is aimed at the indiscriminate economic and moral destruction of all members of the Jewish race living in Germany. The complete passivity of the classes which do not belong to the National Socialist Party, the lack of any feeling of solidarity on the part of those who have up to now worked in business shoulder to shoulder with Jewish colleagues, the ever more evident pressure to draw personal advantages from the free positions created by the purges, the silence about the shame and humiliation imposed on those who although innocent see their honor and existence destroyed from one day to the next: all this is evidence of a position so hopeless that it would be wrong not to confront facts straightforwardly, or to make them appear harmless. In any case, those affected have apparently been abandoned by those who were professionally close to them, and they have the right to think of themselves. They should no longer let the enterprise to which they have devoted their lives determine their actions – unless that enterprise treats them with the same loyalty that it expected of them. Among our colleagues too, the question of solidarity has been raised. My impression was that this suggestion met only a luke-warm response in the management board (perhaps because of its non-homogenous composition); and that if it were to be realized it would take the form of a gesture rather than complete resistance, and as a result would be doomed to failure. I recognize that in the decisive deliberations, differences will be made between different members of the management board who happen to be on the list of proscription. But I have the feeling that although I am viewed as someone whose activity is thought of positively, and although I may be honored as the representative of a now seventy year long tradition, I too will be abandoned once my inclusion in a "cleansing action" is demanded by the appropriate outside authorities. I must be clear about this [...]"[63]

Soon after, with the same mixture of dignity and desperation, he made an extraordinary suggestion to the man in charge of Hermann Göring's Press Office. In a meeting in his own house in Berlin Wannsee, Solmssen argued that German Jews should defend themselves against the accusations thrown at them by the NSDAP by organizing their own National Council, which would "examine all complaints against Jews and organize the emigration of those who prove to be harmful or undesirable [. . .] But we do not wish to be treated as second or third class citizens, we want to be heard when we are accused. That is a simple human right, and the duty of any cultured state." He also tried to arrange a personal meeting with Göring, which fell through at the last moment.[64]

The reform of the bank's supervisory board became in practice an opportunity to renege on the promises that had been made to Wassermann and Frank. It took place on very different lines than those originally suggested during the Depression by Paul Silverberg. In fact, the supervisory board was not so much purged as expanded (from 16 in 1933 to 25 in 1934), to disarm potential criticism by including men from a broader range of business backgrounds. One of the new appointments also held out the possibility of better contacts with the New Germany. Philipp Reemtsma, the Hamburg cigarette magnate, joined not only the supervisory board but also its newly reformed Working Committee. The Deutsche Bank explained to Reemtsma on his appointment that this new body "would be the focus of the real activity of the supervisory board, and would have a deep insight in the bank's business, and would be composed of the most valued and most intimate friends of the bank, who enjoy the highest confidence."[65] Reemtsma was particularly valuable not only because of his powerful position in the Hamburg economy but also because of his good connections with Hermann Göring, which he continued assiduously to cultivate.

The supervisory board's external appearance was also cosmetically retouched for public view. Revolutions often want to rewrite history, and the National Socialist revolution insisted on a vision that would conceal inconvenient reminders of the past. Georg Solmssen remained on the supervisory board until 1938, although he was never listed as a member in the bank's annual report. Max

Steinthal was the most obviously historical personality connected with the bank. He had joined the management board in 1873 and in the Depression, at the age of 80, was still chairman of the supervisory board. Initially, he remained on the supervisory board after January 1933, but he also was not listed in the annual statements after the end of 1934. He was officially dropped from the supervisory board in May 1935. At this time, he noted after a conversation with a member of the management board in which he assured that he would not make "difficulties" for the bank, that "it is painful to see yet another link to the Deutsche Bank cut, but I shall have to come to terms even with this."[66] He did not emigrate and seems to have been completely ignored by the bank, although later, after his death, Emil Georg von Stauss tried to secure better living quarters for his elderly and sick widow. The state authorities harassed Steinthal relentlessly, despite his eminence, age, and deteriorating physical condition. At the end of 1939 he was obliged to sell his house in Charlottenburg to the *Luftgau–Kommando*, moved with his family (including a son crippled as a result of injuries sustained in World War I) to a smaller house, found that that too was requisitioned, and then stayed in a hotel room, where on December 8, 1940 he died.

Meanwhile the supervisory board had to be made to look more representative of the general balance of social forces. In 1937 the bank asked for, and received, permission to expand its supervisory board to thirty members; in 1939 it grew further to thirty-five to continue the policy of making politically useful appointments: "adding some personalities, who might be regarded as semi-public, and in part may be in connection with the territorial additions accomplished in recent years."[67]

Silverberg, who had initiated the discussion of supervisory board reform, was Jewish and left Germany in 1933, so that he no longer attended the Working Committee he had launched. But Stauss, Silverberg's great enemy, moved onto the new body, and the committee originally designed to exclude him ironically gave him a new position of influence in the bank. For the rest of his life (he died in December 1942) he played a crucial part in managing not the bank's financial but its political performance.

Figure 8. Employees of Deutsche Bank during a radio speech by Adolf Hitler on November 10, 1933, in the main counter hall of the Berlin city office.

Source: Courtesy of Deutsche Bank AG.

Bank Employees

Responding to Germany's new political order was not just a matter of changes, however dramatic, in the bank's top management and in the supervisory board. A bank is not simply a policy-making institution but also is driven by internal institutional pressures. National Socialism profoundly altered the climate of work and the internal ethos of the bank. Bank employees, vulnerable in the Depression to layoffs and salary cuts, often hostile to and resentful of their female colleagues, and fearful of a loss of social standing, had provided a capacious reservoir of National Socialist sentiment (Figure 8). At the end of 1932, one tenth of the bank's employees were reported to have been members of the NSDAP (though the source for this figure may well have wished to exaggerate the extent of party

Figure 9. May 1, 1934: Front page of National Socialist Factory Cell Organization for Deutsche Bank newsletter.

Source: Courtesy of Deutsche Bank AG.

membership).[68] Some of the members saw their party allegiance
as a way of altering the behavior of the firm. After January 1933,
the management needed to make concessions to this part of its
work force, to reorganize itself, and pay at least lip service to the
notion of a "works community" [Betriebsgemeinschaft]. Two National Socialist Factory Cell Organization (NSBO) members were
delegated to the supervisory board (Figure 9).

The bank reorganized itself so as to reflect the new German
collectivism (Figure 10). On November 30, 1933, the bank's first
ever general works meeting started with a parade of those employees who were members of the SA, the SS, and the national-
ist paramilitary association, the Stahlhelm. The bank's orchestra
played "Deutschland, Deutschland über alles" and the overture to
Richard Wagner's opera "Die Meistersinger von Nürnberg." 4,000
employees, as well as most of the management board, were present.
The member of the management board with special responsibility
for personnel matters, Karl Ernst Sippell, gave the main address,
praising the "way the new spirit of the age had penetrated the whole
Bank," promising to take into the personnel department "some
gentlemen [. . .] who are especially supported by your confidence,"
and offering new jobs as a result of vacancies created by the return
of female workers to the hearth and kitchen. "Fortunately there
is a healthy turnover of females, who provide for constant fluctu-
ation either through marriage or return to their parental house."
The NSBO representative Franz Hertel also paid tribute to the 324
new positions created by the bank in 1933. Sippell finally stated
discreetly that not everyone in the bank should be expected to be
a National Socialist. "Often it is not the worst people who despite
recognizing the high ethical stance of National Socialism nevertheless cannot reach a complete acceptance, because they see still in it
something that is not yet matured and fully balanced."[69]

A considerable amount of external pressure was applied regarding the bank's personnel policy. Within the bank, Jewish employees,
particularly in prominent positions, were removed either because
of direct party pressure (as in Breslau) or to forestall the possibility of physical attacks (as in Erfurt, where the co-director and his

Figure 10. Visit of Robert Ley, leader of Labor Front, to Deutsche Bank, October 1934 (in center of picture; behind him is the Nazi works representative, Franz Hertel).

Source: Courtesy of Deutsche Bank AG.

two most senior subordinates were Jewish).[70] In Frankfurt, a senior bank official (*Prokurist*) was forced to take early retirement in June 1933 at the age of 55: the memorandum explaining the move only stated that it was "taking account of circumstances."[71]

During the first months of the National Socialist regime, bank branches were occasionally assaulted by revolutionary National Socialists. In Pirmasens, an adjutant of the District Commission appeared to inform the Deutsche Bank's manager that permission was needed for withdrawals by Jewish customers. In Frankenthal (Palatinate) two SA men demanded to inspect a list of Jewish accounts, but the bank manager refused and appealed for protection to the Lord Mayor.[72] In Duisburg, the local party leadership demanded that the bank take down a swastika flag on the grounds that "Jewish enterprises" should not be allowed to raise the banner of the national movement. In Hirschberg in Silesia the local party launched a series of slide lectures with the theme "How they Fiddled – How they Swindled," which included a list of "speculators" from the Deutsche Bank including Stauss and Millington-Herrmann (who were not Jewish), Steinthal, Michalowsky, Fehr, Wassermann, Nathan (mistakenly – he was at the Dresdner Bank), and Solmssen and his father Salomonsohn.[73]

Such pressure from local party organizations and agencies continued through the 1930s. The Labor Front (DAF) in Görlitz responded to the 1935 Nuremberg racial laws by complaining that among the 68 employees of the bank in that city there was a "half-Jewish" female (*Halbjüdin*). A letter from the DAF to the Deutsche Bank works council started with an explanation about the new law, and then added: "Since in addition many thousand fellow Germans are still out of work, and should have access to the advantages of a workplace in preference to non-Aryans, I think it right to demand that you secure a clarification of this issue and an end to this injustice." A few months later, in January 1936, the Deutsche Bank indeed dismissed the employee concerned, with effect from September 1936. The letter of dismissal added that "our efforts to secure a position for you in another branch of our bank regrettably came to naught."[74]

Party hostility came from the center as well as from local party organizations, but for a while at the central state level it was restrained by considerations of Realpolitik. Fundamentally, anything connected with banking and its social world was suspect. In 1934, for instance, the party authorities and the SS turned their attention to a Berlin club, which had traditionally been a meeting place for bankers. The "Gesellschaft der Freunde" (Society of Friends) had been founded in 1792, and its members included Hjalmar Schacht as well as his predecessor as Reichsbank President, Hans Luther, and almost all the past and present managing directors of the Deutsche Bank. The club's president in 1932 had been the speaker of the Deutsche Bank's management board, Oscar Wassermann; and when Wassermann and Frank left the management board, they also left the club, and their places there were taken also by their successors in the bank. Rudolf Hess's office had determined that the club represented an "economic secret society," "which in the economic area represents an almost unassailable because camouflaged and non-transparent bloc – thanks to the composition of its members and their secret cross-contacts." The SS, however, decided that although this was a sinister and unhealthy organization, it could not be banned under the provisions devised for masonic lodges.[75]

The Nuremberg racial laws changed the climate, and the pressure of the party and in particular of the central leadership of the DAF to remove Jews was now universal. In the course of 1936, the bank issued dismissals (usually with a six-month notice period, as in the Görlitz case) to those employees classified as entirely Jewish (*Volljuden*) in the Nuremberg laws. Those employed for over ten years usually received a pension; those employed for less time were given a sum in lieu of pension claims, of up to one year's salary.[76] A list prepared in December 1936 (i.e. after a substantial amount of purging had already taken place) of the bank's remaining Jewish employees lists 103 employees in Germany, and in addition eleven in Istanbul and three in Kattowitz (Katowice), then in Poland. Four employees held the title of director: Richard Heidenfeld in Berlin, Ernst Frankl in Freiburg, Heinrich Mayer in Mainz, as well as Edmund Goldenberg in Istanbul. The personnel director's copy of that list, which survives, is marked with lines through each of the German employees, presumably drawn after each dismissal. Goldenberg was replaced in 1938 but remained in Turkey.[77]

In October 1939, the bank noted that twenty-nine pensions of Jews had been bought out and that there were seventy-two pensions paid to pensioners or widows by the Berlin central office, and another 142 by the bank's branches. The issue had become controversial because of the intervention once more of the DAF and the works council of the Freiburg branch [*Vertrauensrat*], which pointed to a verdict of the Reich court [*Reichsgericht*] in July 1939, reprinted in part in the Nazi newspaper *Der Angriff* in September 1939. The ruling of the court allowed a reduction of pensions paid to Jewish employees dismissed "in the course of the political development," but it was left unclear whether such reductions could be applied to those dismissed (as almost all the Deutsche Bank's employees had been) before the proclamation of the November 12, 1938 decree on the exclusion of Jews from business life [*Verordnung zur Ausschaltung der Juden aus dem deutschen Wirtschaftsleben*]. The bank took the attitude that it should *not* reduce pensions, and the personnel director confirmed this view by meeting State Secretary Hans Pfundtner, the man responsible for drawing up the plan for reduced pensions, in Garmisch. Pfundtner explained the long-term policy but added: "at the moment such a measure is not planned, in consideration of its effects on neutral countries abroad and of our business relations with foreign countries; but there is a firm commitment to abandon this self-restraint. We don't need to be so reticent, but will leave the precise formulation of the policy to a later point in time."[78] The personnel director explained this logic to the works council, which had presented cases in which it claimed the pension payments should be reduced.

A memorandum of 1940 listed twelve Jewish pensioners of the bank as living abroad, and forty-three living in Germany (two of those living abroad, and twenty of those in Germany were female).[79] The 11th Decree on the Reich Citizenship Law of November 25, 1941 confiscated the assets of Jews living abroad (and of those deported), and after this the Deutsche Bank stopped some pension payments.[80] At the beginning of 1943, the central office was still paying twenty pensions, and the branches thirty-one. By the end of April 1944, the respective figures were seven and twelve (and a tabulation explained that the numbers had been reduced by recall (*Widerruf*) of the pension and by death (*Ableben*).[81]

Sometimes, as the pensions debate of 1939 showed, pressure to change personnel policy came not from the outside but from the banks' own employees. A bank inevitably responds to the sentiments and instincts of the mass of its employees and to their conception of the way the institution should function. Some of this anti-Semitic pressure from below also preceded the Nazi seizure of power, and there is some evidence of individual cases of anti-Semitism before 1933. In 1921, for instance, in a discussion about a senior position in the bank in Danzig, a member of the management board wrote: "I note that Herr Heidenfeld is confessionally Jewish, but see no problems in Danzig in the light of the major position occupied by Herr Willstätter; apart from that it is impossible to see that Heidenfeld is Jewish." But seven years later, when the same man, Richard Heidenfeld, wanted to move back to his old home in Leipzig, he was passed over for the senior position, and the bank's Berlin personnel office noted: "apart from other qualities, his confession played a part."[82] Before 1933 many disaffected men and women had joined the party, and after 1933 came the opportunists. It was clearly tempting after the Nazi Revolution to use party membership as part of a bid for promotion. Usually this was not a successful strategy, and the bank's management clearly both resented and resisted it. Karl Ernst Sippell, the senior bank director responsible for personnel issues, reprimanded the offenders quite bluntly. He told one ambitious National Socialist in charge of the Bochum branch: "as a National Socialist he should have increased duties and not merely more privileges," and he refused to allow the inclusion of quotations from *Mein Kampf* in the work regulations for the Bochum branch of the bank.[83]

Such conflicts illustrate the extent to which the German *Zeitgeist* had been transformed. The social and political climate encouraged denunciations, not just on racial or political grounds. Very rapidly, Germany became a country of informers who took their knowledge and their tittle-tattle to the Gestapo and the party, but also to business managers.[84] The files of the Deutsche Bank reflect the challenges faced by the institution in the new age. One of the directors of the Leipzig branch complained that the other director had engaged in an affair with his housekeeper, was driving her to meetings and social occasions, was alienating customers, and was also making bad loans. The denouncer quoted the housekeeper involved as saying: "When Herr V. is sick, she is obliged to lie in bed with him. Herr V. demands the same thing when he comes home drunk. She needs to wean him off bringing street whores back home." The complaint concluded "It is thus not a matter of a 'lady,' but of a 'relationship.'" But Sippell took the line that "the bank cannot concern itself with the personal lives of its branch directors" and

Figure 11. Karl Ernst Sippell: Member of management board 1933–45.

Source: Courtesy of Deutsche Bank AG.

obliged the denouncer (and not the alleged fornicator) to move to a much less desirable branch.[85]

Moral, political, and racial complaints continued to accumulate. It is hardly surprising that Sippell (Figure 11) had soon found the strain of dealing with both the new social climate and the party's personnel demands intolerable. He felt humiliated and burned out and believed that he could no longer continue to manage the personnel department [*Personaldezernat*]. The bank realized that the issues involved required the direction of someone who was himself a trusted party member.[86] In December 1935, a new personnel director was appointed to replace Sippell, Karl Ritter von Halt (Figure 12), who had come from the Munich private bank Aufhäuser.[87] Halt filled the intended role perfectly: he had been a war hero in the Great War, had been wounded on three separate occasions, and had received a Bavarian knighthood.[88] He also was awarded the Austrian Military Cross–Third Class, and the Bavarian Military Cross–Fourth Class.[89] After the war he had

Figure 12. Karl Ritter von Halt: Personnel director, and member of management board 1938–45.

Source: Courtesy of Deutsche Bank AG.

distinguished himself principally as a horseman and athlete; and above all he was a member of the NSDAP. He organized in 1936 the Winter Olympic games in Garmisch and made sports a major part of the life of each Deutsche Bank employee. In Berlin, he frequented the Hotel Kaiserhof, located close to the Reich Chancellery, where many of the most powerful Nazi leaders liked to relax.[90] In 1938, he was promoted to the management board of the bank.

Von Halt's appointment constituted a defensive move by the bank in the face of the new *Zeitgeist* as much as accommodation. The appointment seems to have been a rather well calculated move on the part of the Deutsche Bank. On the one hand, there was no doubt that von Halt would look to the outside world, and to the bank's employees, like a representative of the new movement. On the other hand, he had experience in the bank, and it quickly became clear that he considered his primary loyalty as lying with the institution and not with any external party agency. In this sense von Halt's appointment would bring protection against political pressures for further accommodation. One of his major achievements was to divert party political militancy into athleticism. Some even remember him exhorting the managing directors to become more vigorous physically.[91] Sport was a way of introducing the values of the New Germany and was accompanied by other attempts to raise the productivity of employees. "High achievement," Halt pronounced, "is the Führerprinzip of the German economy." Internal works competitions would promote knowledge of bank economics, foreign languages, shorthand, and typing.[92] Branches also formed sport associations, as well as orchestras and choirs.

Halt successfully tamed part of the National Socialist threat inside the bank. After protracted negotiations with the German Labor Front (DAF) and the Berlin party Gauleitung, he was allowed to dismiss the NSBO representative Franz Hertel (Figure 13), the keynote speaker of the 1933 works assembly, who had tried to make himself the head of a movement to completely reform the bank politically in the sense of National Socialist revolutionary doctrine. After the war, a Deutsche Bank submission to the court [*Spruchkammer*] dealing with Hertel's "denazification" stated that he had frequently worked with the Gestapo. "He managed to declare even slight anti-fascist statements, or the avoidance of a Hitler salute, or the reading of non-Nazi newspapers, or insufficient donations to the party, as the expression of an anti-fascist attitude, and to persecute and even remove such people." To remove Hertel, the bank provided enthusiastic testimonials, and a large cash payment (RM 20,000, over forty times his monthly salary). Hertel rapidly became a "Hauptsturmführer" in the SS and went on to a grand-scale career as an "Aryanizer." At first he worked in the Haupttreuhandstelle Ost, the institution that took over Polish (and Jewish) property in Poland. He then took over for himself a large department store in Prague (the Haus der Geschenke) and then bought Czech Jewish real estate. After the war, he tried (unsuccessfully) to petition for compensation for the loss of his Czech property.[93]

Figure 13. Franz Hertel, NSBO works representative of Deutsche Bank 1933–6.

Source: Courtesy of Deutsche Bank AG.

Hertel was not an isolated case of employee activism within the Deutsche Bank: in Stuttgart, Breslau, Görlitz, and Magdeburg other party members of works councils were dismissed.[94]

A defensive operation alone could not contain the claims of the *Zeitgeist*. In reality, there were many concessions to the New Order. The duties of the bank counter staff were defined so that they became representatives of the state, not the bank, and of what the state taught as propaganda. The clerk was to explain to customers that interest reductions were necessary, were ordered uniformly by the Reich Commissar, and were good for the economy: "these measures would support the economic development of the Third Reich."[95] The NSBO participated actively in the redefinition of the workplace. It instructed, for instance, female employees not to dress fashionably and conspicuously – not to be "fashion ladies." "Everyone should know that simple dresses and blouses can be made and altered for relatively little money."[96]

The change of name and the elimination of the complicated "Deutsche Bank und Disconto–Gesellschaft" in 1937 may have been intended to help the bank's public and political image. The previous title had been cumbersome and commercial; in the widely used shortened form "DeDi Bank" it sounded ridiculous, like a "childish drawl."[97] As the managing director Karl Kimmich noted in 1937: "The name 'Deutsche Bank' is in any case so good that were it not already there, it would have to be invented."[98]

Banks and "Non-Aryan" Business

The government's and party's attitudes, and particularly their anti-Semitic policies, had a major effect on the relationship of banks with the rest of German business. A mixture of official pressure and threats from below led to the removal of many Jewish company directors. Bank directors played their part in this development. In some branches, as in Kassel, they took the initiative.[99] Believed by National Socialist ideologues to be all powerful, represented on many *Aufsichtsräte*, often holding the chairmanship, the Deutsche Bank was inevitably involved in what amounted in practice to a large-scale purge of German economic life.

Two examples will show how the bank became enmeshed in the policies of the new regime. Lorenz Hutschenreuther AG in Selb, where the Deutsche Bank supervisory board chairman Franz Urbig held the chair of the supervisory board, was one of Germany's most famous manufacturers of porcelain, with a substantial and important export market. In October 1933, two NSDAP functionaries replaced representatives of the Weimar Republic work council on the supervisory board. They immediately demanded the dismissal of Jewish members of the board, including the manager of the Mannheim branch of the Deutsche Bank, Ludwig Fuld. The firm felt sensitive because, as it argued, 90 percent of its domestic sales were made through retailers organized in a party retailing organization, the Nationalsozialistische Handels-, Handwerks- und Gewerbe-Organisation (NS-Hago), which might impose a boycott of the firm's products.[100] Urbig responded by attempting to secure the voluntary resignation of the members of the supervisory board who had been attacked, but two refused to give way, pointing out the dangers of compliance (yielding on this issue would be an "ostrich policy"[101]) and adding the commercial argument that obvious and visible acceptance of the National Socialist racial priorities would damage the company's export order book.

For a year, nothing happened and the Jewish supervisory board members stayed in place. Then the party renewed its offensive, through the local party boss. He summoned the manager of Hutschenreuther to come to the town's Brown House and explain himself. When the manager explained that he could not remove a member of the supervisory board, the district party boss (*Kreisleiter*) claimed that this should properly be the responsibility of the Deutsche Bank. "Herr K. [Kreisleiter Kellermann] then asked the question, whether the Deutsche Bank could not decide by itself as a result of its share-holdings or power of attorney [...] Herr K. then explained that one would have to assume that either the Deutsche Bank did not want to intervene – though this was unthinkable – or that because of the capital structure it could not intervene."[102] The tactic of putting pressure on the central office in Berlin to influence local conditions proved eminently successful. As a result of the renewed, and more insistent, pressure from Urbig, the two members of the supervisory board resigned their seats.

The second example concerns Johannes Jeserich AG (Berlin), a major building firm with road contracts all over Germany, especially in the north. Dependency on public sector orders made a company of this sort especially vulnerable to political pressure. On April 1, 1933, the day of a nationwide anti-Jewish boycott, four representatives of the National Socialist Factory Cell Organization walked into a director's office and demanded the immediate dismissal of the company's Jewish employees. The director, Lothar Fuld, who himself was Jewish, responded at once by terminating the contracts of just two workers. But the action of the Jeserich employees turned out to be only the beginning of a much bigger campaign. The company directors were themselves extremely vulnerable. The State Commissar for Building responsible for Berlin, Government Building Master Fuchs, rejected Jeserich bids for road repair work on the grounds that "this was a Jewish enterprise." The NSBO Charlottenburg then demanded the removal of the Jewish directors – Fuld and Stern.[103] The two directors went without making any protest, and at a meeting of the supervisory board on April 13 the bank representatives, who included Ludwig Fuld from the Deutsche Bank Mannheim (who was Jewish), as well as Director Benz from Berlin, agreed "that one should agree to the requests of Fuld und Stern in the interest of the company, since otherwise it would no longer obtain public building contracts."[104] One of Jeserich's remaining directors, Eugen Feuchtmann, then said that it had become clear that the supervisory board required restructuring and that the five Jewish directors on the supervisory board should resign. They did. Both the supervisory board and the management board were in consequence almost entirely depleted. Feuchtmann tried to fill the vacancies with obviously politicized figures, which were at first rejected by Benz. But in the end, Benz was pressed into accepting appointments to the supervisory board which included the leader of the NSDAP party delegation in the Württemberg Landtag, Hermann Kurz, and, as the representative of the Jewish banking house of H. Aufhäuser Munich, the party member Karl Ritter von Halt.[105]

In the cases of both Hutschenreuther and Jeserich, the initial pressure for the purge came from inside the firm. In the porcelain firm, it originated from the firm's employees as reorganized, after the introduction of a new labor law, in a National Socialist "Council of Confidence." With Jeserich, the radical agitation by the workforce ultimately had its source in one of the firm's directors, who self-consciously used politics to take management into his own hands.

The use of physical violence in intimidation that had characterized 1933 diminished as the National Socialist revolution consolidated itself. By the later months of 1933, the anarchical conditions that had characterized the early months of the year were succeeded by the imposition of political centralization and the reestablishment of state authority. For the moment, official anti-Semitism seemed to abate. In the case of the reconstructed department store, Hermann Tietz & Co., where the Deutsche Bank was a member of the bank syndicate that ran a participation company (the Hertie–Kaufhaus–Beteiligungs GmbH), many of the Jewish employees were sacked: by August 1933, 500 out of a total of 1,500. But the party then made peace, and tried to build bridges to the new managers (though these improved relations were to be paid for by the department store). The SA in Karlsruhe, for instance, suggested that "our branch there should sponsor some poorer members of the SA Storm Troopers."[106]

The result of the pressure of 1933 had been that many Jewish firms were purged or sold. More followed in subsequent years. In 1932 there had been approximately 100,000 Jewish-owned firms in Germany (using a religious definition of Jewishness), while in 1935 a contemporary estimate suggested that the number had fallen to 75–80,000.[107] By the end of 1937, two-thirds of small-scale Jewish businesses had already ceased to operate, including five out of six retailers, where Jewish proprietors may have been most visible to the public eye.[108] Many of the larger firms survived until 1938, in part because their earlier elimination by official pressure would have jeopardized Germany's recovery from unemployment and depression, and this would have embarrassed the regime.

Even in the early years of the Nazi dictatorship, however, Deutsche Bank was involved in the transfer of Jewish property. In areas that the Nazi authorities felt to be very politically sensitive, enterprises were subjected to a much speedier "Aryanization." As the owner of a major sector of the German press (including the highbrow and influential *Vossische Zeitung*, the mass-circulation *BZ am Mittag* and *Berliner Morgenblatt*, and the weekly photo magazine *Berliner Illustrierte*), the Berlin publisher Ullstein clearly exercised a direct political influence that the new power elite perceived as threatening. In March 1934, a Nazi journalist, Fritz Geisler, submitted to the Reich Chancellery details of the continuing high circulation figures of the Ullstein press, with the comment: "The style and presentation of the Ullstein papers are more appreciated in extensive party circles, too, and certainly among other sections of the population."[109]

The Propaganda Ministry had already demanded the resignation of Ullstein's general director, the (Jewish) former secretary of state at the Finance Ministry, Hans Schäffer, on March 10, 1933. Hitler himself subsequently took a direct role, and on July 12, 1933 received the new "political director" of Ullstein, the conservative but not Nazi Eduard Stadler, to discuss the "bringing into line" [*Gleichschaltung*] of the publishing house. Reichsbank president Hjalmar Schacht was instructed to produce a plan for a new financial structure. He conducted most of the negotiations with a member of the Ullstein management board, Ferdinand Bausback, who had previously been the director of the Stuttgart branch of Deutsche Bank. The aim was to distribute the new shares of Ullstein widely, throughout the major German industrial and commercial firms. In this way, Schacht concluded, "the influence and predominance of the Aryan shareholder group would be assured." All "non-Aryans," with the exception of one member of the Ullstein family, would leave the management board.[110]

By 1934, the party and government took a much more radical line, demanding the transfer of the publishers to the NSDAP's Franz Eher Verlag under Max Amann, president of the Reich Press Chamber and NSDAP "Reichsleiter für Presseverwaltung." Amann told Max Winkler, who became the critical figure in establishing the nazification of the press: "Goebbels is finishing off the Jewish press."[111] The shares were bought with public money through a trustee firm, Cautio, and left on deposit with Deutsche Bank. Bausback remained as chairman of the supervisory board. The name of the company was later changed to "Deutscher Verlag." The financial details of this transaction were managed by Deutsche Bank. In June 1934, the speaker of the management board, Eduard Mosler, concluded in a minute marked "confidential":

> "Secretary of State Funk (Propaganda Ministry) confirmed today in answer to my question that the transfer of all Ullstein Verlag shares to Eher Verlag has been discussed with the Führer as well as with Dr. Goebbels and has been carried out at his instigation in the Ministry of Propaganda. He told me he had wanted Deutsche Bank to broker the transaction, saying that Deutsche Bank would thus be doing the Propaganda Ministry a great service. Everything as presented to us

had been discussed at the Ministry, he said. At my request he added that he would see to it and discuss with Herr Amann that on no account should the party press attach any disparaging criticism to the deal; he would take steps to ensure that the *Völkische Beobachter* carried an approving article."[112]

As far as can be judged by this memorandum, the main incentive for Deutsche Bank to add a cloak of respectability to this transfer was not so much financial as it was the hope that attacks on the bank from the party press (and perhaps also from the foreign exchange control authorities) would cease, or at least be bought off for a time.

In 1935, the owner of the Aronwerke Elektrizitäts AG, Berlin–Charlottenburg was subject to harassment by the party, repeatedly arrested, and sent to a concentration camp. Under this pressure, he sold his company, a leading manufacturer of radios (under the tradename "Nora") and electrical meters, to the Elektrische Licht-und Kraftanlagen AG, Berlin, which took 3,692,000 shares, and to Siemens–Schuckertwerke AG, which took 1,900,000. In addition, Deutsche Bank kept a further 724,000 shares in its deposit for the Siemens concern. The business was immediately renamed Heliowatt-Elektrizitäts AG. The shares were sold at 83–85 percent of their par value, rather than the 30 percent valuation that Nazis on the supervisory board had been pressing for. Deutsche Bank made a profit on the transaction by selling the shares to Siemens at a price of 86.5, yielding a gain of around 188,000 RM.[113] Deutsche Bank had had no previous business connection with the Aronwerke, which dealt mostly through Commerzbank. Commerzbank also took a lead in organizing the sale.

In late 1935, probably in response to the Nuremberg racial laws, the bank asked its branches to report on the extent of their exposure to credits to "non-Aryan" firms and individuals. At this time, however, irrespective of morality and immorality, there were good "economic" reasons not to "Aryanize" too rapidly. The forced sale of Jewish firms noticeably weakened the quality of German entrepreneurship. Some businessmen noticed and complained about the development. At the Cologne meetings of the

Rhineland–Westphalian *Beirat* of the Deutsche Bank, for instance, a cotton spinner, Emil Engels (of Ermen & Engels AG) stated that the "Aryanizations" had reduced the liquidity of firms in the textile branch, and their capacity to keep up payments. "Until now Jewish elements played a large role in the textile industry. The capacity to pay is sinking rapidly. Aryanization has in part resulted in firms coming under weak management, and he appealed to the bank managements to exercise great caution in managing these transactions."[114]

Virtual full employment after 1936 weakened the force of pragmatic objections to an economically irrational action. It was now the government, not the world of business, that produced a major initiative. In late 1937, Hitler specified Germany's foreign policy goals at the meeting recorded in the Hossbach protocol, explaining that neither autarky nor integration in the world economy would solve the German economic problem. Only the use of force would create an adequate economic space, "Lebensraum." At the same time foreign policy became much more radical, the regime stepped up the pace in implementing its anti-Semitic program.[115] The goal that had been frustrated in 1933 by practical considerations, the removal of those the state defined as Jews from German business life, could now be realized without encountering obstacles or objections.

At the end of 1937, Jewish business activity was restricted by a discriminatory tightening of raw material supplies.[116] On January 4, 1938, a decree defined a Jewish enterprise as one owned or dominated by Jews, in the sense that either one managing director or director was Jewish in the sense of the Nuremberg laws, or that one-quarter of the supervisory board was Jewish. On June 14, 1938 the Third Ordinance on Reich Citizenship reaffirmed the specific criteria for the assessment of what was a "Jewish" enterprise. During the course of the year attacks increased until they reached an apogee in the pogrom of the so-called Reich Crystal Night, November 9, 1938. This was followed (November 12) by an Ordinance on the Exclusion of Jews from German Economic Life, and the imposition of a 25 percent tax on assets (cynically

Figure 14. Karl Kimmich: Member of management board 1933–42, Speaker 1939–42.

Source: Courtesy of Deutsche Bank AG.

termed "Compensation Measure"). At the same time, Jewish enterprises were threatened with prosecution under existing legislation for actual or alleged "capital flight" – attempting to bring their assets to safety beyond Germany's frontiers. The transfer of Jewish property into "Aryan" hands was at first left to private initiative. Reich Economics Minister Schacht had in 1935 defined as one of the tasks that "the economy should solve on its own" "the transfer of Jewish business into Aryan hands."[117]

Throughout 1938, the number of Jewish businesses for sale increased, and banks played a major part in brokering the sales. As was traditional in German business practice, very few of these sales took place on the open market. Bank intermediation made property transfers more discreet. At the beginning of 1938, a letter of the management board to branch managers, signed by Hans Rummel and Karl Kimmich (Figure 14), asked for "a further listing of your non-aryan debit and credit accounts, and of those that would come into consideration for Aryanization [...]. In this regard we are interested in how far the Aryanization process of the respective firm has proceeded, and the extent to which you are involved." The letter added that, in accordance with the decree of January 4, firms were to be counted as Jewish even if there was only one Jewish member of the management board.[118]

The additional credit business generated as a result of "Aryanization" affected the competitive position of the German Great Banks. At a meeting of the Bavarian branch directors in June 1938, the increased "generosity" on the part of the Dresdner Bank in giving credits to allow firms to engage in "Aryanization" was discussed, but the Deutsche Bank's managing directors urged caution: "Herr Rummel pointed out specifically once more that we should not be driven off track in our credit policy. The aim of the management board is that in the foreseeable future the demand for bank credit will be so large that we will have plenty of opportunity to make good loans."[119] But the Deutsche Bank in practice certainly responded to the demand for bank loans, though a few branches of the bank, such as Leipzig, made no "Aryanization loans" at all.[120] In November 1938, shortly before Reichskristallnacht, Kimmich reported that the Deutsche Bank had participated in the "Aryanization" of 330 businesses. "The difficulties, particularly regarding personnel, are substantial. Experts with sufficient capital are thin on the ground." At this time, he estimated the total Jewish capital in Germany to amount to 6–8 billion RM.[121] A separate tabulation of the same month described 599 "major non-Aryan firms" as "dealt with," of which 303 had been "transferred to Aryan ownership or liquidated."[122]

What price was paid for properties subject to "Aryanization"? The Dresdner Bank produced a revealing memorandum in May 1938, after a visit of a bank official to the Economics Ministry, in which the valuation principles were set out. The memorandum began:

> "It is intended within a not too long time frame to either transfer to aryan ownership or liquidate all non-Aryan businesses. The appropriate specialty Economic Group or the local chamber of

commerce will have to decide whether an Aryanization is desirable. In consequence, in cases when there is an overcrowding of businesses, the liquidation of the non-Aryan firm and the transfer of inventories to aryan ownership is preferred. Apart from this the Economic Ministry does not require a forced Aryanization."

The ministry rejected the idea of particular payments to party offices:

"In general, local offices cannot make particular financial demands for the authorization of Aryanizations. It is certainly not the rule that parts of the Aryanization profit have to be transferred to party or other offices. The Economics Ministry only requires payments in cases in which the Aryan purchaser buys at an especially favorable rate because of the absence of the non-aryan seller. In these cases, the purchaser is required to make a payment to the [government owned] Golddiskontbank."

For the valuation, there should be no special calculation of a "good will" content; there should be a reserve to cover "the increased risks to the purchaser." The Gauwirtschaftsberater generally suggested an "estimation" ["Anschlag"] of 20 percent "of the capitalization of the enterprise," "so that Aryanizations are authorized on the basis of between two thirds and three quarters of the original wealth. In part, the party believes that the non-Aryan seller should receive no higher price than if the enterprise were liquidated." This information, the economics ministry official had specified, should not be made generally available "since he did not want to create the impression that a particular bank had been treated favorably."[123]

These "Aryanization" transactions took place in quite diverse circumstances. All except the very largest were managed at the branch level, rather than centrally, and the conduct of the bank's managers varied quite considerably. In most cases, there was a competitive struggle between banks to handle the deal. In that competition, Deutsche Bank's major asset was the extent of its experience as an international bank, which gave rise to hopes among the Jewish owners that the bank might help in transferring assets abroad – in the complicated circumstances of exchange control and discriminatory legislation – as part of the process of emigration.

In some of these cases, the transfer occurred through the agency of the bank because the old owners wanted the help of a reputable financial institution in preserving their life's work and also in securing their position should there by some miracle be a change in regime. In addition, they worked hard to protect their old employees. In the case of the banking houses of Mendelssohn, Berlin, and Simon Hirschland, Essen, the Deutsche Bank worked with the management to prevent the takeover of the house by the state-owned and hostile bank, the Reichs-Kredit-Gesellschaft (RKG).[124] Georg Hirschland, the managing partner of Hirschland, approached the Deutsche Bank after a conversation with a Reichsbank employee. In both the Hirschland and Mendelssohn cases, the NSDAP authorities at first vigorously opposed a sale to the Deutsche Bank. The Gauleiter of Essen, Josef Terboven, insisted that it would have been far preferable to liquidate Hirschland.[125] From the point of view of the banks, a critical consideration lay in the substantial credit lines extended from foreign institutions and which fell under the provisions of the agreements on German short-term external debt, the so-called "Stillhalte-Abkommen" (Standstill Agreements). If the partners of the German banks emigrated, they would continue in law to remain personally liable to the foreign (British or American) creditors. It was therefore essential to secure the voluntary agreement of the foreign creditors to the transfer of the credit lines to another institution. But these foreign creditors wanted the best possible security for their claims, through the liability of an institution with a solid reputation, such as the Deutsche Bank, and not a politically run and state-controlled bank such as the RKG. The Deutsche Bank had a particularly powerful position in the standstill negotiations, as its Managing Director Gustaf Schlieper was the head of the German bankers' delegation.

Mendelssohn was one of the oldest names in German banking. The bank had been created in 1795 by Joseph Mendelssohn, the oldest son of the Enlightenment philosopher Moses Mendelssohn. Franz von Mendelssohn played a major part in the business and industrial politics of the Kaiserreich and the Weimar Republic as President of the "Deutscher Industrie- und Handelstag" and was also a member of the Reichsbank's general council [*Generalrat*]. In the 1920s, for the first time three non-members of the family became partners: Paul Kempner, Rudolf Löb, and Fritz Mannheimer (who, however, conducted most of his business in Amsterdam). But they only held a minority of the shares, and three-quarters of the bank's capital remained in the hands of the family.

Mendelssohn remained a successful bank for the first five years of the Nazi regime and continued to be a member of the syndicate issuing government debt. But it was riven by internal tension, both within the family and among the employees. In 1935 Franz von Mendelssohn and Paul von Mendelssohn-Bartholdy both died, and the internal agreement regarding the distribution of property within the dynasty was consequently reworked. In November 1937 Franz's widow Marie von Mendelssohn (née Westphal) was entered in the commercial register as managing partner [*persönlich haftende Gesellschafterin*], but Paul's widow Elsa was not. Some of the employees began to worry about their future, either fearing that a Jewish-owned bank could not survive or hoping to step into the shoes of the Jewish partners and take over the business.[126]

In the course of 1938, the pressure to exclude the remaining Jews in the bank increased. The vice-president of the Reichsbank, Fritz Dreyse, spoke with Löb and explained that the bank would face increased pressure ("for political reasons, difficulties must increasingly be reckoned with"). The "Reich Commissar for Credit," Friedrich Ernst, also advised Löb to begin immediately with preparations for "Aryanization." Dreyse told Löb that the Reichs-Kredit-Gesellschaft (RKG) was willing to buy the bank, and Löb replied, according to Hermann Abs's account of the transaction, that he would rather deal with Deutsche Bank and Abs (who had only just joined Deutsche Bank, having previously been a partner of Delbrück Schickler). Thus he went immediately from Dreyse's office in the Reichsbank to see Abs.[127]

According to the takeover plan, 68 m. RM in assets and liabilities were to be transferred to Deutsche Bank, and 2 m. RM were not taken over. The customers ("the customer business in its entirety") were all assumed by Deutsche Bank. Deutsche Bank did not pay a particular sum for the new business: the assets and liabilities were simply transferred and the outstanding balance paid. The remaining firm (Mendelssohn in Liquidation) kept the capital of the bank and foreign assets and some German assets that could not be liquidated. In addition it retained the real estate. According to the agreement, Deutsche Bank would also take over the non-Jewish employees, and for a period of three years it would pay them at the higher rates customary in Mendelssohn. (This had been one of the most contentious points in Abs's negotiations with his bank.) Deutsche Bank also took over the pension obligations of Mendelssohn. At the time, the journal *Die Bank* commented: "Meanwhile it would in no way accord with the facts were one to seek by such historical reminiscences to point in the Mendelssohn case to a desire for expansion on the part of Deutsche Bank. As has already been suggested, the causes of the transfer are different here. All the same, Deutsche Bank will welcome the additional business."[128]

The Jewish employees were to be dismissed, and on December 5, three days after the Reich Economics Ministry agreed to the plan, Löb, Kempner, Mannheimer, and Marie von Mendelssohn all left the bank. Löb, who changed his first name to Rodolfo, went first to Buenos Aires, then to the United States. Kempner went via London to New York. As a result of the Reichsbank's judgment that he had been helpful in the question of negotiating the transfer of foreign credits to Deutsche Bank, he was allowed to take some of his personal furniture with him. Otherwise he was left with only 50,000 RM. Löb was permitted to transfer 210,000 RM.

On December 1, 1938, the bank was liquidated. *Bank-Archiv* commented that this liquidation "heralds the final phase of the Aryanization of the private-banking industry," while emphasizing that the special role of Deutsche Bank made this an "exception."[129]

Mendelssohn in Liquidation was renamed in 1943 as *von* Mendelssohn & Co., i.L. In 1941 Elsa von Mendelssohn-Bartholdy, the widow of Paul von Mendelssohn-Bartholdy (after a remarriage now Countess Kesselstadt) left the partnership, as did Giulietta von Mendelssohn, at the beginning of 1942, leaving Robert von Mendelssohn as the only partner, and Ferdinand Kremer as one of the two "liquidators with authority to sign." By 1943, the liquidation had almost been completed, and there remained only some Hungarian investments, real estate, and "compensation claims vis-à-vis the German Reich" on the asset side, with 4 m. RM in liabilities. The bank in liquidation eventually moved to the premises of Deutsche Bank (the Deutsche Bank Kameradschaftshaus at Behrenstrasse 15) after a bombing raid destroyed the previous offices in a Reichsbank building.[130]

When the former "liquidator," Ferdinand Kremer, prepared a report for OMGUS after the war on the takeover by Deutsche Bank (in which he too praised the role of Abs), he mentioned that in the course of negotiations the intention was developed "to revive the firm of Mendelssohn & Co. as soon as the right political and economic conditions obtain." But this aspiration was never realized.[131]

In preempting the RKG in "Aryanizations," the Deutsche Bank assisted the rightful owners of Mendelssohn and Hirschland and enabled them to take a greater part of their assets with them than would have been allowed had they worked through the state banks. But at the same time it also helped to fulfill government expectations of a rapid "Aryanization" of the banking system and thus facilitated the accomplishment of a Nazi objective. By the beginning of 1939, the SS Security Office (Reichssicherheitshauptamt) was able to report: "Aryanizations" in banking have been accomplished successfully, with the help of the private banks, especially the Deutsche Industriebank, the Reichs-Kredit-Gesellschaft, and the Deutsche Bank."[132]

Another example of a cooperative "Aryanization" was the Deutsche Bank's involvement with the German portion of the Petschek concern, a vast empire of coal (primarily lignite) fields controlled by four German–Czech brothers, Ernst, Wilhelm, Karl, and Frank Petschek. The Petscheks' most important property in Germany lay in Upper Silesia and was administered by a trust company, German Coal Trading Corporation (Deutsche Kohlen-handel GmbH), and its assets attracted Germany's biggest and most powerful mining firms: Wintershall, Salzdetfurth, Central German Steel (Mitteldeutsche Stahlwerke), Bubiag (Lignite and Briquette Company), Henckel von Donnersmarck-Beuthen, Gräflich Schaffgott'sche Werke, Deutsche Erdöl-AG, IG Farben, and above all the Flick group. All approached the trustee. The lignite fields were eventually sold mostly to Flick as part of an exchange of property in which Flick would sell hard coal resources to the Reichswerke "Hermann Göring."[133]

But there was also a much smaller Petschek field in western Germany. In this case there appears to have been no rush of interested companies. Of the ordinary shares of the Petschek-owned Hubertus AG, 73.6 percent were owned by Helimont AG Glarus and Deutsche Industrie AG, which formed part of an extensive industrial empire of the Czech part of the Petschek dynasty. Minority participations included 16.2 percent held by the Abs family of Bonn: Legal Counselor Josef Abs, and his sons Clemens and Hermann Abs (who in 1938 joined the management board of the Deutsche Bank). The "Aryanization" started with an accusation from the tax office (Oberfinanzpräsident Hanover) that the Hubertus AG had organized a flight of 70 m. RM. In October 1938, the firm was obliged to present a complete list of accounts, liabilities, and assets held abroad.[134] A decree of the Reich Economics Ministry in January 1939 then obliged the Petschek group to sell Hubertus by the end of February. This transaction was managed by the Deutsche Bank, which sold Hubertus AG to the Abs family interests organized in the Erft–Bergbau AG for the not unreasonable sum of 5,750,000 RM. This represented a valuation of Hubertus shares at 205 based on the current stock exchange quotation (the average bourse notation for the period July 1938 to March 1939 had been 203). For a company whose gross profit in 1937 had been 327,000 RM the stock exchange valuation seems appropriate.[135] In 1950 a West German court established that this sum undervalued Hubertus by some 860,000 RM.[136] There is no doubt that throughout the sale, the Petscheks had confidence in the character and trustworthiness of Hermann Abs, their former junior partner, and that Abs assisted after 1945 in the restoration of their position.

Through the great expropriations of 1937–9, the government also insisted that banks act as its agent in collecting information on Jewish assets. The Deutsche Bank at the same time used the data compiled for this purpose to attempt to buy its own shares from Jewish clients and re-sell them to other bank customers.[137]

Some estimate of the scale of the "Aryanization" business is provided by figures from the Frankfurt branch, which indicate that in 1938 35 m. RM deposits and 15 m. RM of the credits were "non-Aryan." 16.5 percent of the overall business of the branch was regarded as "non-Aryan."[138] This branch undoubtedly saw "Aryanization" as a threat to its business and not in any sense as an opportunity. It weakened the bank, and it brought politics further into the world of finance. For the bank as a whole, we have only data regarding credits. Credits to "non-Aryans" fell rapidly: in October 1935 they had amounted to 13.6 percent of the bank's overall exposure ("incorporated total accounts receivable"), but by July 1937 the sum had fallen to 7.3 percent, indicating the extent to which Jewish business activity in Germany had declined. By the end of November 1938, that ratio had fallen even further, to 3.1 percent (or 69.8 m. RM).[139]

How far was the economic drive against the Jews driven by personal anti-Semitism on the part of bank agents, as well as by a desire for profit? Some bank managers added anti-Semitic invective to their business correspondence. The director of the Hildesheim branch informed his colleague in Hanover in relation to the sale of Metall- und Farbwerke A. G., Oker, that "the content of the same is well-suited to establishing how Jewish infamy has contrived in recent years to exploit this enterprise for itself alone. [...] I am glad, at any rate, to be able to prove that from the start of my managerial activity I have been unrelenting in my efforts to lance this boil."[140] There are at least a few instances of localities where the bank clearly swindled Jewish businessmen. In Rheydt, when L. Stern & Co., a large shoe factory with 2,309 employees, was sold in November 1938 at a cheap price to its managers, the owner repaid to Deutsche Bank the credit secured on his property. But because the new owners could offer no adequate security for their credit, the bank simply retained Stern's mortgage liability.[141]

While smaller transactions remained an affair of the local bank branches, the biggest cases were handled at the bank's central office. The largest and most complicated industrial "Aryanization" conducted directly by Deutsche Bank, and managed directly from Berlin with the involvement of management-board members over years, was Norddeutsche Lederwerke, which was originally called Adler & Oppenheimer. As with Mendelssohn and Hirschland, the legal expropriation of the owners required the participation of a bank with a wide range of foreign contacts and experience. Because of the complexity of the transaction, and because the enterprise was not a purely German one, the "Aryanization" was not completed in peacetime unlike in the vast majority of German cases. The result was that the seizure of the enterprise became enmeshed in the politics of the wartime occupation regime. As with the transfer of the Jewish-owned banks, Deutsche Bank was in a strange semi-competitive relationship with a state-owned bank: in this case, as with Mendelssohn, the Reichs-Kredit-Gesellschaft.

Adler & Oppenheimer (A & O) had been founded in Strasbourg in 1872, became a joint-stock company in 1900, and moved from Alsace to Berlin in 1920. By the 1920s, it had become one of Germany's largest leather producers. It had a nominal capital in 1937 of 18 m. RM and had factories in Neustadt (Mecklenburg) and Neumünster (Holstein). Its business benefited from the recovery of the 1930s, but after 1936 its foreign sales, which had been an important element in the firm's traditional repertoire, fell off very sharply.

Most of the shares were held by the original Adler and Oppenheimer families via a Dutch intermediary, N. V. Amsterdamsche Leder Maatschappij (often called Almy), Amsterdam, that had been founded in 1919 with a modest capitalization of 50,000 HFl to facilitate the import of raw materials.

The leading role in the "Aryanization" of the company was taken by the energetic newcomer to the Deutsche Bank's management board, Hermann Abs, who became chairman of A & O's supervisory board in August 1938. A few weeks before, he had been approached by a newly appointed management-board member of A & O, Ernst Steinbeck, who stated that he would ask the Dutch shareholders of his company "whether and on what conditions sale and repatriation (not to say Aryanization) are possible."[142] Steinbeck had been placed in the company as a result of German pressure to ensure its Germanization, which of course meant "Aryanization." Deutsche Bank, as the lead manager of a syndicate which also included the Reichs-Kredit-Gesellschaft, Delbrück Schickler & Co., and Pferdmenges & Co.,[143] started to buy up shares in A & O at a price of 106 percent of the nominal value from Jewish customers, including many who had emigrated. Between September 1938 and May 1939, a total of 617,000 RM was bought in this way. It is quite surprising that these transactions continued even after the outbreak of war in September 1939 across enemy lines in the "phoney war."[144] In 1940, Deutsche Bank bought another 9,528,000 RM shares belonging to the Adler and Oppenheimer families.

There was a great deal of interest in the future of A & O. The party and especially its representatives in the Reich Economics Ministry who saw their mission as protecting the interests of small and medium-sized business [*Mittelstand*] were hostile to the idea that a major business might form the basis for an even larger concentration of economic power, especially in what had been a classically *Mittelstand* branch of industry. Some suggested that the concern should be taken over by the parastate labor organization, the German Labor Front (DAF). A & O was a major military supplier, and this status allowed the firm to import the leather required for its business. In the struggle that Deutsche Bank conducted against party influence, the military played the part of a helpful ally, as the command was interested above all in securing a continued reliable supply of leather.[145]

Initially, a major part of Abs's negotiations on the transfer of A & O into non-Jewish hands was conducted abroad, during repeated business trips. But there were also many large German businesses interested in acquiring the firm. The big south-German leather and shoe producer Freudenberg was blocked by the Reich Economics Ministry, which wanted to prevent oligopolization in the leather industry. Cornelius Heyl A. G. Worms (a large leather producer with a capitalization of 12 m. RM) wanted to acquire a minority participation to stop the DAF from acquiring the business.[146] The Reich Economics Ministry also blocked the Heyl bid.[147] In 1940 a plan by the Margarine-Union to undertake the acquisition fell through.

At first, the most promising customer for A & O was a large Dutch multinational. At the beginning of 1939, Unilever proposed to take a substantial minority participation in A & O, on condition that Deutsche Bank would also take a participation and thus hold a majority of the shares together with Unilever.[148] At some time in the future, presumably when political conditions in Germany changed, Unilever would be able easily to acquire a clear controlling majority. By July 1939, Abs had reached an agreement with the Dutch representatives of Unilever that envisaged a 12 percent participation of Deutsche Bank and an overall commission of 3 percent for the bank.[149] But when he set out his plan, and the alternatives for German ownership, in a discussion at the Reich Economics Ministry, government officials straightforwardly rejected the plan, explaining that they would not undertake "definitive recognition of the enterprise as a German and Aryan operation."[150] Abs complained that it was almost impossible to find alternatives: he "described it as very hard to find potential buyers as long as the shares remained in Dutch hands and acquisition of them uncertain."[151] From the official standpoint, however, it was crucial to have such a major firm in exclusively German control but at the same time not in the hands of another major corporation. The Reich Economics Ministry thus suggested that Deutsche Bank should form a syndicate to take over the shares and then gradually place them on the market.

Obviously the outbreak of war put a final end to any of the foreign discussions about a sale. But through 1940, there remained a continuous flow of visitors and suggestions to Abs and Deutsche

Bank with proposals about the future of A & O. One leather specialist wanted to pull in the Quandt family to finance the transaction.[152] The Stuttgart branch of Deutsche Bank reported that the big shoe producer Salamander A. G. wanted to buy the company.[153]

In May 1940 the Reich Economics Ministry instructed Abs to drop the name A & O and manage the company as "Norddeutsche Lederwerke."[154] The German invasion of the Netherlands and the integration of the country in the German New Order solved the problem of acquiring foreign exchange to buy out the Dutch interests. On May 3, Deutsche Bank manager Elkmann visited the Reich Economics Ministry to speak with the official responsible in the Jewish Affairs Department, Assessor Möhrke. He added to the minutes: "The Jewish Affairs Department is also in agreement that we should effect the Aryanization in Holland. However, no prior written authorization from the Jewish Affairs Department is necessary for this. All that is required is for us to have been given oral consent." Elkmann explained that the bank was in a hurry to finish the business and had become exasperated with the bureaucratic complexities of the transfer ("we are very keen to speed things up"). The Reich Economics Ministry then explained that it would help if another part of the German bureaucracy became involved and if the bank were to liaise with the NSDAP's "Foreign Organization." Meanwhile, Abs continued to buy up any blocks of A & O shares he could find.[155]

Transferring the shares proved to be much more difficult than the German bankers had initially thought. In October 1940 a meeting at the Reich Economics Ministry took place to negotiate the "Aryanization" of the foreign shares of the Adler and Oppenheimer families. Some shares had been used as a security for a bank loan from the Amsterdamsche Bank and had been deposited in the United States (these were worth about 1.5 m. HFl – almost 2 m. RM). Of those shares held by family members, 9 percent belonged to persons who were now resident in Britain, and these shares could be regarded under German law as "enemy property."

But 30 percent belonged to family members in France, where obviously no similar argument could be made after the armistice. The Dutch representatives of Almy proposed a plan to transfer the family shares to Almy, which would then pay the purchase price from the profits of the company. Abs proposed an alternate solution: that assets and inventories in the United States could be used to make the payments, even though they had been blocked by both U.S. Treasury orders and instructions of the Netherland government in exile in London.

When the Reich Economics Ministry meeting continued it was joined not only by a representative of the Dutch Affairs Department [Holland-Referat] but also by Assessor Möhrke of the Jewish Affairs Department.[156] The owners were in fact in quite a strong position, because neither the German occupation authorities nor Deutsche Bank had access to the shares of Almy.

Clemens Oppenheimer, negotiating for the family from a base in Ascona (Switzerland), stated as conditions for a transfer of the shares that its assets in the U.S. should be released, that the German purchasers should make a substantial dollar payment, and that the family members living in Europe should be given permission to travel to Portugal.[157] At this point, the occupation authorities tried to put further pressure on the Adler and Oppenheimer families through one of the most familiar persecutory tricks of the 1930s: claims for vast tax arrears. In early 1941, the firm faced 4.3 m. RM in tax payments as a result of the calculation of the profit they had taken on the devaluation of the Dutch guilder in 1937. Abs noted: "Impossible to effect placement now."[158] In consequence, the amount of foreign exchange that Deutsche Bank was willing to transfer decreased, but it eventually transferred $600,000 via Switzerland, using a convoluted path to mask the nature of the transaction.

By the end of 1940, Deutsche Bank had thus acquired three-quarters of the total capital of the company (18 m. RM), which it proposed to sell to the German investing public.[159] The bank was rewarded with a commission. Originally a 1.5 percent commission had been proposed, but in the final document on the sale this figure has been crossed out and (with a date of July 3, 1943) 120,000 RM substituted.[160] But there was also a more substantial gain for the bank derived from the issuing of Nordleder shares. The Reich Economics Ministry now stipulated that the shares should be distributed widely to mop up liquidity and offer the investing public something other than war loans and treasury bills. Deutsche Bank disliked this concept, which it viewed as a blocking effort by the Reichs-Kredit-Gesellschaft. Abs was prepared to make concessions such as offering an "Aryanization quota" and putting a Reichs-Kredit-Gesellschaft banker on the supervisory board of Nordleder.[161] Deutsche Bank instructed its branches not to engage in a wide sales effort and not to leave prospectuses for the issue on its counters. Thus the second element of profit from the Nordleder transaction was the difference between the purchase price of shares (106 in Germany) and the issue price of 140. In addition, there was another commission arising from the bank's management of the issuing syndicate. After the sale in the summer of 1941, Deutsche Bank then set about reducing the capital of the firm, as the firm's sales (which lay between 25 m. RM and 30 m. RM annually in the first four years of the war) looked disappointingly small in relation to the capitalization at 18 m. RM.[162]

This was a large transaction that had initially, in 1938, looked relatively simple. The first major difficulty, which postponed the sale, lay in getting government consent, because the Reich Economics Ministry resolutely blocked the involvement of either foreign or large German corporations. Secondly, because the owners held their shares through a Dutch corporation, they were in a powerful bargaining position, quite distinct from the overwhelming majority of "Aryanization" sales.

The occupation of the Netherlands gave the bank a new opportunity to press ahead with the transaction. To do this, it needed to negotiate with more layers of German bureaucracy: with the occupation regime of the Netherlands, with the NSDAP "Foreign Organization," and also presumably (at least indirectly) with the SS over emigration permits. On May 10, 1940, most of the members of the family were already in the United States,

South America, Britain, or Switzerland, but Franz Ferdinand Oppenheimer was still in the Netherlands, in Scheveningen, and Alfred Adler and Anna Luise Adler were in Graulhet, France.[163] In essence, the bank was taking part in what was also a ransom operation, in which lives were to be exchanged for consent to a financial transaction.

The general conditions for such a transaction were the result of government legislation and policy. But at specific moments, the bank forced the pace to wrap up a complex and convoluted transaction – one which was, however, in the end quite profitable for Deutsche Bank, and represents by far its largest "Aryanization profit."

The firm's participation in "Aryanization" in general had brought a terrible moral burden. On the one hand, bank support undoubtedly helped some Jewish owners, especially in Germany in the pre-1938 borders (the *Altreich*): we shall see some occasions in occupied Europe when bank action was much more brutal. Without bank brokerage of property sales, it would have been more difficult for the victims of National Socialist persecution to rescue even the very meager share that state regulations allowed them to retain and transfer out of Germany. The surviving Jewish-owned banks, Mendelssohn and Warburg, in 1937–8 did a large amount of brokering of "Aryanization" transactions, which they saw as helping rather than betraying their customers.[164]

On the other hand, in making "Aryanization" deals, the Deutsche Bank was not only engaged in a relatively well-earning commission business (between 1 and 3 percent was the usual rate) but also facilitating the state's realization of its political, racially motivated, objectives. In this way, banks were being pushed into a subservient role, which the ideological fanatics of the new movement had demanded as early as 1933. An action that in individual cases – as with Mendelssohn or Hirschland or Petschek – may ever appear to have been motivated by a genuine sympathy for former business partners, in its cumulative effect undoubtedly helped to undermine the principles of property, and morality.

Jewish-Owned Bank Accounts

The reason for the discriminatory treatment of Jewish-owned accounts by the German State and by German banks, and then the expropriation through official measures, was the intensified drive, which started at the end of 1937, to exclude Jews from the German economy. One motive lay in using as much of their wealth as could be extracted for the purposes of the Nazi State. Until 1938–9 there was actually no legal way for banks to know which of their customers were Jewish or "non-Aryan" in the sense of the definitions of the 1935 Nuremberg racial law. Working on the basis of "Jewish-sounding" names alone was an unsatisfactory procedure, and in a number of cases it led to difficulties and complaints by customers.

Banks anticipated as well as simply responded to state policy. Soon after the passage of the Nuremberg laws, the Deutsche Bank's head office sent a circular letter to its branches, asking for lists of credits of over 20,000 RM to "non-Aryan" businesses, and some bank branches went further and compiled lists of credit as well as debit customers.[165] These lists, sketchy at first, became more comprehensive in the course of the subsequent three years. They were not compiled in every branch of the bank, and indeed there was no legal obligation or even any general official request for the banks to carry out such an anticipatory registration.

Before 1938, there existed some restrictions on some Jewish-owned accounts. The accounts of emigrants were blocked and could only be converted into foreign exchange at a rate substantially below the official rate (the accounts were treated analogously to the foreign credits frozen in Germany in the course of the economic crisis of 1931). Such blocked accounts [*Auswanderersperrkonten*] could be acquired cheaply for particular specified purposes by foreigners who wished to invest in German securities or make touristic expenditures in Germany.[166] These provisions, however, only applied to those who were emigrating or had already left. The most general way of controlling the disposition of Jewish property was the use of a "security order" [*Sicherungsanordnung*]. Before late 1938, these had been relatively infrequently used, most characteristically in cases where the authorities believed that there existed an immediate plan to emigrate, which might make a partial seizure of assets more difficult.

A decree of April 26, 1938, required German Jews to register their domestic and foreign assets (foreign Jews were obliged only to register German assets) and imposed large penalties for failure to comply.[167] This registration made it easier to impose more general security orders. After the pogrom of November 9–10, 1938, the subsequent imposition on November 12 of a fine [*Sühneleistung*] on the Jewish population, and a surge of emigrants who were liable to pay confiscatory rates of tax under the "flight tax," a tax imposed on those leaving Germany [*Reichsfluchtsteuer*], security orders became quite widely applied.[168] A currency decree of December 12, 1938 required (under #59) those subject to a "security order" to create, within five days, a single account at one bank licensed to deal in foreign exchange [*Devisenbank*], a blocked account: "beschränkt verfügbares Sicherungskonto." Out of this account, a certain amount could be withdrawn monthly for regular payments. Additional releases of funds were permitted for taxes, payments to the Jewish religious community [*Kultusgemeinde*] and other permitted religious and social institutions, for legal and medical fees, for consular fees and the purchase of goods in preparation for emigration, and for the repayment of old debts.

More and more of these payments were made to an institution created in 1939, the *Reichsvereinigung der Juden in Deutschland*, which looked to many Jewish victims of persecution like a valuable self-defense mechanism, in a world in which most Jews were prohibited from following occupations and hence slipped into destitution (by 1940–1, only a quarter to a third of Jews in Germany were living on their own assets).[169] In fact the *Reichsvereinigung* was controlled by the Gestapo and amounted to a channel through which Jews were to pay for their own persecution and its bureaucratic implementation.

Soon after the imposition of the fine, and the new legislation of November 12, 1938 (the *Verordnung zur Ausschaltung der Juden aus dem deutschen Wirtschaftsleben*), the Deutsche Bank's Berlin office called branch offices to explain "that in general Jewish customers could not be allowed to dispose over their accounts in the light of the circumstances created by the new decrees."[170] Some branches reported a police intervention: in Meissen, the political police imposed a general prohibition on payments, but then the same office on Monday stated that "free accounts may be disposed over."[171]

A further decree of December 1938 also provided for the sale of Jewish-owned securities, paid to meet the fine and the emigration tax. The "Economic Sub-Groups" [*Wirtschaftsgruppen*] of the "Reich Group Banks" [*Reichsgruppe Banken*] were to decide themselves about the sales of Jewish security deposits, which had greatly accelerated as a result of the so-called "reparation." But the amounts to be sold were carefully controlled by the banks and the bourse authorities to prevent a sharp dip in the stock market.[172]

One example will show how currency control and pressure to sell Jewish enterprises interacted to produce substantial movements in the accounts of Jewish customers – without, however, producing large or disproportionate commissions or profits for the bank (at least in any of the cases that the author has seen). In the first half of 1938, the machine and apparatus manufacturer M. Eichtersheimer of Mannheim came under increasing pressure to "Aryanize." Part of the enterprise was sold in July 1938 to the Vereinigte Sauerstoffwerke GmbH, for 196,750 RM, which the owner of the firm immediately used to buy securities: mostly German treasury bonds, but also mortgage bonds and IG Farben bonds and shares. The owner seems to have decided to emigrate in November, after the pogrom, and his private house was sold to the German state (Army Administration Mannheim: *Heeresstandortverwaltung* Mannheim) on November 22 (for 61,500 RM). The main enterprise was only sold, to an *Auslandsdeutscher* (German abroad) who was returning from Argentina, in the spring of

1939, when the owner was already abroad. A purchase price of 424,900 RM was agreed on, but the purchaser paid only 45,360 RM in free (convertible at the official rate) foreign exchange to the seller's account with the Deutsche Bank. To secure possession, the Oberfinanzpräsident Karlsruhe insisted that the purchaser pay a further 100,000 RM "without compensation" to the Golddiskontbank and the equivalent of 29,640 RM in foreign exchange, as well as a further sum if the profits of the firm exceeded a certain amount.[173] In June 1939, the assets in Deutsche Bank were subject to seizure to pay taxes: 70,600 RM in IG Farben shares, assessed as being worth 105,489 RM. A total of 290,658 RM was claimed in this way, and the taxes specified included 73,766 RM for the fine imposed on Jewish wealth [Judenvermögensabgabe] and 106,500 RM "flight tax." In August 1940, the Gestapo seized gold coins, watches, and other valuables from the safe deposit box of the owner's wife, which were sold in the course of 1941, and 944 RM credited to the account (the actual goods had been auctioned for more: there was a "surplus" of 586 RM). Almost all of the securities bought by the owner were sold in July 1939, although a small holding (500 RM of preferred shares in the Reichswerke "Hermann Göring") was sold at the beginning of 1942. In the course of 1940 and 1941, the Deutsche Golddiskontbank transferred assets into a blocked account for emigrants [Auswanderersperrkonto] (a total of 190,605 RM was paid in). Of this, 190,184 RM was promptly paid out again, for further tax payments and old debts of the company. But a substantial sum (15,000 RM) was also paid to the purchaser of the machinery factory, and an equally substantial sum was paid to the Heidelberg law firm that had handled the owner's German affairs. If there was any excessive charging in this case, it was by the lawyer acting on the emigrant's behalf. In this way, the account (as well as the securities depot account) disappeared during the war.

In the course of 1940 and 1941, ad hoc expropriations from Jews occurred on the basis of very dubious legality – even in the peculiar legal circumstances of the Nazi dictatorship. There were the payments of Jews to the Gestapo and SS security services dressed up as contributions to Jewish-run organizations. On August 21, 1941, all Jewish communities were instructed by the *Reichsvereinigung* to undertake a complete inventorying of homes and property.[174] There were also direct local actions. On April 4, 1941, the Reichsführer SS announced the confiscation of all property of Jews deported from Baden under the order of October 22, 1940. Similar confiscations took place in Pomerania and the Saar-Palatinate. These were justified simply by reference to the Decree for the Protection of People and State (the emergency decree following the Reichstag fire).[175] On May 29, 1941, Hitler then decided that seized assets should go to the central state (Reich).[176]

The complete and systematized expropriation of Germany's Jewish population came through the 11th Decree on the Citizenship Law (November 25, 1941: *11. Verordnung zum Reichsbürgergesetz*). All Jews living abroad lost their citizenship, as did those who were subsequently to leave Germany. Because under previous legislation from 1933 the loss of German nationality meant an expropriation, deportation outside Germany would now entail a complete transfer of assets to the state. German shares were to be administered through the Prussian State Bank [*Seehandlung*]. Other securities (i.e. bonds and foreign shares) were to be processed by the Reichsbank's securities department [*Wertpapierabteilung*].

But implementing this decree proved to be very complicated for the banks. How were they to know of the movement or deportation of their customers? What happened in the case of Jews who were deported but still remained within the boundaries of the German Reich (Auschwitz, for instance, lay in East Upper Silesia, which had been annexed to Germany)?[177] There were numerous cases in which bank officials demanded some kind of official information or notification on the fate of their Jewish customers. The Commerzbank's Bielefeld branch, for instance, wrote: "Since we do not know to which place the Jew was deported, we cannot ascertain whether it is really a case of a Jew subject to the Decree of November 25, 1941. We inform you, that the transfer cannot be effected until we have the appropriate proof in the form of a decision of the Chief of Security Police."[178]

The Private Banking Group of the Reich Group Banks again acted as an intermediary and as a center for the exchange of information and experience between its banking members on the implementation of the decree. It explained the 11th Decree in a circular, in which it advised its member banks that it was not necessary to inform its customers of their expropriation. The circular added that the general decree about "cession of wealth" meant that "the reluctance of individual banks to transfer confiscated accounts not yet declared as forfeit to an official payments office or other institution, because of fear of foreign legal cases, is no longer justified."[179]

There were indeed such cases of foreign lawsuits. In March 1942, the Deutsche Bank was still complaining that "we have already been threatened by a case based on the argument that the customer did not fall under the terms of the Eleventh Decree."[180] Not all banks dealt with the application of the decree, and the risk of foreign legal action, in a uniform way. In April 1942, the Private Banking Group of the Reich Group Banks noted:

> "from repeated discussions of dubious cases relating to the Eleventh Decree, it is clear that the banks do not proceed uniformly in the question of notifying emigrated Jewish account-holders that a cession to the Reich has taken place. The Dresdner Bank and Commerzbank give a short notice in cases where emigrated account-holders issue instructions or ask for statements, while the Deutsche Bank, because in two cases its conduct was questioned by the Oberfinanzpräsident of Berlin, does not issue such notices."[181]

Generally, however, the major banks were involved in lengthy discussions about the execution of the 11th Decree, managed by the Private Banking Group of the Reich Group Banks. They evolved a common procedure "that they only make the transfer to the Oberfinanzpräsident after a prior ascertaining of the cession of account through the Chief of Security police, and make the notification subject to such instruction."[182] For example, the Deutsche Bank provided a letter from the Oberfinanzpräsident Münster, in which the state agency had added to its request for the transfer of funds:

"Der Jude ist am 27.I.1942 in das Ausland abgeschoben [worden]" (the Jew was deported abroad on January 27, 1942).[183] The general practice was for the regional Oberfinanzpräsident to send lists of "evacuated" Jews and demand the transfer of the assets that were "ceded to the Reich." Inevitably, there were mistakes in which the tax offices demanded the transfer of assets of Jews who had not been deported.[184]

The confusions and complexity arose precisely because this decree appeared to make legal the completely and abhorrently illegal, and in doing so produced endless contradictions. Simple expropriation of every piece of property created a state of absolute rightlessness, a denial in law of the existence of a person (since the person is defined by rights). The complexities were so immense that a further decree on Jewish property was necessary, which made absolutely clear what lay in the future of those Jews in German power. Because it was clear that not all cases were actually covered by the 11th Decree, a 13th Decree stated: "After the death of a Jew his property is ceded to the Reich."

Could there have been in these circumstances, in which the state tried to grasp Jewish funds as completely as possible, "heirless" assets or accounts, analogous to those which in the 1990s created such a furor in the case of Swiss banks? The short answer is yes, but not in any substantial volume. The process specified under the 11th Decree was quite complicated, and not all accounts were actually transferred.

One case serves as an illustration: Emma K. of Böchingen in the Palatinate, who held an account at the Deutsche Bank Mannheim, was obliged to sell her land to the Bavarian Farmers' Settlement Agency (apparently without the intermediation of Deutsche Bank). She received 4,000 RM, of which 1,600 RM was used to pay the imposition on Jewish wealth. Now without a home, she moved repeatedly, first to friends in Mannheim, then to Frankfurt, and then to a Jewish old people's home in Frankfurt (in the Rechneigrabenstrasse). At the beginning of 1942, she paid over what remained of her account, 1,800 RM, to the Jewish office in Frankfurt. Out of this, the monthly charges of the home (120 RM) were to be deducted. On October 6, 1942, the Deutsche Bank Mannheim wrote to the Jewish office to report that on September 26 the Oberfinanzpräsident, Devisenstelle Frankfurt, had stated that the "assets of the account holder have been confiscated." But a few weeks later, on October 26, the bank wrote another letter, to say that the Finance Office letter of September 26 was "to be regarded as void" and asking the Jewish office to obtain the necessary permission of the Gestapo for the transfer of the account to Theresienstadt (to where Frau K. had been deported).[185] There is no reply in the files, and on January 9, 1943, the bank sent a reminder. What had happened between September 26 and October 26, 1942? On October 9, the Private Banking Group had sent a new circular with information about the treatment of Theresienstadt: "Deportations of Jews within the area of the Reich usually take place to Theresienstadt (Bohemia–Moravia)." Accounts of such individuals were not to be treated according to the 11th Decree. Instead, the accounts were to be marked "residence moved to Theresienstadt": "Wohnsitzverlegung nach Theresienstadt."[186] By the end of 1943, there still remained 797 RM in Fräulein K.'s account (790 RM at the end of 1945), and the account was labeled with an addressograph print as "Fräulein Emma K. Frankfurt/M, jetzt Theresienstadt z. Hd. Sekretariat im Hause": "currently Theresienstadt c/o Secretariat of Bank." The account was converted into deutschmarks (DM) after the 1948 currency reform. The conversion was carried out by the bank without a petition by the owner (as was required from German residents), on the grounds that her last recorded residence was abroad. Initially the law provided for a 10:1 reduction, with half the account blocked; the eventual conversion rate was reduced to 100:6.5. As a result, the account now had 50.70 DM, and in 1949 the Südwestbank Mannheim, the successor of Deutsche Bank, deducted 70 pfennigs (Pfg) in fees. On July 19, 1950, a note records, "we request the transfer of the account to the collective account: Owners Not to be Located." The sum of 50 DM was then duly paid one week later into a collective account.[187]

Legally, the postwar situation is clear. The Allied Restitution Law (Military Law 59) required the reporting of assets of victims of National Socialism, and the claims were then transferred to the Jewish Restitution Successor Organization. This organization, to make immediate payments, reached a "global settlement" with the German *Länder*, under the terms of which the Länder paid the restitution and took in return the claims on assets. A later decision of the Federal Court [*Bundesgerichtshof*], in 1955, held that the banks that had managed deposit and security (depot) accounts were still obliged to pay out those accounts without a restitution proceeding. The Deutsche Bank had a number of accounts (not all from victims of National Socialism) that had not been converted at the 1948 reform. The larger accounts (over 100 DM) were paid over to the state: a total of 323 accounts worth 150,000 DM were paid in this way. Smaller accounts, under 100 DM, were simply booked to the general profit and loss account. Thus, by the 1970s, no heirless accounts existed. But some such accounts, for small but not trivial amounts (such as Emma K.S) had been cancelled well before the general cancellation of the 1970s.

The Nazi State had certainly tried to seize every Jewish asset it could identify, but some assets fell through its bureaucratic web and remained a problem after 1945. Such accounts, small as they may be in comparison with Swiss circumstances, are nevertheless rather more than an accounting problem.

4

Emil Georg von Stauss: The Banker as Politician

For the first ten years of the National Socialist regime, the most important high political contacts of the Deutsche Bank were those maintained by Emil Georg von Stauss (Figure 15). His activities were not "typical" of the activities of the Deutsche Bank at this time, but he was quite crucial to its operation in a highly politicized environment. After 1932, he was not even a member of the management board, although he did sit on the most important committee of the supervisory board. The leading Managing Directors – Eduard Mosler, Gustaf Schlieper, Karl Kimmich – concerned themselves with what mattered most to them, the bank's business contacts. They could do this because politics were delegated to Stauss and because they left the politically most sensitive supervisory board positions held by the Deutsche Bank to Stauss. Stauss was, so to speak, the bank's political alibi until his death in 1942. In his view, developed through extensive experience in Imperial Germany, in the Weimar Republic, and with foreign governments, politics meant building links with government, whatever form that government might take. Although he never became a member of the NSDAP, he was well prepared for a National Socialist government in Germany.

Figure 15. Emil Georg von Stauss: Member of management board 1915–32.

Source: Courtesy of Deutsche Bank AG.

In 1930 he was elected to the Reichstag as a deputy for the liberal Deutsche Volkspartei (DVP), but he was soon close to the NSDAP and especially to Hermann Göring. His foreign contacts were attractive to a party preparing itself to seize power, and in December 1931 he introduced, in his house, the U.S. Ambassador Frederic M. Sackett to Hitler (who came under the cover name of Herr Wolf). Earlier in 1931, his hospitality had also brought together ex-Reichsbank President Hjalmar Schacht with Göring and Hitler. In this way, he was a crucial figure in bringing together Nazi leaders and the German financial elite. In 1933, Göring appointed him as a Prussian Staatsrat, and in 1934 Stauss became Vice-President of the Reichstag, although he was still not a member of the NSDAP and was described as a "guest" [*Hospitant*] of the NSDAP party group. Stauss's seat in the Reichstag came to him in a peculiar way. In the election of March 1933, only two right liberal (DVP) deputies

were elected. One of them, a businessman named Otto Hugo,
then wished to dissolve the party and join the NSDAP; the party
chairman, Eduard Dingeldey, on the other hand, who had developed not unreasonable suspicions of the Hitler movement, wanted
to keep the DVP as an independent force. In the course of the internal DVP dispute, Hugo had to resign his position within the
party; but Dingeldey eventually gave up the struggle to maintain the independence of the party. However, it retained the right
to two Reichstag seats as "guests of the NSDAP parliamentary
group"; and Hugo's was taken by Stauss at the suggestion of Dingeldey, as he wrote, "because for financial and political reasons I
place the greatest value on his cooperation at this time." In other
words, Stauss was to act as a bridge between politically and economically active and significant representatives of the old "bour-
geois" parties and the new order – but without joining the party.[188]
Stauss consistently ignored later inquiries from the NSDAP as to
why he had not joined the movement; and in 1942, when Propaganda Minister Joseph Goebbels suggested that he be awarded the
Deutsche Akademie's Goethe medal, the Party Chancellery vigorously objected.[189]

Though not active after 1932 in the conduct of day-to-day business at the bank, he retained an office in the bank's headquarters
and remained very active in the bank's interest. Sometimes he intervened directly to protect the bank's clients. As an example, in
March 1933, at the height of the challenge from National Socialist revolutionaries, he was able to contact Hitler's adjutant and
the Prussian Interior Ministry and prevent the SA from closing
and occupying the Breslau store of the Wertheim department store
chain.[190] Most of his duties after 1933 involved him as a supervisory board member and often as chairman of a large number of
companies, which included some of the firms that became most
politicized under the National Socialist dictatorship. Stauss managed almost all of the Deutsche Bank's most sensitive customers.
Films, aircraft, automobiles, synthetic fibers: these were the high
technology, high visibility, and high prestige lines of the 1930s.
German films, aircraft, and racing cars could all function as political propaganda for the new regime. Stauss had the right contacts

to exploit the plentiful opportunities offered by these industries and to play the part of a political liaison man. He intervened decisively in the affairs of the film company Ufa, Deutsche Lufthansa, Bayerische Motoren Werke, Daimler–Benz, the fiber multinational AKU, as well as a range of cultural and academic associations.

Films and Political Education

From its start in 1917, Stauss had been supervisory board chairman of Universum-Film AG, Berlin (Ufa) and had played a major part in its financial reconstruction after the financial stress of the German hyper-inflation. At the moment of political crisis in 1933, he once more became chairman. Of the 18.8 m. RM shares voting at the 1933 annual general meeting, the Deutsche Bank controlled 8.7 m. Another 910,000 RM were registered personally in Stauss's name.[191]

After the Nazi seizure of power, Ufa stood in a particularly precarious and vulnerable position. Films were obviously political, and the new government had an intense interest in their propagandist use. In the past, however, the business had been heavily dependent on foreign earnings, which accounted for almost two-fifths of revenue. A new political orientation would, and did, ruin this external market. In addition, the firm was concerned that commercial cinemas would face damaging competition from party-run cinemas and from the party's leisure activity organization "Strength through Joy" [Kraft durch Freude]. In March 1933, Joseph Goebbels summoned Germany's leading filmmakers to the Hotel Kaiserhof and explained his ideas for a reorganization of the film industry. Almost immediately, the Ufa management board voted to cancel the contracts of its Jewish employees, and as a result it deprived the company of many of its best actors, directors, and technicians.[192] The combination of all these events and pressures meant enormous operating losses in 1933. Such a performance contrasted with the admittedly small surplus that had been earned even in 1932, the worst Depression year. In the case of Ufa, it was clear that it was political adjustment that was causing the losses.

The response was to toe the party line. But even this was difficult. What was the party line? There were many disharmoniously
competing voices in the National Socialist choir: rustic utopianism
clashed with glorification of modern technology. Then there was
the problem of taste, which also rapidly became political. What
easier way is there to ridicule a movement than to present its ideas
clumsily or unaesthetically? Badly made films on National Socialist themes would appear only as ridiculous. Although it was made
by a Nazi director on the basis of a Nazi script by a Nazi author
(Richard Schneider-Edenkoben), the film *Thou Shalt Not Covet*
[*Du sollst nicht begehren*] for example was attacked by the Agriculture Ministry, by the party press, and in internal party decrees. The
party ideologues accused Ufa of political opportunism.[193] In the
end, 300,000 RM might as well have been thrown down the drain.
Even perfectly political topics such as *The Red Death of Riga* [*Der
rote Tod von Riga*] were endlessly held up by political interventions.

The list of taboo subjects grew ever longer. Scripts based on
books by Jewish authors were obviously out of the question. But
party military and paramilitary organizations, the SA and the SS,
could not be treated either. A planned film called *The Intoxication
of Love* [*Der Liebesrausch*] was called off on the grounds of a "concern that marital conflicts should not be dealt with cinematically,
even if there is no adultery." What was left? "Our secure knowledge
of what cannot be done unfortunately gives no indication of what
can be shown."[194] The uncertainty made the filmmakers ever more
hesitant and above all dependent on guidelines produced by Joseph
Goebbels's new Propaganda Ministry. Resulting films were fiercely
critical of the vices of the old system: they attacked materialism,
individualism, currency speculators, Jews, and capital flight (all of
these were the ostensible targets of Erich Engels's 1933 film *Inge
and the Millions* [*Inge und die Millionen*]).[195] In February 1934,
Goebbels tried to solve the problem by requiring the submission of
all film synopses to a Reich Film Editor.

Light entertainment offered the easiest solution to the problematical question of subjects suitable for cinematic depiction in the
New Germany. It provided the added lure of export earnings in an

economy, which in the process of recovering from the Depression, had quickly run short of foreign exchange. As a result the fees for multilingual actors who could present an attractive nonchalance exploded. A star system was created. It was not the earnest young men who depicted National Socialist heroes, such as Claus Clausen [*Hitlerjunge Quex*] who did well out of the new cinema, but the frivolous and glittering idols of a new vacuity. Hans Albers had the advantage that he could make films in English or German. Zarah Leander looked like other leading actresses: "speaks perfect French and English and plays the roles of Greta Garbo and Marlene Dietrich, whom she resembles." Albers's and Leander's fees shot up. In 1936, Leander received 200,000 RM for three films, two-thirds of which was to be paid in Swedish crowns. In 1933, Hans Albers had been paid 70,000 RM a film, but by 1936 he was receiving 700,000 RM for four films.[196] Filmmakers blamed the government for the fee inflation and pointed to "the speech of Minister Goebbels, in which he announced that actors should be well paid."[197] The average cost of producing a film inevitably rose, from 250,000 RM in 1933 and 275,000 RM in 1934 to 420,000 RM by mid-1936 and 537,000 RM in 1937.[198]

Though its managers claimed that Ufa was still potentially profitable in spite of the additional costs, and that the firm could soon resume paying dividends, in practice the demands of party and state for financial support for a Film Academy and Culture Film Institute meant that there seemed no likelihood of operating as a market-minded producer of pure entertainment. In 1933, the Filmkreditbank GmbH was created with the participation of the leading banks and Ufa, with a pledge by the banks to extend credit, as a way of solving the problem of financing a German film industry. Already in 1935 Ufa's rival, the Tonbild-Syndikat AG (Tobis), had been nationalized. The political pressure on Ufa intensified, including an initially unsuccessful demand for the removal of Production Director Ernst Hugo Correll. In the end, the demands of state and party had their effects. As a result, in March 1937 the majority of Ufa shares held by Alfred Hugenberg's Scherl-Konzern and by the Deutsche Bank were sold at book value to a state-owned trustee company, Cautio Treuhand GmbH. Cautio eventually controlled the whole of the Reich's film business, including Tobis and Ufa as well as a Vienna Film GmbH and Prague Film GmbH. In May 1942 this cinematic empire was eventually reorganized into a single holding company, the Ufa-Film GmbH. But until this moment, and despite an almost complete turnover on the supervisory board, Stauss together with another Deutsche Bank representative, Johannes Kiehl, remained at the helm of the supervisory board of the Ufa AG.[199]

The new cinema did best – at the box office – when it did not try political education. In 1933 the program had included only a few ideological films – *German Border Land in the East* [*Deutsches Grenzland im Osten*], and *Hitler Youth Quex* [*Hitlerjunge Quex*], as well as *Refugees* [*Flüchtlinge*] (depicting Volga Germans fleeing from the Bolshevik revolution) – and instead concentrated on less strenuous themes such as those in *Viktor und Viktoria* or *War of the Waltzes* [*Walzerkrieg*].

Stauss was more than merely a politically influential figurehead for the film company. He involved himself in the commercially critical area of program choice, but he wanted to make political statements, and sometimes aesthetic ones. Ufa had to make money, but it also had to avoid alienating the politically influential. He passed on Ernst ("Putzi") Hanfstaengl's idea for a film based on the novel *People without Space* [*Volk ohne Raum*].[200] In 1939 he supported the making of a film about a colonial theme, in order to underline German demands for better treatment in the matter of colonies. He made (often inappropriate) suggestions as to which actresses to use.[201]

Even more political was Stauss's involvement with the Deutsche Akademie, founded in 1925 with an educational mission that in the course of the 1930s became a political one. In 1932 the Akademie's "Practical Department" had created a Goethe-Institut with the aim of promoting German language and culture. After the outbreak of war in 1939, the Goethe-Institut was given a specific charge. The Akademie negotiated a subsidy from the German Foreign Office to conduct German courses for the natives of Germany's allies or potential allies in the new Europe. Its president set out its mission in a personal interview with Hitler in the following way: "It is most important to work to make the German language *the* world language, or at least a world language."[202] Thus the Goethe-Institut courses of the academic year 1940–1, conducted under the auspices of the Deutsche Akademie, took 600 Italians, Bulgarians, Yugoslavs, Greeks, and Spaniards.[203]

The Akademie held out one way of linking politics and the banking world. Stauss was deputy president and dealt with the very problematical and highly politicized presidents of the 1930s. First in 1934 the geopolitician Karl Haushofer, a friend of the Führer's Deputy Rudolf Hess, was appointed, but it soon became evident that he was mentally and physically sick. He resigned after an outbreak of intense conflict with the Akademie's general secretary about the institution's political future and its virtual financial bankruptcy. At this point, Stauss saved the Akademie by arranging for the appointment of a new general secretary and by volunteering to take over, if necessary, the presidency for a brief transitional period.[204] Unfortunately Haushofer's eventual successor Professor Kölbl soon resigned too, after being arrested for homosexual activity.[205] Then the Minister–President of Bavaria, Ludwig Siebert, stepped in to fill the breach. Even the appointment of a prominent National Socialist politician proved an inadequate form of political protection, and Stauss became involved in personal clashes at the highest levels of the party. Rudolf Hess's chief of staff Martin Bormann complained that the Akademie was violating Hitler's instructions in collecting funds from industry as part of an attempt to move into larger and more representative quarters.[206] Stauss, who had served as the main fundraiser and the organizer of a Berlin association of Friends of the Akademie, could only defend himself by appealing to Siebert; but Siebert's position vis-à-vis the central party authorities was not strong. Stauss then managed to go right to the top and persuaded Hitler personally that "an exception would be justified. He asked Reichsleiter Bormann to inform the Reich Finance Minister as soon as possible."[207] It was all in vain: despite the green light from on high, the army and the Foreign Office joined the party in limiting the wartime tasks of the Deutsche Akademie to the prosaic task of language instruction.

Motors in the Air and on the Ground

Deutsche Lufthansa AG (founded in 1926 as Deutsche Luft Hansa AG) was another enterprise that kept Stauss as the head of its supervisory board. It was owned by the Reich, some of the German states [*Länder*], and the Reichsbahn, with the Deutsche Bank holding over a quarter of the shares on behalf of Deutscher Aero Lloyd. Like air transport companies throughout the world, Lufthansa thrived in the 1930s. Its staff increased from 1,232 employees in December 1934 to 2,415 by June 1939. Its route system in Europe and its airmail lines to South America expanded. The combination of public ownership, public service, and new technology would have meant politics in any system: in National Socialist Germany this fate was inescapable. Many German aviators had been supporters of National Socialism before 1933 and regarded Lufthansa as an appropriate base for the German air force that had been prohibited under the terms of the Versailles Treaty. Erhard Milch left the management board of Lufthansa in 1933 to become State Secretary for Aviation, but he remained on the company's supervisory board. Hermann Esser, a founding member of the NSDAP and in 1933 Minister for Economics [*Staatsminister für Wirtschaft*] and head of the Chancellery [*Chef der Staatskanzlei*] in Bavaria, an uncouth and unsavory radical National Socialist ideologue, was a new arrival on the supervisory board. At his first meeting he stated that "as one of the oldest fellow fighters with the Führer he could declare that Lufthansa had long carried within the spirit of the New Germany and could see this as a justification of its previous work."[208]

Contacts with Milch were crucial for Stauss's other work: the largest part of his time was devoted to being chairman of the supervisory board of BMW [*Bayerische Motoren Werke*] and Daimler–Benz, which both developed in the 1930s into major producers of aero engines. This was an area of armaments production that posed substantial technical problems, requiring difficult choices between different strategies of development. In a highly politicized system, such issues acquired a political edge, as each solution became associated with political clientage networks. Interventions over technical choices over aero-motors reached a dramatic climax during the war, the story of which is told in part below (pages 200–6).

Of all of Stauss's companies, Daimler–Benz most intensively cultivated the National Socialist regime. Stauss had left the supervisory board of Daimler when he had resigned from the management board of the Deutsche Bank, but he returned quickly to become chairman of the supervisory board (on July 4, 1933), almost certainly because of the extent and the warmth of his political connections.[209] Within the firm, the key figure from the political point of view was Jakob Werlin, initially the director of the Munich sales office and an intimate friend of the new leadership. In 1933 Werlin was selling cars on favorable terms to the new establishment, to Joseph Goebbels, to Ministerial Counselor Hanke in the Propaganda Ministry, to Julius Streicher, and to the Nazi economic experts, Wilhelm Keppler and state secretary Feder. This was, at least from a commercial standpoint, not a futile exercise. It brought influence in the new political establishment as well as direct orders.

Werlin was able in particular to extend his contacts with Hitler and to discuss with him at length the consequences of rearmament. He reported back to the firm. "If the size of the army is increased to 300,000, motorization would be carried out with the greatest energy; and our prospects in this case would not be bad. I replied that we would start to operate our Marienfelde plant and would expect to obtain particular support from the Reichswehr."[210] The promised commercial rewards rapidly became a reality: in February 1934, the company received 1.5 m. RM in truck orders from the SA.

Werlin was rapidly rewarded with a seat on the management board of Daimler–Benz, where he behaved in part as prima donna, in part as spoiled child. A letter he wrote in 1935 to Daimler–Benz management board chairman Wilhelm Kissel with the principal objective of pointing out his indispensability to the company is quite typical of the man: "I would like to point out to you already today that if I fail to obtain the necessary support from my own firm, I will have no alternative but to point out how conditions lie to another authority. It is not just a matter of the interests of our firm, but of the needs the state."[211] As supervisory board chairman, Stauss's responsibilities involved both calming Werlin and using him. Stauss did not hesitate to mix himself in the petty politics of automobile bribery, and to play Werlin's own game. Why, he wanted to know in 1934, were Ernst Röhm and Heinrich Himmler still driving Maybachs rather than Mercedes?[212]

But it would be a mistake to see Stauss as nothing more than a politics-playing figurehead tolerated by the Deutsche Bank and commercially useless to the firms on whose supervisory boards he sat. The hand of the banker was visible in the development of Daimler in the 1930s in two ways.

First, Stauss owed his uniquely authoritative position in Daimler to his skill in making the merger of Daimler and Benz in the 1920s. The automobile industry was still in the midst of a large-scale shakeout, with the Depression only increasing the commercial pressure to rationalize. Stauss's recipe for survival in the 1930s included a close working relationship – and perhaps an eventual fusion – with the Bayerische Motoren Werke (of which he was also supervisory board chairman). Franz Popp of BMW sat on the supervisory board of Daimler, and Kissel in reciprocation went to the Munich board meetings. There was some collaboration in manufacture. The bodywork for the BMW 315 and 319 was made in Sindelfingen by Daimler.[213] Popp and Werlin both worked together in preparing the plans for the realization of Hitler's dream for a Volkswagen. Most importantly for the two firms (and, it turned out, most dangerously for BMW) Stauss promoted the idea of a division of aero-engines into different technologies. Daimler would work with water-cooled and BMW with air-cooled engines.

Secondly, Stauss was very keen to apply financially realistic criteria to the firm's management decisions. In the light of the economic uncertainty in the automobile industry, and also the permanent temptation felt by technical experts to undertake interesting but commercially unrewarding innovations, Stauss insisted throughout the recovery period on financial caution. This required a delicate balancing act, between the demands of the firm and the skepticism of the Deutsche Bank representatives. Within the bank, some observers later reported, Stauss was regarded as having used his position on the supervisory board *Arbeitsauschuss* to give excessive credit lines to his favorites in the automobile industry.[214] Daimler was – in the 1930s – a bank-controlled industry, and the experience of the 1920s and the Depression had made bankers very nervous. The firm staged a spectacular recovery in sales and production after the Depression: indeed, it was one of the first German companies to show signs of the upturn, with a significant improvement already evident in 1932. But profitability rose much more slowly, and Stauss insisted on a correction. "In the long run it is of course insupportable that the works should bring no profit worth speaking of from such a large turnover."[215] This was the authentic voice of Stauss the banker rather than of Stauss the politician. An economic recovery should mean larger profits, not just a greater market share, more influence, and more sales.

Multinational Business in Conflict with Nationalism

The roles of banker and politician clashed – less perhaps in the case of Daimler than in the most politically difficult of all of Stauss's operations, the German–Dutch synthetic fiber manufacturer Algemene Kunstzijde Unie N.V. (AKU). This conglomerate, like Daimler–Benz, was the result of a bank-inspired merger of the 1920s. In 1929 Oscar Schlitter of the Deutsche Bank put together a "community of interest" between the dynamic but highly indebted Vereinigte Glanzstoff-Fabriken AG (VFG) and the Dutch producer Nederlandsche Kunstzijde. AKU was formed through an exchange of shares, so that the new corporation controlled Vereinigte Glanzstoffe. As a joint German–Dutch company, it constituted

the first German multinational (as opposed to transnational) corporation. The AKU supervisory board consisted of four representatives (called "delegates") of the Dutch and four of the German
group, as well as one neutral member. The firm owned major foreign subsidiaries: in the U.S., the North American Rayon Corporation, the American Enka Corporation, the American Bemberg
Corporation, as well as companies in Britain, Italy, Czechoslovakia,
and Austria. It also held a participation in Glanzstoff-Courtaulds
GmbH Cologne. Most of AKU's production was still located in
Germany, and its output in the early 1930s accounted for 60 percent of German viscose.

The relationship between the Dutch and German parts of the
enterprise would have been strained in any case. The early years
of almost all multinationals were filled with conflicts, often with
a political edge, about production, sales, taxation, etc., and the
companies were frequently seen by outsiders as being at odds with
national interests. In the 1930s, as a result of the distortions imposed by trade and exchange control, of technical disparities, and
of politics, the climate worsened further. It made work in the AKU
difficult. The VGF was highly indebted to the Dutch company, and
the debt actually increased in the course of the 1930s as the Dutch
bought up VGF bonds issued and owned in the U.S. The result
was that in the course of the 1930s, an ever smaller proportion of
the firm was in German ownership. At the same time, the Dutch
part of the concern lagged in technology, and, despite the installa-
tion of faster double-thread spinning machines, remained relatively
underequipped.

In 1933 the management of AKU became bitterly divided. An
executive director of VGF, Carl Benrath, and Willi Springorum in
the supervisory board were accused of manipulating the account
books and violating the Decree of September 19, 1931 on Share
Law and Bank Supervision. Benrath in turn responded with a fe-
rocious attack on Oscar Schlitter, the Deutsche Bank's foremost
expert on industrial credit, as one of the delegates on the supervisory board, and appealed to Schlitter's more political Deutsche

Bank colleague von Stauss. At this stage, both bankers were no longer active members of the management board but both sat on the supervisory board of the Deutsche Bank. Benrath used the new political language as a way of attempting to rehabilitate himself: "We live in a New Germany in which – thank the Lord – the honor of the individual is protected by a strong hand. I too rely on this protection and I am sure, that I will come into my rights," he wrote to von Stauss. "I am pleased to hear from you that you judge my position favorably from the moral side because of the reasons well known to you."[216]

Even though the accusations against them were eventually dropped,[217] Benrath and Springorum were forced to resign their positions in the AKU, but – as often happens in bitterly internally divided managements – the position of everyone involved in the conflict was damaged, and Schlitter did not emerge unscathed either. Although still joint chairman of the supervisory board of the Deutsche Bank, he was moved to a position as the ninth, "neutral" delegate, and Stauss was placed on the managing German–Dutch supervisory board.

For the AKU, the imposition of Stauss on the reconstructed board facilitated political contacts that were crucial for a concern faced by a demand that it become more national. Its synthetic fibers were needed as a substitute for imported raw materials by an increasingly autarkically oriented regime. To many in the government, it appeared strange that a multinational should be in charge of a policy of import substitution. One of the earliest suggestions from the NSDAP textile experts was that the renationalization of Germany's largest producer of artificial silk should be achieved through a takeover of the company by IG Farben, which was at least an authentically German corporation.[218] Instead, the German delegates of AKU defended themselves from the political charges of not following a sufficiently German course by shifting production to Germany. German synthetic fiber production benefited from government programs, particularly from the import restrictions placed on natural cotton and wool under the 1934 New

Plan. At the same time, production in the Dutch plants at Ede and Arnhem was cut back.[219] In addition, the Deutsche Bank assisted in buying up Dutch shares for the VGF interests.

All this never seemed enough from the standpoint of the Nazi party. After 1936 and the announcement of the Four-Year Plan, the orientation of policy makers towards autarky became much more explicit. In 1937 Göring's office for raw materials asked whether plans existed to nationalize the firm. Stauss gave a temporizing reply: at present it would be "tactically wrong" to move until he could be in a position to make "positive suggestions" on this subject.[220] To avoid retaliation against the U.S. subsidiaries, in particular, the firm had to appear to be non–German-owned with a majority Dutch participation.[221]

But this kind of argument was inadequate for the planners of the Four-Year Plan administration, who saw Stauss and his colleagues increasingly as an obstacle to the implementation of a German solution to the problems raised by the existence of a multinational corporation. In May 1939, the German members of the AKU Delegates Committee, including Stauss, resigned after intensive pressure applied by Hans Kehrl from the Four-Year Plan administration.[222] Göring had reached the conclusion that Stauss had been bribed by the Dutch board members to support an anti-German position, and he cited as evidence the gift of a painting (perhaps appropriately, a Dutch old master) to Stauss. The German delegates were replaced by four new figures, including Hermann Abs of the Deutsche Bank and Baron von Schröder of Bankhaus Stein, Cologne. The Dutch delegates were surprised and outraged, especially when it appeared that the German government wanted to place the suspect managers of the 1933 vintage back in control, including Benrath. This plan was only abandoned at the insistence of Philipp Reemtsma, the cigarette czar, who worked closely in this maneuver with the new men from the Deutsche Bank.[223] In this way, despite the complete change of personnel among the delegates, the AKU survived as a German–Dutch concern until the war and the occupation of the Netherlands. It became the only Dutch multinational corporation whose management the German authorities could directly control.

Shell, Philips, and Unilever had moved their headquarters abroad, and were run under the occupation by trustees. In this way they, unlike AKU, were able at least partially to escape the grasping hand of the New Germany.

Stauss's role was as a kind of political insurance for the bank. After his death in December 1942, relations with the state and the party became much more difficult. The new offensive against the world of finance was in large measure a consequence of the rapid ideological radicalization that occurred during the war. But it was also, at least in part, a result of the bank's inability or unwillingness to find another Stauss adept at the game of mixing business and politics. Perhaps too, as the AKU incident indicated, it was not a game that could be played indefinitely. Within the National Socialist state, there were too many competing hierarchies to make it a very simple exercise, even for someone with little sense of morality and a great penchant for expediency.

The case of the business life of Emil Georg von Stauss holds an interesting and important moral. Stauss's objectives were fundamentally all based on a devotion to doing business and making money, and not on a desire for explicit political power. But he wanted to use politics to further his commercial ends. When, however, entrepreneurial capacities become very explicitly a function of a political system, energies that previously were deployed in business activity are increasingly harnessed to the task of capturing political power and influence. In a purely economic sense, considered in terms of an understanding of agents pursuing a rational individual or corporate self-interest, this development is entirely comprehensible. The development of Stauss's activity from technical wizard in the most modern, twentieth century of industries in the air, on the road, and on the screen, to his role as a broker of political interests in the Third Reich is natural and self-evident from the perspective of a purely business logic. From a different, moral perspective, however, such a development is infinitely more problematic.

5

Foreign Expansion

The Deutsche Bank had always been active internationally. Indeed it was founded with the explicit goal of developing Germany's overseas trade. Before World War I, it founded both the Deutsche Überseeische Bank, for financing trade with South America, and the Deutsch–Asiatische Bank, and it participated in the development of Rumanian petroleum and Turkish railways. International contacts continued to matter in the 1930s, despite the general movement of that decade away from the international economy and towards strategies of autarkic development. After 1931, the Deutsche Bank led the debtor bankers' committee, which annually renegotiated the prolongation of Germany's short-term private sector debts. These discussions of annual Standstill Agreements (called the German Credit Agreements) provided for a gradual and progressive liquidation of the foreign debt; they also dealt with the complex matter of converting frozen debts into other forms of longer term assets in Germany. The constant rescheduling, together with the possibility of debt to equity swaps, bears an obvious resemblance to the international debt negotiations of the 1980s, with the difference that in 1930s Germany a substantial part of the debt was owed by banks and private corporations. The foreign exchange implications of the Standstill Agreements in a country that had almost entirely exhausted its international reserves by 1933 meant that the government and the Reichsbank not only followed the course of the negotiations, but also frequently intervened directly.

In August 1937 Gustaf Schlieper, the highly respected Director of the Foreign Department at the Deutsche Bank, died. His successor, Hermann Abs (Figure 17), was a youthful 36, and he had been a partner of the leading private bank Delbrück Schickler & Co. Abs's principal attraction to the bank was his expertise in foreign dealings, his linguistic fluency in English, Dutch, French, and Spanish, his range of overseas contacts, and his obvious intelligence. Above all, he seemed to the government the obvious choice to replace Schlieper as head of the German Standstill Committee. Abs later believed that Reichsbank President Hjalmar Schacht told the speaker of the Deutsche Bank management board, Eduard Mosler (Figure 16), of the likely successor to Schlieper and of the consequence that the Deutsche Bank would no longer run the Standstill negotiations. From the standpoint of the Deutsche Bank, there was, however, a simple way out, and Mosler told his colleagues that the bank's prestige demanded that this rising star of German finance should be added to its board. Abs developed more and more as a generator of contacts, primarily abroad, where his reach ranged from the world of New York banking to the corridors of the Vatican. He rapidly became the Figaro of German banking: "pronto a far tutto, la notte il giorno sempre d'intorno in giro sta. Ahimé, che furia! Ahimé che folla!" Lothar Gall termed him, appropriately, "A Man for all Seasons."[224]

This was the first major change to the management board since the upheavals of 1933. As long as there had been no new appointments, no one could reasonably complain that there was no party member on the board; but when the very young Abs arrived, it was natural for a bank whose staff had mostly joined the party to encounter questions as to why there was no comrade on the higher floors. Any alteration of the board thus inevitably

Figure 16. Eduard Mosler: Member of management board 1929–39, Speaker 1934–39.

Source: Courtesy of Deutsche Bank AG.

raised the question of its political composition and balance. The bank needed more political support, and it sought this by appointing to the management board someone judged to be a relatively "harmless" party member. Personnel Manager Karl Ritter von Halt – usually described by those who remember him as a banker as decent but ineffective ("a nothing") – was the obvious candidate. On the management board after 1938, he self-consciously took charge of the bank's relationship with the party. He made contributions to a fund supporting the activities of Reichsleiter SS Heinrich Himmler (Sonderkonto "S" at Bankhaus J.H. Stein, Cologne).[225] In 1943 and 1944 the larger German industrial concerns (Siemens–Schuckert, IG Farben, Mitteldeutsche Stahlwerke, Wintershall, Vereinigte Stahlwerke, Braunkohle–Benzin AG) gave 100,000 RM each, and Deutsche Bank contributed 75,000 RM and the Dresdner and Commerzbank 50,000 RM for each year.[226] Halt was also a member of a group of around forty businessmen and officers meeting each month as the "Heinrich Himmler Circle of Friends." By April 1943 there had been thirty-eight invitations, of which von Halt managed to miss only six (Karl Rasche, for the

Figure 17. Hermann J. Abs: Member of management board 1938–45 (and 1952–67).

Source: Courtesy of Deutsche Bank AG.

Dresdner Bank, had an even better attendance record: he was absent from only five sessions).[227] As a banker, on the other hand, von Halt did relatively little and took only insignificant positions on other supervisory boards.

Personnel concessions to the party were overshadowed by the much larger political changes in Germany. The military and political expansion of Germany after 1938 fundamentally altered the climate in which the Deutsche Bank operated. In the late 1930s, the international experiences of the past were set to work in the context of present politics, in large part at the insistence of party and state.

Colonies

Already in the 1920s, Dr. Kurt Weigelt (who in 1928 was appointed as a deputy member of the management board) had dealt with colonial issues. After 1933 he became a member of the NSDAP Colonial Policy Office; he joined the SS in 1934 and the NSDAP in 1937.[228] His public pronouncements indicated a strident advocacy of Germany's right to its prewar colonies: he combined criticism of the exploitative imperialism of the western colonial powers with an economic argument about how colonies would affect Germany's international payments position. "The German Empire requires raw materials that can be paid in Reichsmark." He reckoned that within a few years, the old colonies could sell Germany goods worth 400 m. RM or 10 percent of the German trade balance.[229] In 1933, he had tried to discover, through an intermediary, whether the new German Chancellor had an interest in colonies, but he found it impossible to obtain a clear answer. Weigelt sent a document to Hitler in October 1933 arguing that it would take a long time to create "the possibility of making room for the German people in the East." Might not colonies be a more appropriate and realistic goal? In 1934, he asked Rudolf Hess to support a project to sell coffee produced by German planters in Cameroon and Tanganyika in Germany. Later, he suggested the creation of a Franco–German company to increase German trade with France *outre-mer*.[230]

In practice, these initiatives achieved little. The German government had little interest either in overseas possessions or in cooperation with France. Hjalmar Schacht insisted on colonial demands and argued that it was the stripping of Germany's colonies that had made the country so unstable after World War I. But he found himself isolated in the government and ignored by the party. Germany's overseas colonial plans remained largely on paper. Nor did colonial trade develop as it did in France or Britain in the 1930s: the major expansion in German overseas trade occurred with independent states in South America. Weigelt recognized and appreciated these realities. He seems in fact to have been a rather cautious businessman. His colonial bark was substantially more impressive than his bite. For instance, he advised Siemens not to go ahead with the construction of a major electricity plant in Turkey because of the extent of Turkey's foreign debts and the likelihood that the government would respond by nationalizing Turkish industry.[231] In addition,

Weigelt's position was weakened because of a major scandal in the affairs of one of the colonial companies he managed. But the colonial strategy, though attractive as a long-term ambition, never assumed an immediate priority for the National Socialist leadership that, in the end, determined the direction of German policy and was quite happy to ignore the advice or suggestions of representatives of "finance capitalism."

European Expansion

The immediate objects of German expansionism lay in Europe. The first target for Germany's new-found strength was Austria, joined to the Reich by the *Anschluss* of March 1938. Then came the Sudetenland, ceded to Germany at the Munich conference of September 1938 by a Britain and France that believed giving way to the clamor of the Sudeten Germans might be a cheap way of buying peace in Europe. The Munich settlement began the economic as well as the political reordering of Central Europe.[232] The Sudetenland included a large part of Czech industry, accounting for 37.5 percent of employment in mining and 57.6 percent in the textile industry.[233] But most of the strategically important engineering industry lay in the Czech interior. In March 1939 German troops occupied the defenseless rump of the remainder of Czechoslovakia, and divided it between an occupied Protectorate Bohemia–Moravia and a puppet state in Slovakia. In September 1939 the next act of German expansion – into Poland – brought a new European war.

In some of the newly occupied territories – in the Sudetenland, in the area of Poland annexed as the Warthegau, in the Generalgouvernement, and after 1940 in Alsace–Lorraine – German banks took over branches of existing banks. In other countries, they engaged in a series of strategic links and takeovers of financial institutions in the occupied countries. Viewed in purely business terms, the expansion of Germany re-created that environment long absent, in which, as in the heyday of German universal banking before World War I, banks could respond to new opportunities and

massive transfers of property by organizing huge takeovers and acquisitions. But the new opportunities were fundamentally unlike
those of the pre-1914 world: they were political, and they originated from diplomatic and then, after 1938, from military action.
The sphere of bank activity was fundamentally altered. Banks did
not bother to attempt to conceal these new acquisitions. In 1944,
the U.S. Federal Reserve Board was able to compile an extensive
survey of German banking penetration in continental Europe, fundamentally on the basis of published material. The report noted
that "the banks which have been most active in the penetration
movement have boasted about their expansion, and it has been
an advertising point to show their contribution to the extension
of German influence to foreign countries and to the welding of
the banking systems of the annexed territories to that of the old
Reich."[234] The Deutsche Bank took, as we shall see, an exceptionally cautious position in this regard.

On the whole this principle of avoiding direct involvement was
defended consistently and semi-publicly by Hermann Abs. For instance in September 1941 he addressed the Reichsbank's Stock Exchange Committee. The minutes of the meeting state: "According
to his opinion, it was preferable to develop banking in South-East
Europe through national circles, rather than to attempt to create explicitly German banks. Apart from that there were already in these
countries sufficient banks under a decisive German influence."[235]
German banks could clearly be influential and powerful without
appearing to be directly involved.

Banks did not operate in a political vacuum. One of the remarkable features of the great German trade expansion to southeastern
Europe in the 1930s is that it was accompanied by almost no investment flows. The economic historian Alan Milward has commented
that:

"History indeed records no greater disproportion between foreign
trade and investment than that shown in the economic relationship
between Nazi Germany and south-eastern Europe in the 1930s.
It might be just as logical to ask the question, Why, when the

proportion of foreign trade with Germany was so very high for these
countries, was the level of German investment there so low?"[236]

After the Munich agreement of 1938, German policy makers
changed course and began to devise a strategy that would include
economic dominance through control of capital.

However, the experience of Germany's big banks varied substantially between different countries in occupied central and Eastern Europe. In the course of the war, Deutsche Bank built up a
"concern," based on its ownership of Austrian, Czech, and Slovak
banks.

In Austria after the occupation, there was a powerful political
lobby, based within the Nazi party, to keep Deutsche Bank out of
Austrian banking (there was more sympathy with Dresdner Bank,
which was quickly allowed to take over the Mercurbank). On the
other hand, within the Reich Economics Ministry in Berlin, arguments about the importance of trade finance gradually became
more important, with the consequence that by 1942 Deutsche Bank
was permitted to acquire a majority stake in the largest Austrian
bank, the Creditanstalt.

The Czech case is very different, in that here – from the beginning of the expansion, with the seizure of the Sudetenland,
and as plans were made for a more extensive intervention in
Czech affairs – the German government wanted the two largest
German commercial banks, Deutsche Bank and Dresdner Bank,
to involve themselves in taking over Czech banks, in particular
those banks with a large German-speaking clientele. The banks
appeared as heralds of the German New Order, with a Dresdner Bank manager discussing the reordering of Sudeten–German
banks in the summer of 1938, before Hitler finally stepped up
the pressure on the Czech state. A Deutsche Bank official went
to Prague to negotiate about the future of Czech banking in March
1939, just two days before the German invasion. What did the
banks offer to the German State that apparently made them so
indispensable in economic imperialism directed against Czechoslovakia? What could they do that a state-owned bank, such as the

Reichs-Kredit-Gesellschaft, could not? Firstly, their foreign contacts were essential in financing the transactions: Deutsche Bank's acquisition of the Deutsche Agrar- und Industriebank, for instance, was financed through transactions conducted via Switzerland in blocked marks [*Sperrmark*]. Secondly, they could handle the extensive "Aryanizations" involved in such a way as to win the confidence and cooperation of greedy and hungry German and Czech industrialists, who might in this way be firmly bound into the military economy of the "Protectorate of Bohemia–Moravia."

There was also some German banking activity in occupied Poland, but because the industrial economy here mattered much less for the German war economy than in the Czech case, the pressure from the German authorities to involve the German big banks was not as great. In territories seized from the Soviet Union, industrial management (and hence a banking presence) was even less of an issue. Banks, including Deutsche Bank, established branches in Poland (but not in the Soviet territories). They were of relatively little commercial importance; but they were deeply implicated in the horrors of the occupation regime.

In Austria, the Nazi party – and to some extent the German government – tried to keep Deutsche Bank out, but it wanted to be involved in a major and profitable area of business. In the Czech lands, the government saw Deutsche Bank (and Dresdner Bank) as vital accessories in the process of economic domination. In Poland, banking was of less interest – to both the German authorities and Deutsche Bank.

Austria and the Österreichische Creditanstalt-Wiener Bankverein

The Creditanstalt (Figure 18) was the most famous Austrian investment bank, and it held many important long-term industrial assets. It was founded in 1855, and had a major capital participation of the Rothschild family, so that it was often held to be a "Rothschild bank." Its international fame became even greater after May 1931,

Figure 18. Main building of Creditanstalt, Vienna.

Source: Courtesy of Deutsche Bank AG.

when its failure precipitated a general banking and financial crisis in Austria, which then spread to the whole of central Europe and eventually brought down German banks as well. It was rescued by an expensive intervention of the Austrian government, and in 1934 it was merged with another crisis-torn Austrian bank, the Wiener Bankverein. By 1938, the resulting institution had a capitalization of 101 m. schillings and a balance sheet worth a total of around 700 m. schillings. The estimates for the total cost to the Austrian government of the rescue operation were around 1 bn. schillings.[237]

The Creditanstalt combined two sets of banking business. It was a gigantic industrial holding company, whose assets collapsed in value during the Depression and brought the bank to ruin. This part of the bank would be vital in any plan for the rearrangement of Austrian business. Secondly, the Creditanstalt had wide-ranging contacts in the former Habsburg territories, and beyond, in southeast and Balkan Europe, and played an important part in international trade finance.

Its pre-1938 management was regarded with suspicion by the German and Austrian Nazis because of the extent of the bank's linkage with the Austrian political system. Two members of the management board were Jewish: one, Franz Rottenberg, left the bank almost immediately after the Anschluss; a second, Oscar Pollack, stayed for a few months. Board president Josef Joham also resigned, leaving only one board member, who was an engineer rather than a banker. The chairman of the supervisory board resigned, while the deputy chairman, Franz Hasslacher, as an economics ministry memorandum noted, "is an enthusiastic supporter of the new Greater Germany [*Gross-Deutschland*]."[238] The new Nazi authorities complained that the predecessors had failed to proceed with sufficient vigor against the allegedly criminal actions that had led to the failure of the bank in 1931. As a result, the Creditanstalt was operating practically without any leadership after the *Anschluss*.[239]

In German dealings with Austria in 1938, political arguments consistently overrode any economic logic. In late February 1938, in anticipation of the *Anschluss*, the Reichsbank had rapidly produced a plan for the currency union of Germany and Austria on the basis of an exchange rate of 2 schillings to 1 RM, which corresponded approximately to the Berlin market quotation. The Reichsbank's economists recognized that this rate did not reflect the higher purchasing power of the schilling, but they saw in their suggestion a way of stimulating the Austrian economy.[240] Their view was supported by the Reich Economics Ministry but was eventually rejected on the grounds that it would be unpopular with Austrians, who thus eventually received their marks at the more favorable rate of 1.50 schillings. This rate created a substantial overvaluation relative to productivity of the Austrian currency, similar to that experienced by East Germany after the monetary union of 1990, with a similar consequence of a massive shock to the Austrian economy, and many bankruptcies and subsequent demands for special measures to protect the Austrian [*"alpenländische"*] areas. How could Austrians be reconciled with the newly composed "Vaterland"? Göring envisaged an immediate, massive work-creation program to absorb Austria's 600,000 unemployed.

As an additional response to the Austrian difficulties, Göring arranged a bank syndicate to give credit to Austrian business (including agriculture) with the intention of "rehabilitating Austrian enterprise and performing functions that will serve the Foreign and Four-Year Plan in the land of Austria."[241] The syndicate was to be led jointly by the Creditanstalt and the Mercurbank, which absorbed the Austrian subsidiary of the Parisian Banque des Pays de l'Europe Centrale, known in Austria as the Länderbank, to become the second major Austrian bank. The Mercurbank was already owned by Dresdner Bank. Deutsche Bank and Dresdner Bank were eventually also brought into the syndicate and each took a share equal to those of the two leading banks. In the first year, a total credit volume of 25 m. RM. was envisaged; this was extended by 1940 to 65 m. RM.

Immediately after the *Anschluss* (March 12, 1938), Mosler, the speaker of Deutsche Bank's management board, tried to see Bank Commissar Ernst, to tell him "that we are currently considering establishing branches in Austria on the basis of annexation by Germany."[242] A few days later, Deutsche Bank sent Abs, together with Helmuth Pollems and Walter Pohle from the Berlin secretariat, a young man who quickly emerged as a major figure in dealing with the banking consequences of the military reordering of Central Europe. The attractions of the Creditanstalt did not lie principally in its Austrian business alone. For Deutsche Bank, the acquisition of the Creditanstalt would be the beginning of a drive to build contacts in an area of Europe that was increasingly subject to German political and economic pressure. But participation of Deutsche Bank in the Creditanstalt ran into opposition from the new Nazi government of Austria.

Economics Minister Hans Fischböck announced his reservations. (Fischböck, a member of the NSDAP and a former manager of the ill-fated Bodenkreditanstalt and of the Creditanstalt in Austria, had been the economic adviser of the Austrian Nazi leader Arthur Seyss-Inquart; in March 1938 he was appointed Economics Minister and in May became Minister of Finance.[243]) This impression was confirmed when a board member of Mitteldentsche Stahlwerke, Otto Steinbrinck, told Abs of his interview with Wilhelm Keppler, Hitler's economic adviser and "Reichsbeauftragter für Österreich," on April 12: "very nasty atmosphere against Deutsche Bank," he noted. Keppler had said to him, "D.B., with robbery in mind, has arrived in Vienna with 20 men to take over the C.A."[244]

Deutsche Bank representatives were certainly quick off the mark in establishing the appearance of control. The general meeting of the Creditanstalt on March 25, 1938 was chaired, in the absence of Hasslacher, by Abs. One day later, on March 26, a contract was drawn up regulating relations between the two banks, according to which, "given a corresponding material relationship between Deutsche Bank and the C.A., Deutsche Bank is prepared to conduct its southeast Europe business as far as possible through Vienna."[245] Branches of Deutsche Bank in the "Altreich" immediately began to advertise their close connection with the Creditanstalt ("we are able to say that we have at our disposal exact knowledge of all relevant circumstances within Austria").[246]

Keppler blocked this agreement while Fischböck claimed that Schacht had told Abs that Deutsche Bank could not take the Creditanstalt. Abs noted in response that he had had no meeting with Schacht at all in 1938. Instead, the Creditanstalt started to discuss the sale of a stake to the state-owned Viag. Deutsche Bank was "disappointed" at the decision taken by the Economics Ministry. Abs noted that "the southeast European business that I have so often stressed met with no appreciation whatsoever."[247] The 35 percent stake in the Creditanstalt owned directly by the Austrian state was sold to the Reichs-Kredit-Gesellschaft, and another 39 percent, owned by the Österreichische Industriekredit A.G. and the Österreichische Nationalbank, was sold directly to Viag, which thus controlled 71 percent of the Creditanstalt stock.[248]

A Deutsche Bank executive, Helmuth Pollems, contacted Rudolf Brinkmann, the Vice-President of the Reichsbank, as well as the Reich Economics Ministry, and obtained some support for the idea that Deutsche Bank was best placed to develop business with southeast Europe.[249] But this was just before Brinkmann had a catastrophic nervous breakdown, which led him to distribute bank notes to the amazed public in the streets of Berlin before he was removed to a sanatorium. Deutsche Bank's argument was that it was unfair to let Dresdner Bank take the Mercurbank and not to give Deutsche Bank some equivalent business.[250] In May 1938, Deutsche Bank produced a lengthy memorandum in which it emphasized the longstanding nature of the contacts with the Creditanstalt (going back to 1873, when the three-year-old Deutsche Bank had held two seats on the board of directors of the four-year-old Wiener Bankverein). It complained that the Viag sale had led to "elimination of its [Deutsche Bank's] activities in Austria" and again suggested a merging of foreign activities of the Berlin and the Vienna banks. "Above all, however, bringing together the foreign business of the Creditanstalt and the Deutsche Bank would make it possible to process the main provision and marketing areas of the south east in a very special way." In addition, establishing a link between the Creditanstalt and a Berlin big bank would facilitate the flow of credit and capital to Austria.[251] By the autumn of 1938, the Reich Economics Ministry supported the idea of a close cooperation between the Reichs-Kredit-Gesellschaft and Deutsche Bank in the Creditanstalt, with a roughly equal capital participation. It concluded that Viag should sell its share in the Creditanstalt to Deutsche Bank; but if that were not practicable, because of the opposition of Viag, Deutsche Bank should conclude a friendship treaty with the Creditanstalt "that secures the co-operation of both banks' systems."[252] In return, Deutsche Bank would not set up its own branches in the Austrian territories.

In fact, the leading managers of Viag were quite prepared to cooperate closely with Deutsche Bank in order to be able to use the latter's considerable expertise in commercial banking and trade finance. The Reichs-Kredit-Gesellschaft proposed to Abs a division of southeast Europe into spheres of influence: Hungary and Yugoslavia would be managed by the Creditanstalt, through the branch in Budapest and a majority in the Allgemeiner Jugoslawischer Bankverein; Bulgaria and Turkey would be managed by Deutsche Bank, through the Kreditbank Sofia and the Deutsche Bank branch in Istanbul; while Dresdner Bank would be left with Greece "in order to develop a certain equality in terms of settlement."[253] By this stage, Deutsche Bank's plans were also supported by State Commissar Josef Bürckel, who noted that "both banks' representations in the south east complement each other exceptionally well." The Creditanstalt should sell its industrial holdings and concentrate on trade finance.[254]

The Nazi politician Fischböck became chairman of the Creditanstalt management board, but in practice he played a little role in banking business. His major official function lay in dealing with the bank's personnel. In any case, his attention was rapidly engaged by the business of "Aryanizing" the Netherlands, on the model that he had developed in Austria.

Most of the Creditanstalt's major industrial holdings were stripped out in 1938 and sold to the Reichswerke "Hermann Göring," which took over controlling shares in the Steirische Gussstahlwerke AG, the Kärntnerische Eisen- und Stahlwerksgesellschaft, Feinstahlwerke Traisen AG vorm. Fischer, Steyr-Daimler-Puch AG, Maschinen- und Waggonfabrikations AG in Simmering vorm. H. D. Schmid, and the Erste Donau-Dampfschiffahrtsgesellschaft. But in the course of the very rapid "Aryanization" of the Austrian economy in 1938, it acquired a substantial number of new shareholdings, including companies in paper, stone, bridge-building, and foreign trade.

The Creditanstalt played a significant role in the process of Austrian "Aryanization," even though that development was driven – much more clearly than had been the case in Germany – by the state. It registered all the Jewish assets in its deposit accounts. It asked to buy Jewish assets paid into the Prussian State Bank

[*Seehandlung*] in Germany as part of the "Jewish property levy" of November 1938. It attempted to buy Jewish-owned firms, notably the large paper producer Bunzl and Biach A.G.,[255] but this was a highly complicated transaction and the Creditanstalt was frustrated by a rival syndicate organized by Dresdner Bank. It had to be content with a smaller stake (36 percent) in the enterprises.[256] There were also Creditanstalt loans to "Aryanized" companies, such as the leather case and purse manufacturer Brüder Eisert A.G. This enterprise required Creditanstalt credit lines, even though their owners had "made their shares available," as the report prepared by the Deutsche Revisions- und Treuhandgesellschaft for the Austrian credit syndicate euphemistically put it, "partly for nothing, partly against payment of a small sum (max. 10 RM per share)."[257]

All businesses in Austria, not just Jewish-owned businesses, were negatively affected by the choice of an inappropriate exchange rate in the Austro–German monetary union. There was thus a demand for new capital from Germany, which became increasingly urgent in the course of 1938 and 1939. These circumstances made the political authorities suddenly more sympathetic to Deutsche Bank plans that they had previously rejected.

Deutsche Bank and Viag decided in a "syndicate agreement" of December 30, 1938 to sell 25 percent of the Creditanstalt's share capital, 48,500 ordinary and 35,000 preferred shares, to Deutsche Bank. Viag would have three representatives and Deutsche Bank two on the supervisory board of the Creditanstalt; each would supply one vice-president for the supervisory board, which would be under the presidency of Franz Hasslacher.

Deutsche Bank sent bankers to supervise the restructuring of the business, and it recommended that the Creditanstalt send its managers to study the banking practice of branches of Deutsche Bank. In November 1940 (i.e. after the German occupation of Belgium), Deutsche Bank bought Creditanstalt shares of a nominal value of 525,000 RM from the Société Générale de Belgique, and of 262,500 RM from the Compagnie Belge de l'Etranger, so that its holding now increased to 36 percent. The Société Générale welcomed the opportunity to dispose of southeastern European assets, which had been in fact very costly since the Depression. At the end of 1941 preliminary discussions began about the purchase of some or all of Viag's 51 percent stake in the Creditanstalt. The critical argument that Deutsche Bank made in discussions with German officials rested on the proposals for a coordinated economic development of southeast Europe: "If things develop as Deutsche Bank wishes and has described, then Deutsche Bank welcomes the strengthening of the Creditanstalt's south-eastern business, even at the cost of Deutsche Bank." As part of the conditions for Deutsche Bank's ownership, the sale of further industrial participation was discussed.[258]

Already in 1940, the Creditanstalt had started to develop as a major player in the financial reorganization of Austria's neighbors. Without consulting the German banking authorities, and to their astonishment and irritation, it bought the Slovak branches of the Czech Böhmisch-Mährische Bank (Legiobank), which had been attacked by the Slovak government.[259] At the same time, at the initiative of Fischböck, the Creditanstalt took over the Cracow branch of Deutsche Bank. In May 1942 an agreement was reached under which Deutsche Bank would acquire a majority holding, by buying 17,675,000 RM worth of Creditanstalt shares and then selling the rest of the Viag holding (amounting to about 10 percent of the total capital) to small shareholders. Viag was paid with the industrial holdings from the Creditanstalt. At the same time, the Creditanstalt was restructured as a vehicle of financial control in central Europe. It was to take 30 percent of the shares of Banca Comerciala Romana, Bucharest, 30 percent of the Deutsch-Bulgarische Kreditbank, Sofia, and a third of the shares of the Böhmische Union-Bank (BUB), a major Deutsche Bank subsidiary in the Czech lands. The BUB deal was authorized by the Reich Supervisory Office for Banking in October 1942.

Abs explained the philosophy of control in a meeting of the working committee of the Creditanstalt in August 1941, when he argued that a branch of the Creditanstalt in Budapest could never be effective on its own.

"Since [he said] the business could not for the most basic reasons be run with its own funds alone, consideration must be given to borrowing funds, which a bank that looked externally like a Hungarian institution might be able to do. As regards the partner, Mr. Abs is of the opinion (and all the members of the working committee agree with him) that only the highest-ranking institution could be considered for this, which would be the Pest Commercial Bank of Hungary."[260]

The banks that would form a Deutsche Bank–dominated network in southeastern Europe were in addition to be linked through interlocking directorships. The Creditanstalt would send a delegate to each of the boards of directors of the Bucharest and Sofia banks, and two to BUB. In addition, a BUB banker would be on the supervisory board of the Creditanstalt. The completion of the 1942 deal marked the completion of a major Deutsche Bank–led banking group in central Europe, which was already earlier frequently referred to by German officials as a "Konzern" or "group."[261]

Abs had seen the Creditanstalt's role as part of a Europe-wide investment banking network, in which the Creditanstalt would work closely with the Deutsche Bank as well as with the Société Générale de Belgique. His first efforts, before the outbreak of war, involved urging the Creditanstalt to sell shares in "Zorka" (First Yugoslav Chemical Company) to the Belgian chemical giant Solvay.[262] The Société Générale had large holdings in the Jugoslawischer Bankverein, which the Göring authorities wished to transfer to German banks, but Abs resisted this business and the matter rested until the occupation of Belgium.[263] Then the memory of the apparent sympathy of the Deutsche Bank to Belgian interests subsequently led the Société Générale to try to deal with more enthusiasm with Abs in disposing of eastern and southeastern European assets than with rival German bankers.[264] The Société Générale eventually gave up its Yugoslav holdings. Payments for the sale of the Jugoslawischer Bankverein were made, in the usual fashion, over the German–Belgian clearing account. The Creditanstalt took 51 percent of the Yugoslav stock, and German banks held minority stakes: the Deutsche Bank and the Dresdner Bank each had 12.5 percent, the Commerzbank and the Reichs-Kredit-Gesellschaft had 6.25 percent each, and the Böhmische Union-Bank had 4 percent.[265] The Yugoslav bank was subsequently divided up along the lines of the new political settlement into a Bankverein für Kroatien and a Bankverein Belgrad AG.

The Creditanstalt also expanded its direct Yugoslav operations, lending to Südost-Montan and the Mines de Bor, a major source of copper (with substantial reserves of zinc, lead, antimony, and chromium ores). By March 1941 a majority of shares had been bought from their previous French and Belgian owners.

The Böhmische Union-Bank and Czech Banking

The dismembering of Czechoslovakia[266] in 1938–9, through the September 1938 Munich Agreement and then the invasion of March 1939, was a crucial part of German economic expansion. Czechoslovakia had an industrial base that represented a substantial addition to Germany's armaments economy. To use this new potential, German policy makers aimed at a restructuring of ownership. The Czech lands were also home to a number of banks with German-Jewish histories, and with substantial industrial holdings. These banks, and indeed the whole Czech banking system, had been weakened by the Depression, and there were many complaints that the country was overbanked. During the Depression, many banks had acquired substantial industrial holdings as their customers found themselves in difficulties.[267] In the eyes of the German economic planners, the Czech banks might lend themselves to the goal of a reorientation of the Czech economy and its integration in German economic mobilization for war. A strong German position was built up in the months following the first stage of the dismemberment of the Czech state at Munich: this provided a base for further economic imperialism after March 1939. After Munich, the German government sent lists of Jewish firms in the Sudetenland to the banks together with a demand that the banks should manage the process of "Aryanization."[268] In addition, Deutsche

Bank prepared a detailed guide on the industrial structure and the character of the major companies of the Sudetenland, as well as of the rest of "Bohemia and Moravia."[269]

The economic guide to the Sudetenland was published very quickly in October 1938, and must already have been prepared before the Munich agreement. Dresdner Bank had been even more provocatively explicit in its preparations for economic imperialism. On July 25, 1938, the director of its Dresden branch, Reinhold Freiherr von Lüdinghausen, had organized a meeting of Sudeten-German businessmen, including many board members of the two most important German-language Czech banks, the Böhmische Union-Bank (BUB) and the Böhmische Escompte Gesellschaft (Bebca), in the home of a glass manufacturer, Walter Riedel, in Polubny (Unter-Polaun). At this meeting, the businessmen discussed the potential for taking over the Czech banking system.[270]

Expansion did not halt here. Just three weeks after the German invasion of the Sudetenland, on October 21, 1938, Hitler ordered preparations by the army that would enable Germany "to conquer 'rump-Tschechei' at any time, if it were to pursue, say, a policy hostile to Germany."[271] After the German occupation of March 15, 1939, "Aryanization" became such a transparent device for the establishment of German preponderance and the "Germanization" [Eindeutschung] of Czech business that for that reason – more than from any deep-seated moral objection – Czech industrialists and the Czech government of Emil Hácha voiced increasing hostility to the German policy, and they demanded measures for the confiscation of Jewish assets "where disturbances of public order might occur."[272] The resulting clashes between German and Czech concepts produced a further brutalization in the Jewish policy in the Czech territories.

There can be no doubt that the German political authorities provided the ultimate driving force in this process of establishing German control. The major German banks, especially Dresdner Bank and Deutsche Bank, played an important part as accessories. Their motivation was complex. In part, they were driven by competitive calculations: if they neglected expansion in the new territories, they would lose out to their German rivals. Deutsche Bank noted and complained about each instance when it felt that the military regime or the party was favoring the Dresdner Bank unfairly. In some part, the banks were also driven by tax concessions and other subsidies from the German government. Thirdly, the process of expansion developed a dynamic of its own: as the German banks established their hold over Czech business, the young, ideologically driven managers who were now placed on the frontier of German imperialism saw a chance to make a name and reputation, and so they developed their own initiatives. Such spontaneous ideas, emanating from the middle levels of the banking hierarchy rather than from the Berlin executives, eventually fitted in perfectly with the turn to radicalization in occupation policy in September and October 1941, after Reinhard Heydrich came to Prague.

After the Munich Agreement of September 30, 1938, and the annexation of the Sudetenland by the German Reich, Deutsche Bank took over sixteen branches of a Czech bank with a large German-speaking customer base, the Ceská Banká Union or Böhmische Union-Bank, as part of a reordering of Sudeten banking under the direction of the Reich Economics Ministry. Deutsche Bank had originally been interested in acquiring the Sudeten-German branches of a larger and more successful Czech–German bank, the Böhmische Escompte Bank; but in early October 1938 German Bank Commissar Friedrich Ernst agreed to allocate the branches of the Escompte Bank to Dresdner Bank.[273] The Commissar was responsible for granting permission to take over branches and for decisions on the closure of individual branches.[274] In discussions within the German political authorities imposed on the Sudetenland, BUB was regarded with the least sympathy. A discussion in November 1938 about which banks could be used to extend German influence concluded that BUB "is ruled out as a point of concentration, being a purely Jewish bank."[275]

Deutsche Bank had already been in contact with a Czech bank. Bankers sometimes have finely tuned political antennas: the first contacts occurred before the Munich meetings. Rösler and Abs of Deutsche Bank started negotiations with Viktor Ulbrich of the

Deutsche Agrar- und Industriebank AG, Prague (DAIB). At the start, the German bankers do not appear to have been very enthusiastic about the new business prospects. Abs noted on the cards he kept detailing his business contacts: "our intentions, in which connection we need to make it perfectly clear to him that a full takeover of the branches, let alone of the whole business, is out of the question."[276]

On October 14, 1938, the bank commissar agreed that Deutsche Bank might begin negotiations with BUB, as well as with the DAIB "for the purpose of taking over the Sudeten-German business of those banks." The suggestion was that Deutsche Bank should take over the whole business but might make reductions in the number of branches.[277]

BUB was founded in 1872, with a capital of 10 m. Austrian florins. It was substantially weakened by the Depression, but it was in a far better position than the much more exposed Agrarbank. Because of the German character of the BUB and the Bebca, and of other Sudeten banks, and because they were believed to have substantial assets in Germany, these German banks were subject to depositor losses of confidence and bank runs after the banking crisis of July 1931.[278] Both BUB and Bebca had a substantial number of Jewish customers and employees and managers. The takeover of the Sudetenland branches of BUB proceeded according to a document dated January 4, 1939, but was to take effect retroactively from November 1, 1938 (Figure 19). But even earlier, individual Sudeten BUB branches put out signs saying "Deposits for Deutsche Bank accepted here" – to the irritation of the German authorities.[279] Eventually, Deutsche Bank took twenty-three branches in all. The assets and liabilities of these branches were transferred to Deutsche Bank, and BUB kept only a few named customers. Separating the branches from the Prague bank was a complex financial operation. It had major implications for the profitability of the remaining rump of BUB, which had lost branches in the most dynamic industrial areas, with substantial loans to the textile and glass industries. A memorandum of December 1938 presented to the Czech Finance Ministry listed 53 firms in which

BUB had previously held sizeable stakes. Of these, 32 had been lost in the Sudetenland. Of the Sudeten firms, the financial positions of 16 were said to be "good," 11 "had prospects," and 5 were "bad." Of the 19 firms that remained in the Czech state, however, only one was classed as "good," 9 "had prospects," 6 were "weak," and 3 were "bad." The bank had lost its best enterprises and was in a "catastrophic state."[280]

After the invasion of March 15, 1939, Bohemia–Moravia remained legally separate from Germany, although it was clearly intended to be part of a German economic imperium in which the German people should "secure for itself the sources [. . .] of the raw materials so important for its well-being."[281] By October 1940, Bohemia–Moravia was linked to the Reich by a customs union. But long before that the banking system had been used to tie the Protectorate's economy to Germany through ownership.

The German authorities generally assumed, after the experience with the Sudetenland, that Deutsche Bank would continue to work with BUB. But one official in a meeting in the banking Commissariat immediately objected that "Union Bank [of Bohemia, i.e. BUB] being a strongly Jewish-infiltrated enterprise, it therefore seems intolerable that Deutsche Bank should allocate orders to it on a preferential basis."[282] Together with Dresdner Bank, Deutsche Bank sent to the Reich Economics Ministry on March 14, 1939, one day before the invasion, a new plan for the reordering of Czech banks. Whereas the Reich Economics Ministry had tentatively given Deutsche Bank permission to buy the Tatra Bank's holding of the Escompte- und Volkswirtschaftliche Bank, Bratislava, the banks now proposed that Dresdner Bank and its affiliate the Vienna Länderbank should carry out this transaction and that a purchase of Bebca's share in the Bratislava Handels- und Kreditbank A. G. Half of the Handels- und Kreditbank shares acquired in this way then be transferred to Deutsche Bank or the Vienna Creditanstalt.[283]

After the actual invasion, Deutsche Bank sent (under the signatures of Rummel and Rösler) a letter to the Reich Economics

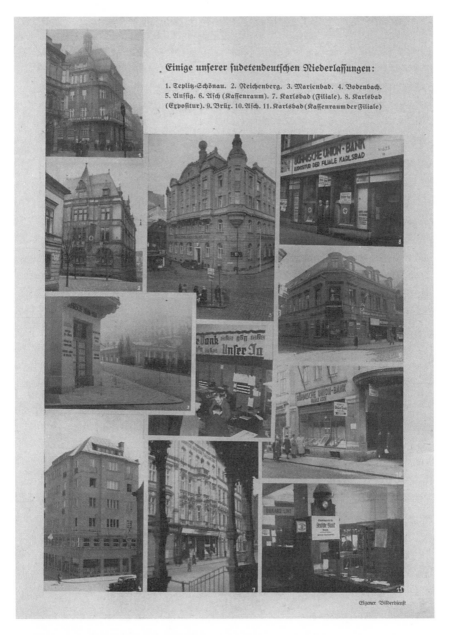

Figure 19. Branches of Böhmische Union-Bank in Sudetenland, 1938.

Source: Courtesy of Deutsche Bank AG.

Ministry about the Czech banking situation. It would suit the goal of integration in the German economic sphere if

> "in future one or more regional banks of a Czech character remain in existence for the time being. However, this is possible only on condition that those banks adapt themselves to the general German interest [*gesamtdeutsche Interesse*], in which connection it may turn out to be necessary that sooner or later German banks themselves participate in such institutions. [...] Another thing to be borne in mind here is that, of the partially transferred Czech banking industry, various institutions will need to disappear for racial reasons or because they are currently insolvent. In connection with the restructuring and liquidation of such institutions it would be necessary, where enterprises of significant size are concerned, to think of involving German big banks, since a regional bank would scarcely be in a position to cope with the problems that will arise in this connection."[284]

The Deutsche Bank was still looking for more attractive Czech alternatives to the BUB. Rösler originally wanted to continue to work on a 50:50 basis with Dresdner Bank in taking over Bebca. The Reich Economics Ministry pushed Deutsche Bank to take over BUB instead, and in practice Deutsche Bank continued to work with BUB in Bohemia and Moravia. It took 23 more branches (out of a total of 34), the 28 branches of the DAIB, and 5 of the Mährische Bank (BUB's Slovakian branches were incorporated into the Union-Bank Pressburg, which was jointly owned by BUB and the Wiener Creditanstalt-Bankverein).

There exists an account of the events of the German invasion of the Sudetenland in September 1938 and then of Czechoslovakia in March 1939 and the takeover of BUB prepared by the bank's *Prokurist*, F. Kavan, who remained in this position through the whole of the occupation. Walter Pohle appeared in BUB in Prague on March 13, 1939, two days *before* the German invasion, declared himself to be a senior official and "confidential agent" of Deutsche Bank, and started negotiations about the financial claims of Deutsche Bank following the transfer of BUB's Sudeten-German branches. Clearly, the political atmosphere was already growing tenser. On March 10, the federal Czech government in Prague tried to launch a preemptive strike against Slovak separatism and to dissolve the Slovak government. By March 11 and 12, there was street fighting in Bratislava, and German minorities flew swastika flags and staged riots in Jihlava (Iglau) and Brno (Brünn). On March 13, Hitler summoned his ally, the Slovak separatist leader Father Tiso, to Berlin.

At least to Kavan, in retrospect it was clear that Pohle, who subsequently came to be the dominating personality in the BUB, knew about the impending invasion. Immediately after the invasion, German military officials demanded a greater German influence over BUB. On March 16 or 17, Pohle put in another "forceful appearance, saying that BUB was a Jewish enterprise and must therefore, both in its own interest and in that of Deutsche Bank as major creditor arising out of the transaction of the cession of the Sudeten branches, be pronounced an aryanized enterprise as quickly as possible." Pohle's rival at Dresdner Bank, von Lüdinghausen, behaved in a similar way, arriving in military uniform in the Bebca offices shortly after the German invasion.

Pohle, according to Kavan, was protected by the Gestapo. He immediately dismissed the Jewish directors and appointed the previous director of the auditing division, Joseph Krebs, who had German nationality, as the new director. The supervisory board meeting of March 16, 1939, began with a declaration by Otto Freund "that his service contract is not being renewed and that he will remain at the bank's disposal as long as it wishes." Such an action was certainly not legal under the bank's existing articles of association. Who had the legal authority not to renew the contract? Freund also stated that Stein and Schubert "have resigned, which information was registered with regret." At the next meeting of the supervisory board, the existing eighteen members resigned en bloc; only four members returned in the reconstituted supervisory board.[285] Freund, the previous principal director, was arrested fourteen days later by the German police and soon died in prison, allegedly by his own hand. The board members were replaced by Deutsche Bank officials, or by people who were acceptable to the occupation regime.

The *Tantiemen* (payments to directors by virtue of their membership on other supervisory boards) of the former Jewish directors
were now to be paid directly into the bank. In June 1939, Pohle
announced the dismissal of the non-Aryan members of the auditing department. But in January 1940, he still reported that, of the
917 employees, 38 were Jewish.[286] After the war, the Deutsche
Bank estimated that in all some 400 Jewish employees had been
dismissed.[287]

To foreign bankers, however, Deutsche Bank carefully camouflaged the events of March 1939. When Sterling Bunnell of the
National City Bank of New York visited Deutsche Bank in May
1939, he was told that in the reordering of Czech banking, "the
removal of the Jewish members of the board of directors was effected without coercion by mutual agreement. To our knowledge
[he said], the persons concerned had resigned their offices volun-
tarily in the light of the altered political circumstances."[288]

In April 1939, the Reich Economics Ministry in Berlin demanded "final clarification of the question [...] whether Union
Bank of Bohemia [BUB] is to be seen as an Aryan or as a Jewish enterprise." Some of the companies in Bohemia and Moravia
in which BUB held participations found themselves in difficulties
because they were treated by the German authorities as "non-
Aryan" by reason of BUB's engagement. Deutsche Bank was required to prepare "at the earliest opportunity a memo concerning
the current circumstances, both financial (with regard to capital)
and personal, [...] which is then to be forwarded to Prague for
checking."[289]

Accordingly, Deutsche Bank sent a paper to the Reich Economics Ministry in which it attributed the necessity for a "restructuring" of BUB to the actions of the German government. On the
basis of such an argument, the BUB was granted a "certificate of
Aryan-ness" [*Bescheingung über den arischen Charakter*] on July
5, 1939.

In his 1950 affidavit Kavan claimed that Deutsche Bank deliberately made BUB appear to have large losses. "In the circumstances,
Deutsche Bank representatives decided to make the BUB balance

sheet look so bad that it in fact showed a loss and could be uti-
lized for their further plans." In March and April 1939, Deutsche
Bank submitted to the Reich Economics Ministry estimates of the
losses on the basis of an audit by the Czech firm Revisni Jednota
Bank, and of its own – more generous – estimates. The Jednota
concluded that the bank had lost all its reserves, as well as 40 m.
CKr of its capital. Deutsche Bank initially estimated the losses as
at least 200 m. CKr. It argued that the Jednota had not taken into
account the likelihood of losses in Slovakia, Carpathia–Ukraine,
"losses to be expected on non-Aryan accounts receivable," and
"reordering costs/dealing with non-Aryans."[290]

The main German aim was to reduce the capital by a ratio of
1:10 to make it possible for Deutsche Bank to acquire a majority
of the shares. The Czech bankers had originally preferred a smaller
capital reduction of 1:4 (Kavan mistakenly claimed 1:5), but the
larger scale German plan prevailed.[291] In March 1939, the capital
of BUB had amounted to 150 m. CKr (nominal), in 750,000 shares
of 200 CKr. Of these shares, 100,000 belonged to the British Overseas Bank, London (which also held an option on another 25,000);
70,292 belonged to the Société Générale de Belgique, Brussels;
130,000 belonged to the bank itself; and 80,000 belonged to an
enterprise controlled by the bank, the Petschek sugar refinery.[292]
Of the other shares, 264,000 were domiciled in the Protectorate,
106,000 in the Sudetenland and Austria. Kavan noted that "in fact
a substantial number of those shares were owned by non-Aryans."
In addition there were, as an internal memorandum of Deutsche
Bank noted, further "quite substantial amounts [...] in the possession of Sudeten-German industrialists."[293] In May 1939, it was
reported that about 3 percent of the shares were in "non-Aryan
hands."[294]

The Sudeten-German owners were bought out at a price of 25
percent of the nominal value of their shares. In the politically tur-
bulent months of August and September 1939, Deutsche Bank also
tried unsuccessfully to buy shares from the London and Brussels
banks at a price of 10 percent of their nominal value.[295] The Société
Générale refused to go along with this plan. Having failed in its

move to establish complete legal control, Deutsche Bank instead bought the 210,000 shares of the bank that BUB controlled (at a low price of 20 CKr, although the shares were valued in the books at 77.27 CKr). This purchase was only ratified by the Reich Economics Ministry on March 16, 1940.

An extraordinary general meeting was held on December 12, 1939, to agree on a capital reduction to one-tenth of the previous value. Deutsche Bank had 216,000 shares, and in addition it had bought another 6,100; 85,448 were in trustee accounts. It asked the Belgian Société Générale to vote for its proposals; but the Belgian bank cabled back with the instruction that its votes should be used to abstain: Pohle expressed his extreme irritation about the Belgian decision. (Two months later, the governor of the Société Générale, Alexandre Galopin, told Hermann Abs that his bank was "not under any circumstances prepared to lend retrospective support to events in Czechoslovakia by taking part in supervisory board meetings or general meetings of BUB."[296]) Only 1,449 shares were represented by individuals, who Kavan believed to be members of a shareholders' protection association. Again, Kavan's affidavit is quite damning. When Kavan warned Pohle that many of these individuals had detailed inside knowledge of the finances of BUB, Pohle replied: "These people should think long and hard about their protest plans, because steps will be taken to ensure that, at the general meeting of December 12, 1939, people from the Gestapo or persons very close to the Gestapo will also be present." At this extraordinary general meeting, Deutsche Bank was sold the shares held by BUB "at the price, laid down by the German foreign-exchange authorities, of 100. − K = 10. − RM."[297]

Pohle explained the capital reduction as the *quid pro quo* for bringing in Deutsche Bank and its support. He also told the general meeting: "We believe that, in our area of responsibility, we can build a bridge from the Protectorate to the Greater German Reich and even farther afield."[298] The latter objective involved Pohle in increasingly ambitious plans for economic and financial reordering, some of which brought him eventually into conflict with the

German authorities, as well as with Deutsche Bank's Berlin headquarters.

Deutsche Bank then wanted to turn BUB into a commercial bank and to sell off its industrial holdings.[299] It believed that the BUB had not originally been constructed as an industrial holding company, but had acquired its substantial shareholdings largely as a result of Depression-era difficulties. Deutsche Bank also seemed to the Prague bankers to be striving for greater direct control of Czech affairs. In his postwar memorandum, Kavan claimed that Deutsche Bank applied the "Führerprinzip" and centralized all decisions in Berlin, so that BUB "was an independent institution in name alone; in reality it was a subsidiary of Deutsche Bank."[300]

In 1939 the BUB was in a sorry state. Its commercial position had been eroded by the Depression. It was illiquid. Its management had been in large part German–Jewish, and the departure of its senior managers left the bank effectively leaderless. It remained vulnerable to anti-Semitic purges. Its most valuable industrial holdings had been in the Sudetenland. At lower levels, in November 1939 the firm was still employing a large number of Jews.[301] Many of the banks' depositors were Jewish, and many of the credits and industrial assets related to Czech–Jewish firms. In August 1939, a candid letter to a member of Deutsche Bank's supervisory board stated:

> "In addition to the partitioning-off of Sudeten-German business, the formation of the Protectorate of Bohemia-Moravia was in the nature of things a further heavy blow for what was left of BUB, for its continued existence as a German-Jewish bank became impossible. On top of the general difficulties of economic reordering in the Protectorate, BUB was particularly affected by the fact that it was almost exclusively Jewish-run and that even today much of its clientele also consists of Jewish firms, whose future is in doubt."[302]

And finally, the BUB had lost 2,461,000 CKr through "speculation at bank risk."[303] It survived by borrowing large sums from its own pension fund (the 20.5 m. CKr were repaid in 1942).[304]

After the outbreak of war, a further source of weakness emerged. Some of the bank's safe-custody accounts were held abroad, where they were vulnerable to legal action. In November 1940, Pohle reported "on the seizure that has occurred of safe-custody accounts in New York because of actions brought by Jews who have emigrated to the USA for release of their stockholdings and on the only partly completed transfer of such accounts with Dutch banks to Swiss banks; he points out the possibility that in certain circumstances the bank might successfully be sued by customers for damages."[305]

The reordering of BUB had involved a 10:1 capital reduction, so that 150 m. CKr capital was reduced to 15 m. CKr. The capital was then increased to 100 m. CKr, through the issue of 212,500 new shares at a nominal value of 400 CKr. This required the consent of the Reich Finance Ministry, which was requested in January 1940 and granted on January 18.[306] The capital reduction was followed by an offer from Deutsche Bank to buy out existing shareholders at a price of 25 percent of par value. Jewish shareholders were explicitly excluded from this option. 60 m. CKr were to be issued to Czech shareholders, and Deutsche Bank already held 25 m. CKr. With the assistance of the private bank Delbrück Schickler & Co., Deutsche Bank eventually acquired 76,740,000 CKr worth of shares and thus owned 75 percent of BUB.[307] (In a subsequent capital increase of 50 m. CKr in 1942, the Vienna Creditanstalt took a significant minority participation. As a result, in 1943 Deutsche Bank held 58 percent of the shares, the Creditanstalt 33 percent, the British Overseas Bank and the Société Générale 2 percent, and "other banks" 7 percent of the capital.[308]) Deutsche Bank received permission to buy up Jewish-owned shares at the much lower rate of 11 percent of their value.[309]

The new management of the bank came from Deutsche Bank in Germany. The main figure, Walter Pohle from the Berlin office, was an energetic young man, 31 years old, who had briefly been employed by the Reich Economics Ministry before joining Deutsche Bank, at first as an intern [*Volontär*]. At the outset, Deutsche Bank believed that it might be very helpful to employ someone with good contacts with the Economics Ministry department responsible for regulating banking (*Geld- Bank- und Börsenwesen*). Pohle was promoted with exceptional rapidity, from the position of intern with an annual stipend of 300 RM to that of holder of power of attorney (*Prokurist*) in 1937. In 1938 he became a deputy director, with a salary of 15,000 RM. This promotion occurred despite an odd interlude in January 1937, when he was arrested by the Gestapo and held for two days. The Gestapo eventually informed Deutsche Bank's legal department that Pohle had "without his knowledge become involved in a stupid business and the affair is now provisionally closed."[310] Pohle had already worked with Abs in the attempt to take Adler & Oppenheimer into "Aryan" hands. He asked Deutsche Bank to keep open the possibility of his return to his old bank at the end of his adventure in Prague. The other former Deutsche Bank representative on the management board, Max Ludwig Rohde, was older, and came from the Saarbrücken branch.[311]

Taking over the management of BUB and installing new directors[312] involved substantial costs for Deutsche Bank. Because the operation had been conducted at the insistence of the German government, Deutsche Bank demanded a public subsidy. Its initial strategy was to try to extend the procedure using discounted blocked mark accounts that had also been employed to acquire the DAIB.[313]

Eventually, in December 1939, the Reich Economics Ministry agreed to the provision of a subsidy on the grounds that "BUB had [...] always been a German institution. Its collapse would therefore represent a political setback for German interests [*das Deutschtum*]."[314] As a result, the German state agreed to meet 55 percent of Deutsche Bank's losses arising out of Sudeten debtors of BUB through the extension of a Reich guarantee up to a total loss of 16.9 m. RM. The guarantee and loss account, it was agreed, would be credited by any gains to Deutsche Bank arising out of a revaluation of the Czech assets of BUB.

From the standpoint of Deutsche Bank, few aspects of this transaction could hold any attraction. In November 1939 the bank explained to the German government that it would not have been interested in the business "if we had been completely free in our decision-making."[315] Internally, it justified the takeover on two grounds: first, that the initiative had lain not with the bank but rather with the Reich Economics Ministry; secondly, that without any response from Deutsche Bank to the new situation, the expansion of Germany would in reality mean enhanced business for the politically better-connected Dresdner Bank and thus a diminution of the business of Deutsche Bank.[316]

From the beginning of 1941, as BUB's profitability revived dramatically, Deutsche Bank tried to obtain a cancellation of the Reich guarantee of BUB claims. The bank explained: "[it does not suit] Deutsche Bank to have within its group a Reich guarantee for its commitments and even less to receive payments in consequence of that guarantee that might be seen as subsidies. The reputation of BUB will also suffer if it is deemed to be in some way underwritten by the Reich."[317] Deutsche Bank now proposed to take the risk of BUB losses, provided the full amount of the loss could be written off against taxes: "[that] no tax disadvantages accrue to it as a result, i.e. if in its profit-and-loss account it can write off against tax, just like any other accounts-receivable loss, the loss it will now incur in its entirety rather than merely at 45 percent, and if for example waiving its right vis-à-vis BUB to draw on reserves is not put down against it as taxable income."[318] In the end, the Reich guarantee was only cancelled in February 1942, with retroactive effect from the end of 1941. Deutsche Bank at the same time bought the Reich's income and adjustment bonds [*Besserungsscheine*] of Liebig & Co., Reichenberg, and J. Ginzkey, Maffersdorf.[319]

The extent of the losses tells us a considerable amount about BUB's position. The initial subsidy from the Reich included a provision for 40 m. CKr (4 m. RM) claims against "non-Aryans." In November 1939, Deutsche Bank estimated its total likely losses as 20.6 m. RM, of which 4.2 m. RM were covered through the transfer to Deutsche Bank of assets from DAIB. In April 1941, a foreign-exchange audit report came to the conclusion that the losses on debtor accounts amounted to 141,138,000 CKr.[320] The eventual losses indeed were considerably lower than this estimate — 5.9 m. RM, of which the Reich guarantee had covered 3.23 m. RM.[321] This was because, after 1941, a quite dramatic turnaround in the bank's fortunes, scope of business activity, and profitability occurred. The overall balance sheet of the bank grew from 5,426.1 m. CKr at the end of 1942 to 7,074.5 m. CKr at the end of 1943.[322] In November 1941, the Prague subsidiary (Revisions- und Organisations-Gesellschaft m.b.H.) of the Deutsche Revisions- und Treuhand AG prepared a comprehensive audit of BUB for the Reich Economics Ministry in which it adjusted some of the rather conservative valuations of BUB.

What was the source of the new profitability that allowed the government guarantee to be paid off? By the beginning of 1943, Rohde stated "that on the other hand it is possible to speak of a positive growth in business in the past year."[323] The main source of income was the participation of the bank in a dramatic reordering of Czech and more generally Central European business life.

The uncertainty about the extent of BUB losses arose in large measure because of the threat that the party and Sudeten-German nationalists would use compulsory "Aryanizations" as a way of stripping BUB's assets, which had largely been acquired as a result of non-performing loans. Thus the Reich Ministry of Food proposed in April 1939 to seize the Troppauer Zuckerfabrik, on the grounds that BUB, which held a majority of the shares, had remained a Jewish bank. "The interests of the farmer are so urgent that any bank interests have to take second place." In 1940, the Four-Year Plan authorities took over the operation of the Kupferwerke Böhmen, in which BUB had a substantial holding.[324]

The BUB quickly created an "Aryanization" office, under the direction of Ernst Gaertner of the Freiburg branch of Deutsche Bank.[325] It repeatedly acted as an intermediary, first buying property on its own account, and then reselling the business.[326] In addition, the bank regularly gave credits for "Aryanization" sales.[327] The bank was also active on its account and used "Aryanization" as a way of disposing of financially weak customers. Textile firms especially had frequently fallen into difficulties in the Depression of the early 1930s, and BUB had come to hold a controlling interest in a number of companies. Usually "Aryanization" therefore involved a writing-off of part of the loans and a consequent realization of long-past losses.

One "Aryanized" factory, the "Bohemia" ceramics works in Neurohlau (Nová Role) near Karlsbad, which had been owned by the Prague investment and banking house of Petschek and which held substantial assets in Germany, was sold by BUB to the SS in 1940. It had paid no dividend since 1922 and had large inventories that were difficult to sell. Deutsche Bank noted that "a purchase-price demand based solely on balance-sheet figures would need to be at what for third parties would be an unacceptably high level."[328] Negotiations for the sale had begun as early as August 1939. Like many struggling Czech firms, "Bohemia" had substantial debts to its bank, and the sale involved a reduction of the outstanding credit from 601,195 RM to just over half that figure. The loss was shared equally between Deutsche Bank and the German government.[329] These terms were firmly opposed by the only one of BUB's directors who had been part of the pre-1939 management: Krebs. In the end, the sales contracts were signed by the new men from Deutsche Bank while Krebs was absent on leave. Its chief attraction for the SS lay in its capacity to provide high-grade china artifacts designed in the form of SS kitsch. An SS report listing the SS economic enterprises described the firm as "in qualitative terms the most important porcelain in the whole of Czechoslovakia, for both crockery and figurative porcelain, notably such specialties as underglaze blue (indistinguishable from Chinese and Japanese ware) and what is called 'ice glaze.'" 5 percent of its production was reserved, at Himmler's command, "to provide gifts for SS newlyweds, bomb-damage victims, and other needy persons." In 1942 the factory provided spare capacity for use in the armaments economy.[330] The SS management ran the works in Germany as the Porzellan-Manufaktur Allach-München, with a labor force composed in part of prisoners from the concentration camp at Dachau. Allach was one of the first parts of what by the end of the war became a gigantic economic empire under the control of the SS.[331]

Already in the national emergency of September 1938, the Czech government tried to mobilize foreign assets and ordered a partial opening of bank safes to convince citizens to comply with their patriotic duty in surrendering foreign assets. On March 25 and 31, 1939, under the occupation, the Finance Ministry ordered that the safes of Jews be opened and inventoried. Czech currency was to be transferred to a "tied – non-Aryan – account," and objects of value and precious metals were to be left in the safe but sealed.

The administration of Jewish accounts produced a voluminous and incriminating correspondence with the Gestapo, especially after the change in the occupation regime and the beginning of Jewish deportations in the autumn of 1941. On September 27, 1941, SS-Obergruppenführer Reinhard Heydrich took over the functions of "Reich Protector in Bohemia–Moravia" from Konstantin von Neurath, who was placed on sick leave. Heydrich's major mission lay in the "Germanization" of the new territories, and the erosion of the power of the Czech government under Emil Hácha. On November 24, 1941, the occupation authorities conducted the first deportation of Czech Jews to the ghetto in Theresienstadt (Teresin). Theresienstadt occupied a unique position in the world of the Nazi camps: in part designed as a model or display institution, it was intended to lull the Jewish victims of Nazi persecution into a false sense of security. In fact, on January 9, 1942, deportations from Theresienstadt to the killing camps of the occupied East, mainly to Auschwitz, began.

Deportations had obvious financial implications. Banks, including BUB, were presented with numbered lists prepared by the "Central Office for Settlement of the Jewish Question in Bohemia and Moravia." In these lists Czech Jews were given registration numbers. The banks had instructions not to take action regarding the account until a second number was placed behind the name: the deportation number. Once Jewish names appeared with these two numbers, the corresponding accounts would be compulsorily transferred.[332] Under the terms of a decree of October 12, 1941, the "Emigration Fund for Bohemia–Moravia" would administer the accounts of Jews listed for deportation. The main Emigration Fund account was held at the Böhmische Escompte Bank, and other banks were ordered to make the transfer of assets to this account.[333] But BUB also held two very substantial accounts for the Emigration Fund. These accounts also held some of the proceeds paid as part of "Aryanization" transactions, especially those arising out of small and medium-sized firms.[334] Valuables, including jewelry, works of art, and precious metals, which had been left by deported Jews in safe-deposit boxes, were sold to the German trading company Hadega. Up to July 1942, BUB administered an estimated 364.5 m. CKr worth of Jewish property.[335] The Gestapo ordered the bank to report the assets of Jews "who died in the concentration camp" and to block the accounts in favor of the Gestapo. Some of the funds resulting in this way were transferred to other party institutions. Thus one account of a Czech Jew was transferred by order of the Gestapo for the use of Lebensborn e.V., Munich, an institution devoted to the breeding of a superior German race.[336]

In November 1943, the list of the bank's "unstable creditors" (sight accounts) amounted to 943,584,000 CKr (or 94 m. RM), which included "emigration monies" and "resettlement accounts" (of expelled and "resettled" i.e. murdered Jews) worth 271,527,000 CKr and an account of 284,109,000 CKr in the name of the "Jewish Autonomous Administration" of Theresienstadt concentration camp.[337] In addition, there were two term accounts of 312,172,000 CKr each for the "Jewish Autonomous Administration" of Theresienstadt. Thus a total of 908,000,000 CKr was on deposit for the victims of Theresienstadt. It demonstrated clearly how BUB's major business lay in the administration of the property of the victims of National Socialism for the benefit of the German State. Again, most of the true owners of this property were the murdered victims of the National Socialist genocide. There was some movement in these accounts, and they were discussed by the bank's credit committee. In November 1944, Director Ulbrich gave a report on the general state of the bank. "He pointed out the big reductions in the investments of financial institutions and the Emigration

Fund as well as the resultant diminution of the balance-sheet total and investments in stocks and shares."[338] A final statement (survey of debtors and creditors) produced for February 28, 1945, showed assets consisting mostly of government papers, and liabilities still shown as 287,693,000 CKr in short-term deposits and 617,432,000 CKr in term deposits held by Theresienstadt.[339]

Initially, however, the economic future of occupied eastern Europe seemed to lie less with the SS than with the gigantic state-run but privately financed holding company, the Reichswerke "Hermann Göring." The initial expansion of the Reichswerke "Hermann Göring" outside Germany's 1937 frontiers began with large-scale "Aryanizations" in Austria; it continued in Bohemia with the takeover of the Petschek lignite mines.[340]

The banking connections of the Reichswerke "Hermann Göring" had from the beginning been concentrated with Dresdner Bank. Deutsche Bank had complained frequently and quite insistently about its relative handicap in what promised to be a very rewarding business, and about the apparent favoritism on the part of the state concern.[341] The Reichswerke "Hermann Göring" manager, Paul Pleiger, told Deutsche Bank's Karl Kimmich, with some irritation, "that the disagreements between the two banks could not possibly continue indefinitely."[342] Pleiger in 1937 had asked Kimmich to do the investment-banking work connected with the launching of the new firm, to prepare a list of companies that would be prepared to work with the Reichswerke "Hermann Göring," and to prepare a financial plan for the Reichswerke "Hermann Göring" conglomerate. Kimmich arranged a meeting between Pleiger and Germany's major steel industrialists Flick and Klöckner. But Deutsche Bank was subsequently ignored, and Pleiger instead promised the leadership of the issuing syndicate to Karl Rasche of Dresdner Bank.

History repeated itself with a surge of investment-banking activity in Bohemia–Moravia, and Kimmich again complained bitterly to Pleiger that the big transactions of the Sudetenland and the Protectorate had eluded Deutsche Bank. The sale of the major industrial concerns – Witkowitz Bergbau- und Eisenhüttengesellschaft (three-quarters owned by the Rothschilds of Vienna and London), Skoda (where French firms held a significant equity stake), and Brünner Waffen – to the Reichswerke "Hermann Göring" via the Reich Economics Ministry had initially been entrusted to Dresdner Bank.[343] (Although BUB congratulated itself when in 1940 it succeeded at least in establishing a business relationship – if only a deposit account, on a credit basis – with Witkowitz.[344]) At the beginning of 1940, BUB secured for itself a 20 percent share in credits to the Reichswerke "Hermann Göring" for the takeover of the Erste Brünner Maschinenfabriks-Gesellschaft (the share amounted to 4,575,758 CKr) and the Brünn-Königsfelder Maschinen- und Waggonfabriks AG (1,952,194 CKr).[345]

The transfer of property by sale was central to the Reichswerke "Hermann Göring"'s strategy for the wartime reordering of occupied Europe in preparation for a postwar New Order. A sale would have made the transfer much more permanent than the alternative of a German military imposition of trustees to manage foreign or alien property, but it posed major legal difficulties that would have taken years to resolve. The eventual transfer of Witkowitz to the Reichswerke "Hermann Göring" took place only in 1942, and then under a ten-year renewable contract.[346]

Retrospectively, these operations appear hard to comprehend, a bizarre mixture of astonishingly punctilious legalism and insistence on the following of correct procedures with, underlying these, a simultaneous profound immorality and criminality. It is, for instance, a constant surprise for the historian to discover the amount of time and care devoted to finding and transporting often torn and damaged share certificates in occupied Europe and registering the transfer of ownership, with payments made through the reparations and occupation accounts. From the invasions of 1940 until well after the fighting in France began in the wake of the Normandy landings, bank couriers shuttled from Paris to Berlin with sealed suitcases, engaged in the paperwork of creating legality for the New Order. This mixture of correctness, honesty, and order (what the historian Jonathan Steinberg has termed the "secondary virtues") with an ignorance and neglect of the human and moral issues involved was a characteristic of the conduct of institutions and businesses in the National Socialist dictatorship.[347]

In spring 1940, when Göring's prestige in the National Socialist hierarchy temporarily declined, Kimmich believed that there might be a new set of transactions forthcoming as part of a breaking-up of the gigantic Reichswerke "Hermann Göring."[348] But as long as the Reichswerke "Hermann Göring" existed, Deutsche Bank believed that it was necessary somehow to establish a relationship with it. In April 1939 Deutsche Bank had sold to the Reichswerke "Hermann Göring" its holding of Bayerischer Lloyd to facilitate the integration of transport on the Danube with the strategic and political priorities of the Reich. BUB appeared to be the ideal instrument in managing such a connection of the bank with the monopoly enterprise in eastern Europe, and in the summer of 1939, for this reason, Deutsche Bank pressed BUB to investigate the possibility of taking charge of the sale of the Witkowitzer Eisenwerke and the Brünner Waffenwerke.[349]

In fact, far from breaking up the Reichswerke "Hermann Göring" in 1940, Hermann Göring launched a new phase in its expansion. On June 22 Göring ordered Reich Economics Minister Walther Funk to prepare the "integration of the areas incorporated in the Reich and the occupied areas into the Greater-German economy" to begin a "reconstruction of the German-led continental economy." Funk promised that the New Order would bring the "beginning of an unsuspected economic flowering." As part of the reorganization, the structure of industrial ownership in Europe would be rationalized.[350] In the wake of the spring invasion of the Netherlands, Belgium, and France, in September 1940 Göring instructed German banks to negotiate the transfer to German control of the major foreign assets of the defeated states. In the National Socialist "New Europe," Germany's "big banks" were to be given back their old function as industrial brokers who built and remodeled vast industrial empires. The difference was that these enterprises were now to be overwhelmingly controlled by the German State.

By 1941 in the Netherlands alone, foreign participations worth over 65 m. RM had been acquired "in the wake of private-enterprise negotiations" [original emphasis].[351] These purchases occurred at such a rate that they began to interfere with government-directed purchases. In April 1941 the Reich Economics Ministry official in charge of banking supervision ordered the banks to slow down the rush of their private customers to seize Dutch assets. "It was therefore the duty of banks, in the way they advised the public, to recommend unconditional restraint in buying Dutch shares and annuities."[352] The private acquisition of shares in Western Europe was to be slowed down; and in the meantime, the state-managed program to reorganize the structure of Europe concentrated on east-European assets held by residents of western states.

BUB, which had by now established reasonably cordial relations with the Reichswerke "Hermann Göring" in Eastern Europe, as well as with the SS, was an ideal agent for this operation. It bought shares of Czech and also Polish works from west-European stockholders: Witkowitz Bergbau und Eisenhüttengesellschaft, Janina, and the Huta Bankowa, which in turn held shares in the Sosnowitzer Bergwerks AG, Sosnowitzer Röhren AG, Radomsko Metallurgia, and Kuxe Renard.[353] These commercial transactions followed quite logically from the extension of German military rule. As BUB's Walter Pohle wrote in 1940, at the height of German successes, concerning the purchase of shares in the Berghütte from Schneider-Creusot: "If it was possible to buy Schneider-Creusot shares – cheaply, too – this was ultimately a triumph of German arms."[354] In all, Pohle organized the purchase of 110,454 Berghütte shares in France, at a price of 137.10 RM per share; and in addition another 19,170 shares were purchased from "Jewish owners resident in the protectorate, which we are to purchase at the demand of the Reich Economics Minister and the Protector." On this transaction, the BUB earned a commission of 2 percent.[355] Pohle repeatedly emphasized in reporting on the French transactions that they were "by agreement with the Reich Economics Ministry" and that there was no risk to the bank: "the bank [he said] will be indemnified by the HTO [see pages 160–161] in every respect and the funds presented will enjoy full cover."[356] When Pohle reported the purchase for 333 m. FF (16,759,309.31 RM) of shares in the Huta Bankowa and the Französisch-Italienische AG der Dombrowaer Kohlengruben, he added: "this is not a personal transaction but a confidential commission for the government."[357] Such transactions were conducted principally for the Reichswerke "Hermann Göring," but BUB also carried out similar sales on behalf of private German corporations. Pohle spoke about "the purchase of shares of steel rolling-mills in which Mannesmann is interested."[358]

The shares of central and east-European enterprises bought by the government or by public-sector institutions in occupied western Europe were sometimes paid through the reparations account, but some were also bought out of the proceeds of sales of French and Belgian domestic securities that had fallen into the hands of the German authorities. The latter included substantial quantities of securities seized from Jews in occupied Europe, most importantly in the Netherlands, where a new office in the Sarphatistraat of a formerly Jewish bank (Lippmann & Rosenthal) was used as a front for collecting shares turned in to the occupying power on the basis of Decree 141 of 1941 issued by the "Reich Commissar for the Occupied Dutch Territories." This operation was conducted in extreme secrecy, and like the rest of such operations, channeled through BUB rather than Deutsche Bank.[359] (Deutsche Bank was not directly a part of this arrangement, although its management knew of the operations: in 1943 a memorandum noted "that the agreements with BUB had been possible only as a result of the fact that Deutsche Bank had for general purposes made a substantial contribution by making securities available, though without wishing to be identified with the Prague business."[360]) The transactions continued until 1944, when in March Pohle told BUB's credit committee: "all French commitments have been wound up, though the individual write-offs have yet to be made. After a projected trip to Paris, it will be possible to close the accounts."[361]

It was BUB rather than Deutsche Bank that had the closest links with the Reichswerke "Hermann Göring." At the height of his influence, BUB's director Walter Pohle was chairman of the

supervisory board of Berghütte and ran the key firms in the
Berghütte complex (Berg- und Hüttenwerksgesellschaft Karwin-
Trzynietz, Berg- und Hüttenwerksgesellschaft Teschen (Tecin), and
Berg- und Hüttenwerksgesellschaft Wegierska Gorka); in addition
he sat on the board of directors of the Böhmisch-Mährische Stick-
stoffwerke explosives factory, Coburg-Werke, Bandeisen + Blech-
walzwerke AG Karlshütte, and Friedeck bei Mährisch-Ostrau
(Ostrava).[362] Politics here as elsewhere brought dangers to management, and BUB was quite exposed to periodic political interventions.

The first object of Nazi party and Gestapo hostility on the BUB's
board was Joseph Krebs, who was accused of political unreliability,
membership in a masonic lodge, and contact with Jews. Already in
July 1940, the bank had to write to the security service (Sicherheitsdienst) in Prague in defense of its director: "His frequent dealings
with Jews are probably an inevitable outcome of his having occupied a high position in an almost exclusively Jewish-run bank with
a large Jewish clientele. We ourselves have come to know Mr. Krebs
as a man of whose German cast of mind we are not in any doubt."
The letter concluded by stating that he was indispensable to the
bank's business.[363] In 1941, he was refused a visa to undertake foreign travel, and a large part of his business transactions then became
impossible, so that his duties were redefined as lying exclusively
in the Protectorate.[364] Deutsche Bank's Berlin directors consistently tried to defend Krebs against the political and police attacks.

Oswald Rösler (Figure 20) in particular consulted with the director of Deutsche Bank responsible for personnel matters, the
party member Karl Ritter von Halt, and urged Krebs not to proceed
with a conflict with the Gestapo but instead reconcile himself to
a reduced sphere of activity.[365] Rösler was right in that the attack
on Krebs was only the preliminary to an attack on the rest of the
bank's management, especially Walter Pohle.

In 1942, as part of the restructuring of Germany's economy to
meet the demands of total war, Pohle was pushed out of his influential positions by Major-General Hermann von Hanneken (head
of the Reich Economics Ministry's "Hauptabteilung II": Mining,

Figure 20. Oswald Rösler: Member of Deutsche Bank management board 1933–45, Speaker 1942–5.

Source: Courtesy of Deutsche Bank AG.

Iron and Steel, and Energy Economy). Pohle had consulted the Reich Economics Ministry after he had been asked to buy the IG Kattowitz and Berghütte for a new Göring monopoly organization designed to encompass formerly Soviet as well as Polish metallurgy works.[366] The ministry rejected the indirect control of Reichswerke "Hermann Göring" shares by Berghütte: "The Reich Economics Ministry wants [...] 'Berghütte' to remain tied to the Reich in terms of capital as well, so that the influence of the Protectorate will be that much less."[367] This one false step of attempting to extend BUB's industrial interests at the expense of the Reichswerke "Hermann Göring" cost Pohle his functions in the Berghütte industrial enterprise.

The Reich Economics Ministry managed the situation by approaching Rösler and explaining that Deutsche Bank "could do itself a favor by persuading Mr. Pohle to resign his seat." [original emphasis] Kehrl of the Four-Year Plan was much more explicit:

"Mr. Pohle, on the other hand, felt he could handle the "Berghütte" question as he thought best, and he constantly placed himself in conflict with the Economics Ministry by holding talks with political authorities in Prague or Upper Silesia without the ministry's knowledge or getting involved in discussions that had caused the ministry endless problems. The ministry had therefore increasingly been forced to accept that Mr. Pohle's conduct had been shady and dishonest."

Rösler then spoke with Pohle and persuaded him to give up the supervisory board positions. He also wanted Pohle to apologize to Kehrl (he made the point very emphatically in a letter). Pohle was replaced on the supervisory board of Berghütte by Ambassador Hans Adolf von Moltke, a man of great reputation and decency who was trying to leave the Foreign Office but who died within a year as a result of an unsuccessful appendix operation.[368] Moltke was succeeded by someone whose sympathies lay close to Deutsche Bank, Karl Blessing, director of the strategically important Kontinentale Oel, which had been set up in 1941 as a model for a future "planned economy using private capital," the intention of which was to "create the situation that, as a great power, Germany needs and deserves."[369] Until 1939 Blessing had been a director of the Reichsbank; he was dismissed after signing the Reichsbank memorandum of January 7, 1939, condemning government policy.

Private capital may have competed with the state concern to acquire east-European assets, but the competition was complicated by the fact that both the Reichswerke "Hermann Göring" and its private competitors were producing the same goods, namely armaments, designed for the same monopolistic consumer, the German military moloch. In the early phases of the war, even private concerns had to negotiate with the Reichswerke "Hermann Göring" in attempting to build up industrial assets. In 1940, the Graf von Ballestrem'sche Güterdirektion Gleiwitz established a powerful position in Upper Silesia, using Deutsche Bank and Delbrück Schickler & Co. to repurchase shares in formerly German enterprises that had passed into the hands of the Polish state after 1918: the coal field operated by Rudaer Steinkohlegewerkschaft, Friedenshütten (which had been ceded under the Versailles Treaty to Poland, with Ballestrem retaining a minority of shares), and machine-tool and boiler-making plants in Sosnowice, Dombrowa, and Kattowitz/Katowice.[370] The price paid was 12 m. RM, but of this only 4 m. RM was paid immediately, and the rest was to be paid out of future profits; the initial down payment could be made out of the profits made in Upper Silesian works since September 30, 1939.

After 1941, as Göring's political role came under attack and his importance in the National Socialist hierarchy waned for good, German private capital could attempt to assert itself further. The Reichswerke "Hermann Göring" conglomerate began to break up. Metallurgia Radomsko, which bought its raw materials from Berghütte Dombrowa, part of the Berg- und Hüttenwerksgesellschaft Teschen (Tecin), was leased to Oberhütte, despite opposition from the Cracow Armaments Inspectorate.[371] The end of the Reichswerke "Hermann Göring" as an industrial conglomerate came only later, as a result of military developments. It needed to use its complex holdings system to minimize the extent of its financial liabilities, and by the autumn of 1944, the Reichswerke "Hermann Göring" refused to give any guarantee for the debts of companies affiliated in the concern and now being overrun by Soviet armies.[372]

BUB's share-purchasing activities were not confined to central-European assets with west-European owners. It bought up Jewish-owned shares in Hungary. In Yugoslavia, it built up a participation in the Bankverein AG Zagreb and the Bankverein für Serbien AG. Its position within Deutsche Bank's southeast-European banking system was confirmed through an exchange of shares and seats on the supervisory board with the Creditanstalt-Bankverein Vienna.[373]

Much of BUB's investment-banking business took place on behalf of state or SS purchasers looking for an apparently respectable financial intermediary to regulate transfers of property. But the war economy, though state-dominated, was not entirely socialized, and some private concerns used the same methods.

As the course of the war changed, with a German defeat appearing ever more probable, and as the intense involvement of BUB in the economics of imperialism in the East became ever clearer, the Bohemian bank appeared as more and more of an embarrassment to the Berlin managers of Deutsche Bank. The Berlin bank had been dragged in on the crest of the wave of expansionist euphoria in 1938–9 and could now see no way out. In July 1943, Oswald Rösler of Deutsche Bank, the chairman of the supervisory board of BUB, wrote an extensive memorandum about the poor quality of BUB's business, which he attributed to the disruptive consequences of "Aryanization" and the impossibility of finding adequate management.[374] But just at this moment, the bank started to become profitable.

The BUB represented the clearest and most direct case of Deutsche Bank's involvement in a brutal elimination of Jewish managers and personnel, in dubious share transactions, and in the confiscation of Jewish assets. It is not surprising that the bank tried to distance itself from the BUB after the war. One of the BUB's managers, Wilhelm Hirschmann who had worked in the sensitive personnel department of the bank, on secondment from Deutsche Bank, was not denazified, and the Deutsche Bank refused to reemploy him because of his wartime record. Hermann Abs, who had been on the supervisory board of the BUB, and bore some measure of responsibility, told his American interrogators about the share purchase operations of the BUB but also added in an attempt at exculpation: "Messrs Roesler and Kaiser attended all meetings at Prague while I took part only once annually. I am, therefore, not very intimately acquainted with the details of the Union-Bank."[375]

Slovakia: The Union-Bank Bratislava

At the beginning of 1939, Deutsche Bank had suggested to the Reich Economics Ministry that even before the final dismemberment of Czecho–Slovakia, it should be allowed to buy a branch in Bratislava: it wanted the Escompte- und Volkswirtschaftliche Bank, while Dresdner Bank would take, in a parallel operation, the Allgemeine Handels- und Creditbank. The purchase of 90 percent of the stock of the Escompte Bank was to be a joint operation with the Creditanstalt.[376] The Slovak authorities resented and feared Czech influences. Minister President Vojtech Tuka was still complaining in the middle of the war that the personnel of the former Czech banks were responsible for "constant agitating." In December 1939, the Slovak government correspondingly resolved to turn BUB's Bratislava branch into a "German-type institution."[377]

So it was that in October 1940 the Bratislava branch of BUB began a separate existence as the Union-Bank Bratislava (UBB) and established its own network of branches by taking over other bank branches. The Sillein (Žilina) branch, for instance, was bought from the Böhmisch-Mährische Bank or Legio-Bank. The capitalization amounted to 60 million CKr: 50 million CKr capital stock and 10 million CKr capital reserve.[378] At an initial general meeting, executive-committee [*Verwaltungsrat*] chairman Ludwig Fritscher (from the Creditanstalt, Vienna) gave a speech in which he emphasized the bank's German character:

> "UBB works with German equity. It operates here in Slovakia, where borrowed funds will flow into it in the form of investments of all kinds. Those facts place the bank under an obligation vis-à-vis the Reich and Slovakia, yet these are not two conflicting obligations; they both flow together into one: to serve the Slovako-German economic relations that shall bring like blessings upon both peoples, already such close mutual friends. The new bank is not being founded on a private-capital basis; it has not come to Slovakia to exploit the country but in order to assume the necessary role of intermediary in Slovako-German economic intercourse."[379]

Its business looked similar to that of the Prague bank, its most profitable transactions involving the sale of Slovak companies to German firms. Philipp Reemtsma acquired the Vereinigte Holz und Industrie AG, Bratislava, and left UBB as a trustee. The Coburg mining complex was integrated into the gigantic Reichswerke "Hermann Göring" company Berg- und Hüttenwerke. The Antinom Berg and Hüttenwerke AG, Neusohl (Banska Bistrica) was integrated into the Berghütte as well.

As with Prague, and for similar reasons, Jewish credits looked uncertain. The bank's executive committee, on which

German bankers sat – Ludwig Fritscher (Austrian, Creditanstalt-Bankverein), Hermann Kaiser, Max Ludwig Rohde (both Deutsche Bank), and August Rohdewald (Creditanstalt-Bankverein) – noted among others cases of credits where the securities for credits involved liabilities of Jewish businessmen (as in the firm of M. Rippers Söhne, in Sillein/Žilina).[380] But the extent of weak loans was infinitely less than for BUB, and there was no collapse of profitability followed by an "Aryanization"-driven resurgence. Jewish-owned accounts were also handled in a different way in Father Tiso's puppet state. Many Jewish-owned deposits were simply transferred to the state-run postal savings bank system, where the Slovak state rather than private banks – or the German police – could reap the financial rewards of racial persecution.[381]

Deutsche Bank and the Creditanstalt in Poland

With the exception of Silesia, which was part of the area brought into the German Reich, industry formed a much less crucial part of German military planning. The military machinery did not need banks in the way they had been required in the Czech case.

There had been a German banking presence in interwar Poland. Both Deutsche Bank and Dresdner Bank had kept branches in Polish Eastern Upper Silesia, in Katowice, under the terms of the 1922 Geneva agreement,[382] which expired on July 14, 1937. Dresdner Bank then closed its branch, and the German authorities suggested that Deutsche Bank should act similarly. Reichsbank President Schacht stated that "the German banks that still maintain branches in Katowice would do well to consider selling those institutions." The speaker of the management board of Deutsche Bank, Eduard Mosler, then proposed to sell his branch as part settlement of Polish claims against Germany from transit traffic in the "Polish corridor." But the Polish authorities wanted the German banks to stay, because of their importance in the financing of Silesian heavy industry, and Deutsche Bank remained as the largest branch in Katowice (Figure 21).[383] There were also similar pressures from

Figure 21. The Katowice branch of Deutsche Bank.

Source: Courtesy of Deutsche Bank AG.

the German government. In 1936, a Reich Economics Ministry official told Deutsche Bank: "of the necessity that the Deutsche Bank should be more interested in economic relations with Poland than it was up to now, and as the Dresdner Bank has already become active in connection with the new economic agreement."[384]

Immediately after the German attack on Poland on September 1, 1939 and the German occupation of the western parts of the country, Deutsche Bank executives looked enthusiastically at the economic opportunities offered by military expansion. They wrote to the German supervisory authorities: "Presumably, then, the Polish banks will have to go into liquidation, particularly since (simply in the light of their many Jewish and Polish accounts receivable) most of them will be unable to avoid forced bankruptcy or at least insolvency proceedings."[385] At this time, the Katowice branch of Deutsche Bank had a staff of ninety, of whom at least eighty were "*Reichsdeutsche*" or "*Volksdeutsche*." Even before the flight of the Polish government (on September 17), or the capitulation of Warsaw (September 27), Deutsche Bank had started to open new branches. It rapidly inaugurated sub-branches in Bielitz (Bielsko-Biala; September 11), Teschen (Tecin; September 11), and Oderberg (Bohumin; September 14).

What did these new sub-branches do? Why was it so important to establish them so quickly, even during the military conflict? The main concern of the German authorities was to seize financial assets – gold, silver, share certificates, foreign exchange, and Polish and Czech currency – that might otherwise be taken from the area under their control. On September 7, 1939, officials of the Foreign-Exchange Tracing and Search Department [*Devisenfahndungsamt*] visited the major towns in the Upper Silesian industrial area (Figure 22). They later noted: "Findings made here showed that banks were almost without exception closed and their owners or managers had fled into the interior of Poland, taking the ledgers and all movable assets with them. The same findings were made regarding wealthy Jews formerly resident in these towns." On the following day, September 8 Regierungsoberinspektor Fischer of the Foreign-Exchange Tracing and Search Department noted: "The

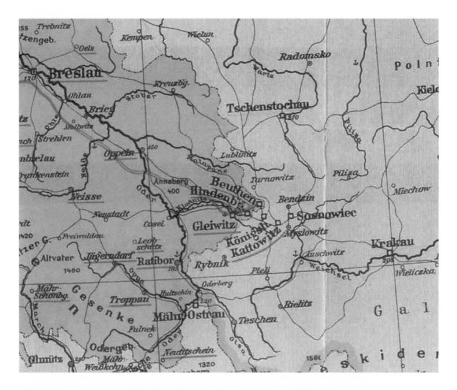

Figure 22. Deutsche Bank branches in Upper Silesia, 1939.
Source: Courtesy of Deutsche Bank AG.

Reichsbank representative with the Head of Civil Administration, Councilor Behrbohm, today instructed Deutsche Bank Berlin to buy up the said assets in the Olsa District. Deutsche Bank will immediately set up purchasing offices in the largest towns in the district to enable the order to be carried out." But he also saw that the Germans had come too late: "According to the findings made hitherto, the wealthy Jews formerly resident in the Olsa District have fled to Cracow with their assets. Because of the rapid occupation of Cracow, they were probably no longer able to move their property farther into the Polish interior." Behrbohm would consequently also establish a Devisenbank in Cracow. The subsequent detailed report of the Foreign-Exchange Tracing and Search Department noted that "after Deutsche Bank had at the instigation of

Councilor Behrbohm established branches in Teschen, Oderberg, and Bielitz and been authorized to purchase assets required to be handed over, the order was put into effect in the Olsa District on September 9, 1939." There were further plans for the expansion of the bank in eastern areas: "The intention is to set up branches of Deutsche Bank in those towns (Tarnow, Rzeszow) that will then take over the purchasing of assets."[386] But these further plans were never realized.

The conquered territories were divided up by a decree of Hitler's of October 8, 1939. Four areas were designated as "occupied eastern areas" and integrated into Germany: the "government district" [*Regierungsbezirk*] of Zichenau, in the north (including the Polish district of Suwalki); the "Reichsgau" of Danzig and West Prussia; the industrial areas in Silesia, which were simply added to German Silesia; and "Reichsgau" Posen (later renamed Reichsgau Wartheland), which included the industrial city of Łódź. The remaining territories were run under an occupation regime designated as the "Generalgouvernement."

At this time, several German banks raced to establish a banking presence in the newly acquired territories. The banks complained about each other's "aggressive" business methods, and the Reich Economics Ministry tried to preserve Polish banks that the German authorities might then influence and control directly. For instance, Deutsche Bank, Commerzbank, and the Deutsche Genossenschaftsbank complained about the behavior of Dresdner Bank in Łódź (renamed by the Germans as Litzmannstadt). The Reichsbank office reported that Dresdner Bank was managing the payments of the Zentral-Textil-Gesellschaft, which was then influencing its clients to establish accounts with the bank. In addition, Dresdner Bank had organized a "beer evening with food" in the rooms of the Grand Hotel, "to which we are told more or less all the industrialists of Litzmannstadt and the surrounding area, including ones that do not have accounts with Dresdner Bank, have been invited."[387]

The Reich Economics Ministry also expressed its dissatisfaction with the plans of Deutsche Bank. Deutsche Bank had tried to establish a grip on the officials of the major administrative agency responsible for the reordering of industry in the East, the "Haupt-treuhandstelle Ost" (HTO: Central Trustee Office for the East). By 1941, Deutsche Bank's successful takeover of HTO was such that, at the bank section of HTO's Katowice "Treuhandstelle," all seven or eight administrators had come from Deutsche Bank.[388]

The HTO administered a large number of sequestered companies and sold some of them, often to the administrators who were provisionally charged with running the firms. Since most of these administrators lacked their own resources, they often required bank credit for the purchase. The Katowice branch of Deutsche Bank dealt with a substantial number of such cases.

At the same time, the new bank branches in the East had little room to maneuver. They were obliged to give credits when the state decided to offer a guarantee for a particular project, and, given the wartime conditions, there existed few other businesses or loan prospects in the region. Deutsche Bank angrily rejected Reich Economics Ministry complaints that it had unpatriotically refused such credits. In the late summer of 1940, a bank memorandum noted:

> "This enables us to ascertain that the charges leveled do not, so far as Deutsche Bank is concerned, hold any water whatsoever. None of our branches has refused a loan for which a Reich guarantee was available; they have all acted dutifully in implementing the conditions laid down by the government on issue of the guarantee. [. . .] That we have furthermore not shrunk from making considerable sacrifices, particularly in the Katowice district especially mentioned, is proved beyond doubt by the past history of our Katowice branch, which is also well-known and generally acknowledged."[389]

The most sinister of such credits involved lending by the Deutsche Bank's Katowice branch to building firms engaged in the construction of the concentration camps at Auschwitz, as well as direct credits to IG Farben for the construction of its huge synthetic rubber (Buna) plant near Auschwitz, which was constructed and later operated with slave labor. One such construction firm was Wilhelm Riedel of Bielitz, which from 1942 received a credit line of 300,000 RM for the construction of pipes, canals, bridges, and drains at the IG Farben plant, and for concrete construction for the Waffen-SS at Auschwitz. In all, the credit reports of the Deutsche Bank indicate that the firm had some 2 m. RM in orders from the SS and another 2 m. RM from IG Farben, in addition to some smaller scale work for the Reichswerke "Hermann Göring" at Brzeszcze.[390] In 1943, the credit line was overdrawn by 160,000 RM secured by claims against IG Farben and the SS in Auschwitz.[391] Another building firm, with a smaller (100,000 RM) credit was Hermann Hirt, which from 1941 had been building for the SS.[392]

Deutsche Bank Katowice from 1941 provided a credit of 250,000 RM to IG Farbenindustrie Werke Auschwitz (the credit line was raised in December 1943 to 500,000 RM). These very substantial credits were of course reported to the Berlin offices of Deutsche Bank.[393] A bank official also visited the site of the IG Farben plant in Auschwitz in April 1943 and reported:

"On the occasion of my visit yesterday in Auschwitz [...] I could convince myself on the basis of documents willingly supplied to me that 80% of the current financial business is done by us. Apart from the district savings bank, IG Farben Auschwitz works exclusively with us. The savings bank deals with wage payments, but these are not substantial as the building firms finance most of the wages on the construction site themselves. [...] IG Farben was particularly grateful that we use the form of the company to make money transfers, which creates a considerable saving for them (but additional work for us)."[394]

The Katowice branch seems in all to have been rather proud of its association with a building site that had already become the largest site for murder in European history.

Deutsche Bank established, as well as its new branches East-Upper Silesia, Bielitz-Biala, Teschen, and Oderberg, a major branch office in Łódź in Reichsgau Posen (Poznan), and in Cracow, in the Generalgouvernement. The head of the Katowice branch of

Deutsche Bank in addition requested the establishment of a branch in Sosnowice.[395] In April 1940, the Cracow branch was transferred to the Creditanstalt, after an initiative from Fischböck: "that the Credit-Anstalt should set up branches in Cracow, Tarnow, Rzeszow, und Przemysl and Deutsche Bank cede to the Credit-Anstalt the branches it has established in Bielitz and Cracow. Mr. Abs reserves his position after discussion within the Deutsche Bank board."[396] After the German military offensive against Russia in 1941 brought all of prewar Poland under German control, the Creditanstalt also established a branch in Lvov (Lemberg). The German supervisory authority [*Reichsaufsichtsamt*] disliked the push of the big German banks into the Generalgouvernement. As early as October 1940, it declared its opinion that, "from a purely organizational point of view, probably the sensible thing to do would be to limit branches of 'Altreich' banks to Cracow."[397]

By the end of 1940, both the Creditanstalt and Deutsche Bank were discussing the idea of establishing branches in Warsaw. At first, one proposal was to take a Polish regional bank in joint ownership.[398] The Creditanstalt discussed the possibility of an "expansion of our Polish business," perhaps by taking over the Allgemeiner Bank-Verein.[399] Deutsche Bank wrote to the Creditanstalt rather brusquely: "We once ceded the Cracow location to you after we had established a promising branch there. It is our conviction that, so far as Warsaw is concerned, for the above-mentioned reasons our interests must be regarded as paramount."[400]

In April 1942, Johannes Kiehl of the Deutsche Bank board was proposing to take over the Bank Handlowy, the most significant Polish bank. Bank Handlowy had a capital of 25 m. zloty (12.5 m. RM), and a substantial foreign ownership. Foreign owners included the British Overseas Bank, London (5.5 percent); Hambros, London (3.1 percent); the Banca Commerciale Italiana (4.8 percent); and the Banque de Bruxelles (3.2 perscent).[401] It continued to do a significant amount of business with foreign enterprises in wartime Poland: there were, for instance, substantial movements in the accounts of International Business Machines Corp., New York, and of Watson Business Machines.[402] At the outbreak of war, about half of its deposits came from Polish Jews. Kiehl reported to Consul-General Winkelmann in Danzig (Gdansk):

> "Mr. Bechtolf and I intend to travel to Warsaw on 30 April and possibly also stay there on 1 May. The object of our journey, apart from generally informing ourselves about circumstances there, is particularly to make further preparations in connection with our endeavors to establish a branch of our bank in the Generalgouvernement or, in line with previous tendencies of the competent government agencies, to take over a Polish bank and run it as a regional subsidiary of our bank. This is a matter we have often discussed before. The first potential candidate for such a takeover is the Warsaw Bank of Commerce as being by far the largest institution."[403]

In 1945 the president of the bank council of Bank Handlowy, Stanisław Wachowiak, wrote an account of the negotiations with Deutsche Bank. He described 1942 as the beginning of "a war on the fundamentals of Polish banking": the bank Control Commissar in Cracow, Reichsbankdirektor Paersch, who was also the director of the Polish Issuing Bank (the wartime replacement for the National Bank of Poland), told Wachowiak that Economics Minister Funk had issued an ultimatum to merge the Polish banks with German banks. Wachowiak thought that he and his council would resign or be dismissed. Then, on May 1, came the visit of Bechtolf, who was accompanied at first by a secretary and then later spoke alone with Wachowiak.

> "When we were left alone, to my amazement, he told me that Deutsche Bank with a one hundred year tradition does not, for the duration of the war, agree with the stand of the Economics Minister of the Reich. Deutsche Bank would not agree to the merger, and, in order to gain time, would send a so-called "observer." Asking me to maintain discretion, he assured me that Bank Handlowy would in no way be threatened by the observer. Indeed, with a delay of half a year, the observer arrived, stayed in the Hotel Bristol [the best hotel in Warsaw] and visited us twice."[404]

Deutsche Bank was not of course operating in a vacuum, and the rival Dresdner Bank consistently expressed its own interest in acquiring Bank Handlowy. In August 1943, Glathe of Dresdner Bank visited the bank supervisor in Cracow and asked whether his institution could not take over Bank Handlowy. He "inquired whether we should be prepared to alter the standpoint communicated to Dresdner Bank in writing if, for example, the Polish Bank of Commerce were to continue to operate in Warsaw under its old name and the influence of Dresdner Bank remained invisible."[405] In these circumstances, the continued declarations of interest by Deutsche Bank combined with practical inaction amounted to a protection for Bank Handlowy.

One of the issues from the point of view of the German authorities was that the Reichsbank and the Polish Issuing Bank were reluctant to see both the Creditanstalt and Deutsche Bank with branches in the same city: "Mr. Paersch is said to have stated in this connection [. . .] that he could not license Deutsche Bank and the Creditanstalt in the Gouvernement alongside each other but that in that case Warsaw would need to be combined with Cracow and Lvov under one institution."[406]

The Creditanstalt in Cracow was meanwhile engaged in a quite lucrative business. The extent of its credits reduced its liquidity so much that the bank supervisor in the Generalgouvernement several times expressed his unease. What were the credits used for? To a considerable extent, credits were taken to buy firms under trustee administration. Under a decree of September 24, 1940, the property of the Polish State was subject to trustee administration. In addition, private property might be confiscated, or, if declared to be without an owner [*herrenlos*], taken over [*eingezogen*]. By 1942, 3,296 enterprises were administered by trustees: 1,659 were industrial firms, and 1,036 were trading or artisanal units. These enterprises were in part prepared for sale. A 1942 report in the *Krakauer Zeitung* noted that:

> "The sale of the trust businesses can proceed only slowly in view of the state of prewar indebtedness and the poor performance ascertained particularly in connection with formerly Jewish businesses. Where at all possible, the sale will take account of the interests of

German soldiers at the front. This presupposes, however, that the businesses are developed in such a way that they are able, after the war is over, to stand comparison with corresponding enterprises in the Reich."[407]

The Cracow Creditanstalt carried out transfers of money from relatives of concentration-camp inmates. It is clear from the scant surviving documentation that the Cracow bank knew about the massive mortality in these camps.[408] In addition, the same bank administered some of the accounts of the trustee administration, which dealt with confiscated Jewish-owned property.

As the German military situation deteriorated, the risks of lending increased. In July 1943, Walter Tron, a director of the Creditanstalt, spoke about the risks posed by the bad loans:

> "The special review of accounts receivable now introduced has shown that certain commitments need to be terminated or rearranged – with no certainty yet as to whether and in what amounts losses are to be expected. On the basis of this information, the working committee reiterates the opinion expressed earlier that, in the light of these risks, converting the branches into an autonomous bank would be desirable."[409]

In October 1942, Tron spoke of negotiations with Deutsche Bank about joint ownership of a Polish subsidiary.[410] In August 1943, Tron told the supervisory authority that he would prefer to turn the branches of the Creditanstalt into a separate bank: "It is difficult to handle and supervise business from Vienna." He added that he had already spoken with Deutsche Bank, "which may possibly take a holding in the new regional bank." Such a bank might take over Polish institutions later ("Director Tron remarked that starting up a regional bank in no way anticipated the subsequent takeover of a Polish bank.")[411]

Discussions about the creation of a Polish regional bank were only completed in March 1944, by which time of course the German armies were in full retreat. In April 1944, Tron reported that in Cracow and Lvov "the process of making branches independent [...] is already under way."[412] The "Creditanstalt AG,

Krakau," was established in May 1944, with Walter Tron from the Creditanstalt as chairman of the supervisory board, and another Deutsche Bank banker, Hermann Kaiser, as a member. It never took over a Warsaw bank.

In June 1944, it seemed that deposits in the Generalgouvernement were still increasing.[413] But some significant accounts were now being closed. On July 27, 1944, the SS "Wirtschaftsamt" transferred its deposit on the account of the "Reichsführer SS" (8 m. zloty, or 4 m. RM) to the Kommerzialbank, the Cracow subsidiary of Dresdner Bank, where the Reichsführer had a larger account (79 m. zloty), which the SS also tried to withdraw. The man responsible for these withdrawals was SS-Standartenführer Erich Schellin. Was it more than an arithmetic coincidence that the total in the bank accounts, 87 m. zloty, was close to the 101 m. zloty that Schellin acquired in "spoils" [*Beutemittel*] from the genocide of "Aktion Reinhard"?[414] After protests from the bank supervisor, the SS took only 30 m. zloty from the Kommerzialbank.[415] By September, the business from the Cracow Creditanstalt had moved to Breslau (Wrocław), and the Kommerzialbank had moved to Leipzig. These moves ensured that – at least in the case of the Cracow Creditanstalt – the overwhelming majority of its files cannot be located. Consequently, the documentation of its activity and an important part of the story of the economic aspects of the persecution and expropriation of the Polish population, including the genocide of Polish and European Jews, are still missing.

Bechtolf's failed negotiations in Warsaw were obviously in part a product of his personal conviction, in 1942, that Deutsche Bank had no business taking over a major Polish bank. But the fact that the Generalgouvernement banking authorities were prepared to tolerate his deliberately dilatory approach indicates a comparative indifference of the authorities to the issue of German bank involvement. For Deutsche Bank and the Creditanstalt, there was no massive financial control of the key elements of the Polish economy, analogous to the system that Walter Pohle had established in the Protectorate of Bohemia–Moravia. Instead there was an engagement in some relatively small-scale but nevertheless lucrative side

business generated by the occupation regime, at the expense of the
Poles (including of course Polish Jews).

The Netherlands

The Deutsche Bank was much more hesitant in attempting to take
over new banks in occupied Western Europe than it had been
in its campaign of acquisition in the east. In France, Denmark,
and Norway, the Deutsche Bank played almost no part in any attempt to consolidate German economic power. There was, however, rather more activity in the occupied Netherlands and Belgium
after 1940. Here the strategy involved building on existing business contacts. Like many German companies and banks, Deutsche
Bank had established a presence in the Netherlands in the inflationary aftermath of World War I, for currency and tax purposes. In
1936 the bank tried to disguise its Netherlands subsidiary Handel-
Maatschappij H. Albert de Bary & Co. N. V. Amsterdam as a Dutch
company through the transfer of stock to a nominal Dutch ownership. After the outbreak of war in September 1939, the bank dismissed a substantial part of its German staff. Only after the invasion
of the Netherlands were the shares repurchased by the Deutsche
Bank and did the Germans return to their positions. By 1941,
Deutsche Bank owned all the stock of de Bary and raised the capital
of the bank. The Reich Economics Ministry noted that Deutsche
Bank was "the strongest German position in Holland."[416]

Almost immediately after the occupation of the Netherlands,
the Reich Economics Ministry also asked the Deutsche Bank to
take over shares in the Rotterdamsche Bankvereeniging, but the
bank responded with great hesitance. Karl Kimmich replied "that
since at present the Dutch are rather stiff in their attitude to
German influence, such cooperation can only be imagined with
great difficulty and can only be achieved very slowly in a voluntary way."[417] The Economics Ministry then tried to divide up the
newly occupied countries between German companies and allocated Dutch banks to the Deutsche Bank and Belgian banks to the

Dresdner's sphere of influence. The plan was to divide Europe between the banks, rather than permit bank competition in each occupied territory.

Again the Deutsche Bank protested. Kimmich told the State Secretary in the Economics Ministry, Neumann, that: "Such a process is contrary to any commercial view, and can only lead to a fiasco."[418] The Deutsche Bank's main commercial interest lay in Belgium, not the Netherlands, and the bank remained cautious about attempts to generate a greater German direct participation in Dutch business. One year after the German invasion, the Deutsche Bank's director in Den Haag wrote skeptically that "a German-Dutch economic inter-penetration on a larger scale can only be accomplished if the Dutch no longer believe in a final victory of the English."[419] But the Deutsche Bank did engage in some major share purchases in the Netherlands, buying for instance most of the Dutch shares of the Algemeene Kunstzijde Unie and the 75 percent of the Norddeutsche Lederwerke AG that before 1940 had been held by Dutch owners.[420]

Belgium and the Société Générale

The Economics Ministry's attempts to make banking spheres of influence and to award the Deutsche Bank Dutch banks but not those in Belgium was particularly irritating because Kimmich believed that the dominant Belgian bank, the Société Générale, wished to work closely with the Deutsche Bank but not with the more politicized Dresdner Bank.[421] The Governor of the Société Générale, Alexandre Galopin, had been the exponent of the theory of the "lesser evil" (known in wartime Belgium as the "doctrine Galopin") – that it was better to work with Germany and supply products (even semi-military products such as boots or steel) than to allow the Belgian population to starve. To do this, he needed to have a reliable and non-political German partner. At the same time, from September 1940, through the Vice-Governor of the Société Générale, Félicien Cattier, Galopin kept contacts with the Belgian exile government in London. From 1941, the bank tried to reduce the extent of its collaboration with the Germans, and in February 1944 Galopin was assassinated on his own doorstep by a member of a Flemish fascist group, the Veiligheidskorps, that specialized in counter-reprisals against attacks by the Belgian resistance.

The Société Générale was a vast holding company, with a wide range of assets both in Belgium and abroad. By the summer of 1940, it had ensured that an important part of its overseas assets, notably the important mineral holdings at Katanga and elsewhere in Africa, had been transferred to management in London and New York. On the other hand, the bank was not at all unwilling to dispose of its holdings in southeast and Balkan Europe, which had brought enormous losses and had substantially contributed to the very poor performance of the Société Générale in the 1930s. After 1940, in consequence, it rapidly sold to Germany its shares in the Österreichische Eisenbahnverkehrsanstalt, the Creditanstalt in Vienna, the Istituto Nazionale di Credito per il Lavoro all'Estero, the General Yugoslav Bank Association, and the Banque Commerciale Roumaine.[422] On the other hand, the deal proposed by the Société Générale for a sale to the Deutsche Bank of half of the shares of the Banque Générale of Luxembourg, with an option on the purchase of the other half, was much more complex, with tacit provisions for annulment at the end of hostilities.

In late August, a race for Belgian contacts and assets between the German Great Banks took place. Carl Goetz of the Dresdner Bank believed that he could rely on Funk's order and on the sympathy of Major von Becker, the German occupation official in Brussels in charge of banking. Goetz visited Galopin and the Société Générale's President, Willy de Munck, but was told by Galopin that he could make no arrangement as "political conditions did not allow him to form a clear idea about the future of Belgium and the Société Générale."[423] Suddenly on the evening of August 27 Hermann Abs appeared unexpectedly in Brussels and set out the details of his own bank's negotiations with the Société Générale. The Deutsche Bank's local representative noted: "His unexpected appearance caused visible confusion in the office of the Commissariat."[424] Abs's intervention apparently was not enough. Ex-Economics Minister Schacht, still officially in the German government as a Minister without Portfolio, was called in by the Deutsche Bank, spoke on the telephone with Goetz and Funk, and then wrote a letter to Funk in which he explained that the two German banks had come to an agreement. "The banks agreed with him in thinking it right to leave individual deals in Belgium and the Netherlands to themselves, but to inform the Reich Economics Minister about 'larger business'."[425]

After this initial skirmish had apparently been won by the Deutsche Bank, major German industrial firms visited Galopin, expecting to acquire their own Belgian assets: Vereinigte Stahlwerke, Mannesmann, Otto Wolff. Some German firms, notably IG Farben, had drawn up their own preliminary studies of the Belgian economy in the summer of 1940. Otto Wolff had made an agreement in August with the metal exporting firm Société Commerciale d'Ougrée, with which Wolff had worked before 1939, in which Wolff took over export shares to central and eastern Europe. But Galopin criticized the Wolff agreement, and stated to the Deutsche Bank that it would never come into force during the war.[426] Even for those firms such as Mannesmann which had historically been very intimately connected with the Deutsche Bank, the bank's representatives in Brussels were strikingly unhelpful. Director Alfred Kurzmeyer of Deutsche Bank made it clear that his institution could not help with the task of acquisitions. They were, it soon appeared, simply too complex for the bank to handle.

The biggest single transfer of industrial ownership in the case of occupied Belgium involved the Luxembourg steel works ARBED, which had French, Belgian, and Luxembourg owners. In November 1940, the Société Générale proposed to the Deutsche Bank the transfer of half of its shares in a holding company for ARBED stock, as well as a sale of some of its shares in the German chemical company Dahlbusch to IG Farben. But in practice the transaction was postponed to the end of hostilities. Instead of the legally highly complicated process of rearranging a jumble of interlocking holdings with an untransparent ownership structure, the ARBED was run throughout the war by a German military commissioner.

Would direct banking participations be any easier? On September 20, 1940, the Economics Ministry authorized twenty-two German firms to undertake capital participations [*Kapitalverflechtung*] in the Netherlands, Belgium, and occupied France. But the political circumstances of the occupied countries remained unclear: King Leopold of Belgium visited Hitler in Berchtesgaden in November 1940, but the Führer disliked the monarch, and no peace treaty resulted. As a consequence, even Baron de Launoit of the Banque de Bruxelles, generally thought to be more sympathetic to the Germans than Galopin, explained to the Dresdner Bank that a German participation in a large Belgian bank would be counter-productive, as it would undermine the confidence of the population in that bank.[427]

In November 1940, the German Military Bank Commissariat in Brussels produced a paper recommending greater commitment by German banks. They should, it suggested, establish subsidiaries in Belgium to give credits to factories producing armaments for German orders, and to deal with "the task of penetration" arising in the question of the readjustment of the ownership of European industry. This exposé was followed by negotiations in the Economics Ministry in Berlin, in which the banking expert suggested that there should be a series of joint German–Belgian banks. These would acquire the assets of "enemy property" in Belgium, such as branches of British and French banks, as well as "Aryanized" banks (Phillippson et Cie, Banque Lambert, Banque Cassel). The Dresdner Bank responded by creating a "Banque Continentale" in the offices formerly occupied by the Banque de Paris, and the Commerzbank used the Brussels "Hansabank." The Deutsche Bank declined to engage in this exercise and to take over the Banque de Commerce as the German authorities suggested, because it believed it needed no subsidiary. Abs pointed out that the Deutsche Bank intended "to base its business in Belgium on its very old and good relations with the foremost Belgian bank, the Banque de la Société Générale, and before making further decisions to wait for further political development."[428] Abs clearly looked at the foreign involvement of Deutsche Bank in terms of an overall vision of the longer term development of the European economy. The main focus of his interest in the Société Générale lay increasingly not so much in Belgium as in the bank's southeast-European assets.

Southeast and Balkan Europe

The division of Southeast Europe into spheres of influence between competing banks was carefully planned and calculated by the Reich Economics Ministry.[429] It reflected expectations about the future trading as well as financial connections of a re-ordered Balkan Europe. Trade with Southeast Europe was complicated by systems of exchange control: payments were made by means of clearings through the central banks of the countries involved in trade. Managing these payments meant in effect directing the pattern and course of trade.

Much of Southeast Europe was to be managed by Deutsche Bank through the Creditanstalt, but there were some exceptions. Greece lay outside the Creditanstalt's area. In the summer of 1941, the Deutsche Bank worked with the Reich Economics Ministry in buying the Société Générale's shares in the leading Greek commercial bank, the Banque Nationale de Grèce, while the Dresdner Bank was left to build up a participation in the much smaller Banque d'Athènes.[430]

Rumania and Bulgaria also lay outside the economic orbit of the Creditanstalt. Here too the Deutsche Bank acquired a major direct equity participation. By 1941, it controlled 88 percent of the Banca Comerciala Romana SA (formerly owned by French and Belgian banks) and over 90 percent of the Bulgarian Kreditbank Sofia, historically a correspondent bank of the Disconto–Gesellschaft which had financed German–Bulgarian trade. In the August 1940 meeting with the Board of the Creditanstalt, Abs had spoken quite candidly about obtaining an "enrichment of the Deutsche Bank" in Rumania.[431]

Rumania had played a major role before 1939 in German economic diplomacy vis-à-vis Southeast Europe. It had had a powerful bargaining advantage, in that Germany was dependent on petroleum imports and found the development of a substitution through synthetic gasoline to be both extremely slow (and thus useless from the standpoint of Germany's military ambitions) and highly uneconomic. Rumania attempted to use its strategic advantage as a major oil producer by increasing its refining capacity, so that four-fifths of native petroleum would be exported as refined products.[432] In 1935 the Deutsche Bank participated in negotiations to establish a joint German–Rumanian refining company that would pay for the import of German machinery with petroleum products, but the plan faced hostility from the German authorities.[433] Instead, Rumania cut back on exports to Germany and imposed a special tax to compensate for the overvaluation of the RM in the clearing arrangements. Only after September 1938 and the Munich conference did Rumanian policy become more sympathetic to the Reich: in November 1938 King Carol spoke with Hermann Göring about a "systematic cooperation for the development of economic relations."[434]

At the beginning of 1939 Helmuth Wohlthat of the Reich Office for Foreign Exchange led a mission charged with the expansion of German–Rumanian trade. It produced an agreement after the fall of Czechoslovakia that was widely regarded as a model for future economic relations in the "greater economic area." Germany would sell agricultural equipment, tractors, and seeding machines, in exchange for oil. Already before the outbreak of war, Wohlthat promoted the establishment of companies in which banks and industry as well as state and party would work to develop relations with the states of Southeast Europe. Again, as in the case of the Low Countries, there was an intended official division into spheres of interest between the two major German commercial banks. The Dresdner Bank's director Professor

Emil Meyer was to become President of the German–Yugoslav Society, and Abs of the Deutsche Bank was to become President of the equivalent Rumanian Society.[435] By the end of 1940, a ten-year plan had been agreed upon, in which Germany would provide long-term credit for the delivery of machinery to Rumania. The argument was now made that "Rumania will in the long run only be able to solve the pressure of rural over-population through industrialization."[436]

This scheme provided the basis for a much more elaborate proposal worked out after consultations between businessmen on both sides, and it was eventually incorporated into a new German–Rumanian agreement of February 2, 1943. A German–Rumanian Experts Committee included, on the German side, Abs; Karl Blessing, formerly a Director of the Reichsbank and after 1941 head of Kontinentale Oel AG; and (as chairman) Max Ilgner of IG Farben. The Committee drew up an "Immediate Programme," whose main features were the relocation of consumer production from Germany to Rumania; the production of synthetic fibers from reeds in the Danube delta and from beech wood; the production of artificial fertilizers (phosphates and nitrates), natural gas, bauxite, and aluminium; hydroelectric works, and electrification of major railway lines. The total cost of this ambitious industrialization drive was estimated at 150–200 m. RM, of which half would be financed from Germany and would cover the supply of German equipment and expertise; the rest would be raised in Rumania, where the German-owned Rumanian banks would play the major role.[437] Kontinentale Oel had by this stage become the major Rumanian petroleum producer, thanks to the purchases by the Deutsche Bank of the French Rumanian holdings in the Colombia and Concordia companies.[438]

The Deutsche Bank also bought holdings in other foreign countries on behalf of a variety of private companies. The Otavi metallurgy company required inputs of aluminium and rare metal ores, but found its African mines useless because of the military conflict. As substitutes it acquired Zinnbergbau Sudetenland GmbH, the Bauxit-Trust AG (which had substantial Hungarian ore sources),

Donautal-Tonerde AG Budapest, and the Gravia bauxite mine in Greece. It also tried to buy Rumanian companies from the portfolio of the liquidated Rumanian Jewish bank, Marmarosch Blank & Co., but found it difficult to circumvent Rumanian legislation limiting foreign ownership of industrial enterprise.[439] And despite the war, Otavi also purchased mines in the Congo from Belgian owners.[440]

Gold and Securities

Did the Deutsche Bank perform tasks that other, more directly state-dominated, institutions would have found hard or impossible, and in this way did it perform a useful service for the regime? We have already seen that the greatest comparative advantage of the bank lay in the range and diversity of its international contacts.

On at least one occasion, German military intelligence (the Abwehr) tried to use Deutsche Bank as a front for intelligence operations. In 1941, the bank hired a new press and information director [*Leiter der Nachrichten–Abteilung*], Claus Morgenstern, who had previously worked for the corporative organization of German industry, Reich Group Industry [*Reichsgruppe Industrie*]. An internal note on the new appointment explained that he traveled frequently in Europe, and that this would be an asset ["*Aktivum*"] for the bank. In 1941, Morgenstern wrote a memorandum for Deutsche Bank in which he explained that he had met a member of the Swiss Nazi organization Erneuerungsbund, a Dr. Keller, who had explained that the owner of the *Neue Basler Zeitung* was trying to move the paper away from supporting Germany and did not want to receive German official support any longer. So Morgenstern proposed that Deutsche Bank might offer a guarantee and take over the assets of the *Neue Basler Zeitung* in Germany. He ended his report with the statement that "Minister Schmidt of the Press Department of the Foreign Office as well as the Reich Economics Ministry is interested in this business."[441] The bank does not appear to have reacted positively to this suggestion, and by the next year

the bank's managers were themselves worried about Morgenstern's attempted politicization of the bank. In March 1942, Lt.-
Col. [*Oberstleutnant*] Schmidt from the Münster intelligence office
[*Abwehrstelle Münster*] visited Deutsche Bank and asked that Morgenstern continue to use his foreign trips to supply intelligence information. The bank's reply was quite hostile: the bank would have
no objection to Morgenstern using his military leave for this purpose, but he should not use his title from Deutsche Bank, or his
calling cards, in pursuit of such information. The bank stipulated
that "the performance of his military orders must under all circumstances be separate from his task as head of the information
office of Deutsche Bank." The next month, when Morgenstern visited the Basel trade fair, the bank instructed him to contact only
German journalists, and not (as Morgenstern wished) Swiss journalists. Soon after, Morgenstern resigned from the bank, although
Deutsche Bank continued to pay him until June 1943.[442]

But the bank undoubtedly served German national objectives
in less direct ways. In the 1930s, Deutsche Bank was one of a
number of banks registered as *Devisen* banks, licensed to perform
foreign exchange transactions and to receive on account of the
Reichsbank the precious metals and foreign securities that were
subject to registration and then to compulsory purchase as a consequence of new state legislation. A wholly owned subsidiary of
Deutsche Bank, the Aktiengesellschaft für Vermögensverwertung,
was used to manage the repatriation of foreign securities (often
deposited in foreign banks) held by persons domiciled in Germany
after this was required by Germany's exchange control apparatus (under the terms of the seventh foreign exchange ordinance,
Durchführungsverordnung zum Devisengesetz, of November 19,
1936). Such assets were to be surrendered to a German *Devisen*
bank, and the AG appeared as a useful intermediary institution.
Later, after the outbreak of the war, the same company was used to
camouflage German ownership of assets in Dutch and other foreign
banks.[443]

Ever since the financial crisis of 1931, private dealings in gold
had been subject to control. Just how sensitive the gold issue was

is demonstrated by the fact that two bank officials in Deutsche Bank's Krefeld branch were arrested for having sold between 1931 and 1936 22,495 RM worth of gold coins to dentists who actually had permission to acquire such gold but not from a private bank because "the branch was not entitled to sell gold, since it only acts as in the commission of the Reichsbank in foreign exchange transactions."[444]

Gold played a peculiar role in Nazi economic thinking. Officially, the regime regarded gold as an outdated relic of the liberal international world of the nineteenth century. The German currency was now supported, according to this view, not by internationally convertible reserves, but by German labor. One of Hjalmar Schacht's first acts, as the reinstalled President of the Reichsbank in 1933, was to pay back the international central bank loan of 1931 that had been used to bolster reserves during the currency crisis of 1931. With that, Germany's gold reserves shrank dramatically. The officially published reserve level remained constant at a mere 70.8 m. RM. But during this period, the Reichsbank also accumulated additional, non-published reserves, so that the real total of the Reichsbank's own gold stock at the outbreak of war was 387.2 m. RM. In addition, the Reichsbank seized the gold reserves of Austria and Czechoslovakia.

During the war, the German authorities, and the Reichsbank, became increasingly obsessed with the need to acquire gold sufficient to pay for the imports of strategically vital materials such as petroleum, wolfram, and manganese ores. The Minister of Economics, Walther Funk, stated bluntly in 1941 that "by the end of the war, the gold which we need will be ours."[445] Of the total gold at Germany's disposal, $483.2 m. (or 1,208 m. RM, at the official gold price) came from foreign central banks looted during the war, and a staggering $82.0 m. (212.5 m. RM) came from individuals, expropriated by so-called Currency Protection Squads [Devisenschutzkommandos] in the framework of Hermann Göring's Four-Year Plan Organization. This figure also includes at least $2.9 m. taken from the victims of Nazi extermination camps in Poland in Operation Reinhard. Of this stock, $298.9 m. was recovered in Germany at the end of the war, while $565.5 m. (or three-quarters) was sold abroad, mostly to the Swiss National Bank but also to Swiss commercial banks.[446] A relatively small part of the Reichsbank gold was sold to the two largest German banks, Deutsche Bank and Dresdner Bank, as well as to two small specialty banks that handled the Four-Year Plan's secret business in occupied Europe, H. Fetschow & Sohn and Sponholz & Co.[447]

What was the role of the commercial banks, and why did they want to buy the Reichsbank's tainted gold? From 1941, Deutsche Bank ran a small-scale but quite lucrative business in supplying gold to German diplomats and others resident in neutral Turkey. Its major customer was the German Ambassador, Franz von Papen, who had been a long-standing customer of Deutsche Bank and who kept his personal papers in a safe in the Berlin bank. At first, Deutsche Bank had a monopoly on this business, and in the summer of 1942 it refused to share its business with the Istanbul branch of Dresdner Bank (still named the Deutsche Orientbank). Initially, the bank bought gold in Switzerland and sold it in Turkey against dollars, Swiss francs, or "free" (convertible) Marks. But in the summer of 1942, the Swiss National Bank, worried about the possible loss of Swiss reserves, started to control the Swiss market and restrict Swiss gold exports. Finally, in December 1942 the Swiss government restricted gold sales and purchases to the official price, and it laid down the rule that all gold transactions in Switzerland had to be conducted through the National Bank. Deutsche Bank's Istanbul branch then looked for an alternative supply of gold. At the moment when the Swiss business was becoming more difficult, the leading managers of the Reichsbank's precious metals and foreign currency department, Albert Thoms and Karl Graupner, visited Istanbul. The Deutsche Bank branch's director produced a memorandum in which he suggested that the Reichsbank should provide gold for the arbitrage business. The Reichsbank accepted, probably because this would be a quite profitable transaction, in which the Reichsbank would sell gold at prices substantially higher than the pre-1931 parity, which was still the official gold price in Germany.

In all, the Reichsbank sold 4,446 kgf to Deutsche Bank (of which 2,456 kgf was in bar form) and 5,762 kgf to Dresdner Bank, including 2,136 kgf in bars (the Dresdner Bank was eventually admitted to this profitable business, probably because of its strong political contacts).[448] The Deutsche Bank's gold was worth 12.5 m. RM at the official price but considerably more on the free Turkish market. In addition, Deutsche Bank bought in Switzerland, so that 4,143 kgf (out of a total of 4,967 kgf) was sold on the Istanbul market during the war.[449]

This gold was almost entirely sold to private individuals, mostly Axis diplomats from Bulgaria, Italy, and Rumania (Hungarians and Japanese worked more with the Dresdner's Deutsche Orientbank). One of the Deutsche Bank's Istanbul managers explained after the war: "Since the gold transactions were very profitable, each bank attempted as much as possible to increase its business, and this naturally involved a certain stimulation of the customers."[450] The Turkish gold sales, however, did not form a part of the large-scale operations of the German war economy, and they were not essential for national defense. Germany was desperate for Turkish chrome ores, which were essential for high-grade steel production, and offered to buy Turkish ore for gold, but the Turkish government declined and the trade was financed in a different way. Neither is there any evidence that the commercial banks' gold arbitrage operations were used as a source of payments for German espionage (as is claimed in the Second Report of the U.S. State Department on Gold Transactions).[451] The most important German spy was actually paid in forged British bank notes. The truth is much more mundane: dealing in gold was one way that German and other diplomats in Turkey enriched themselves, and the Deutsche Bank and its managers were keen to participate in this attractive and lucrative semi-private and semi-official business.

The most problematical aspect of the gold transactions lies not in the use of the gold in Istanbul but rather in the gold's origin. Thanks to the account books of the Reichsbank (which exist only in a microfilm copy in the National Archives in Washington and were rediscovered by historians in 1997), and the smelting registers of Degussa, the precious metals smelting and refining company, it is possible to be quite specific about where the Deutsche Bank's Turkish gold originated. A surprisingly large share of that gold (744 kgf) came from gold bars that were labeled by the Reichsbank as "Melmer" bars. These were part of, in all, 76 deliveries of gold and precious metals by SS-Obersturmbannführer Bruno Melmer, to the Reichsbank. This was "victim gold," taken from live or dead (largely Jewish) victims of the killing fields in Poland, who were murdered in the course of the so-called "Operation Reinhard." This was not the only victim gold. In addition, 3.2 kgf of gold sold to the Deutsche Bank probably originated from an SS massacre in Stanislau (Ukraine).[452] The explanation of why so many of these bars originating in gold stolen from the victims of genocide went to the Deutsche Bank (a smaller amount went to Dresdner Bank) is in part a product of the chronological chance that the Reichsbank's agreement to sell gold for transport to Istanbul occurred just before the main tide of delivery of "Melmer" gold. But there were also far larger sales to the Swiss National Bank at this time, which involved relatively few of the "Melmer" bars and came for the most part from gold seized, largely from the Dutch and Belgian central banks, but also from individuals in western Europe. These very much larger quantities were simply resmelted in 12.5-kg bars, which was the standard for gold operations between central banks. The more personalized Turkish transactions required smaller quantities of gold: either coin (largely from western European sources) or single-kilogram bars. A large share of these bars were the result of resmelting the "Melmer" gold deliveries.

There is, nevertheless, no way of knowing what exactly happened to the physical gold delivered by the SS under the supervision of Bruno Melmer. The most recent research on Degussa's smelting operations suggests that the gold delivered to a customer was not physically the same as the gold sent for smelting and also possibly refining.[453] There is thus no necessary physical connection between the gold of the East European killing fields and the Deutsche Bank's deliveries to von Papen and others. Few people in

the Reichsbank knew about the SS transactions, although Thoms
and Graupner certainly did. We can only speculate as to whether
they let slip some details of their secrets either in Berlin or when
visiting German banks in Istanbul.

The Turkish gold history had a peculiar aftermath, which suggests that Hermann Abs felt uncomfortable about the gold transactions and feared that even a small part of the gold might create
publicity about the whole of the Deutsche Bank's wartime Turkish business and the circumstances around it. The gold bars, as
a result, remained in a Swiss bank vault until the 1990s. Alfred
Kurzmeyer (Figure 23), a Swiss citizen and a Director of Deutsche
Bank, at the end of the war administered 307 kg of gold for the
Istanbul branch of Deutsche Bank, as well as cash in Swiss bank
notes. He registered these for a time under his own name (in order to escape the freeze on German assets imposed by the Swiss
government in February 1945). The gold bars were unfrozen under the terms of a 1952 treaty between Germany and Switzerland
and were subject to one-third being paid to the Swiss government
(Kurzmeyer had tried to avoid this payment on the basis of an
argument that the gold belonged to Germans in Turkey, i.e. not
domiciled in Germany and thus not liable for the payment). The
actual bars, however, remained in Switzerland as the property of the
Trinitas Vermögensverwaltung, a wholly owned subsidiary of the
successor institutions of Deutsche Bank. This gold was only sold
in 1995, after Abs's death, for 5.6 m. DM. In 1997, the Deutsche
Bank gave these proceeds away, half to the World Jewish Restitution Organization and half to the Foundation "March of the Living." Jonathan Steinberg, in his report on the gold transactions of
the Deutsche Bank, speculated that Abs and Kurzmeyer may have
known the secret of the Reichsbank's gold.[454] Abs's hesitation in
the postwar period to deal with the Trinitas gold may have sprung
from an awareness of its taint.

Kurzmeyer himself had direct contacts with the SS, and he seems
to have played the role of fiduciary for that sinister organization
in a way analogous to his actions on behalf of Deutsche Bank. At
the beginning of 1945, the SS opened a numbered bank account
with the Credit Suisse (Schweizerische Kreditanstalt) in Zurich for

Figure 23. Alfred Kurzmeyer, director with power of attorney, 1939–45.

Source: Courtesy of Deutsche Bank AG.

its extensive economic enterprises (Deutsche Wirtschaftbetriebe), to which not only the SS economic managers Oswald Pohl and Georg Lörner had access, but also the SS emissary who had set up the Swiss accounts, Leo Volk, and Kurzmeyer. He was also well known to the Swiss police and intelligence services, who from September 1944 reported on his trade in jewelry, from a base in the Hotel Savoy on the Zurich Paradeplatz.[455] Abs must have known that Kurzmeyer was also working for the German Foreign Office and the Reichsbank, since Kurzmeyer's advantages stemmed largely from these connections; it is impossible to say whether Abs was aware of the SS connection, but it would have been reasonable to suspect any range of contacts in the case of that seedy operator of backstairs and hotel-room finance.

Abs's particular strengths and knowledge before he entered the Deutsche Bank had lain in the field of Germany's foreign debt negotiations (the yearly renegotiations of the debt standstill agreements originally concluded in the aftermath of the great banking crisis of 1931). One of the most lucrative financial opportunities of the 1930s involved buying up German bonds that had originally been bought by foreign investors in the 1920s, and which traded at very low prices (between 10 and 50 percent of the nominal value) after the default of 1931. These bonds were then repatriated to Germany, where they could be resold at close to par value. Such transactions required foreign exchange, which the Reichsbank guarded jealously. Soon after joining Deutsche Bank, Abs carried out such a transaction, on his own account (not that of the bank). In 1940, he bought $40 m. bonds from the large so-called "Kreuger loan" of 1929 (a total of $125 m. had been issued). The price was 40 percent of the nominal value, and Abs bought the bonds from the Wallenberg-owned Stockholms Enskilda Bank (the Wallenbergs had been the great rival of the "Swedish Match King," Ivar Kreuger, and the main beneficiaries of his financial collapse and suicide in 1932). Abs was acting as an agent directly for the Reichsbank, which provided the gold for the transaction but obviously wanted to conceal its role because it was quite contrary to the public rhetoric about conserving Germany's gold reserves. He found the deal so lucrative (he had a commission of 293,052 RM, only slightly less than his entire annual earnings from Deutsche Bank) that he proposed to buy back more Kreuger bonds. The Finance Ministry refused to agree to the use of further German gold reserves for this purpose.[456]

Abs also did other currency business during the war for the Reichsbank through the Deutsche Bank's subsidiary Deutsche Ueberseeische Bank or Banco Alemán Transatlántico (DUB). German payments to South America, a good part of which had been conducted through New York banks, became much harder after the United States imposed a general freeze on continental European assets on June 14, 1941. The Lima branch of the DUB had opened an account for $100,000, nominally for the Banco Central de Reserva del Peru, with the Chase National Bank of New York.[457] Already in February 1941, another Deutsche Bank subsidiary, the Deutsch-Asiatische Bank in Shanghai, had taken a credit from Credit Suisse's

New York branch. In all the Credit Suisse lent 6 m. CHF to the Deutsch-Asiatische Bank.[458] In April 1941, the Reichsbank proposed that it create a U.S. dollar account with the DUB.[459] After the June freeze, the DUB confirmed that it would handle on behalf of the Reichsbank a shipment of $90,000 in banknotes and gold certificates to Buenos Aires.[460] The DUB was also employed to pay quite substantial amounts to Switzerland, especially in the final stages of the war, when the Allied supervision of Swiss banking practices was becoming ever more intensive. In October 1944, the Reichsbank created a Swiss franc account with the DUB.[461] The francs were used to pay for war material, and perhaps also for espionage purposes. At the end of 1944, the DUB was used to make a payment of 1 m. CHF to Major Gaefgen, the head of the German Industrial Commission in Switzerland [*Leiter der Deutschen Industriekommission in der Schweiz*]. On the payment note, alongside the 1 m. CHF on account of the Auswärtiges Amt, there is also a figure of 682,325.90 CHF "for use as service money for the office Hames (Political Dept.), previously Winzer, on the orders of the Reichsführer SS and Minister of the Interior [Himmler]."[462] In January 1945, 4.7 m. CHF was paid to the German Consulate General in Zurich.[463] In March 1945, a further 1.3 m. CHF went to Major Gaefgen. How did the money arrive in Switzerland? It no longer came directly from Germany but was transferred, at the instruction of the DUB, from the Spanish Instituto de Moneda Extranjera. The cash – a total of 6,769,550 CHF – was then kept by Kurzmeyer at the Credit Suisse in safe box XXXII.[464] The DUB became in this way a mechanism for the concealing ("cloaking") of German payments.

The Kreuger business is not the most problematical private activity of Abs during the war. In the last months of the war, Abs also seems to have conducted some business on his own behalf. In September 1944, he made a lengthy (one week) trip to Switzerland, where he gave his address as care of his mother-in-law, Doris Schnitzler, at Küsnacht near Zurich. While he was there he was sent 746,800 CHF through the Zurich office of the Schweizerischer Bankverein by the Dresdner Bank. It is not certain what he did with this sum, or why it was paid.[465] The nature of this transaction is mysterious, but it was certainly contrary to his conditions of employment at Deutsche Bank, which forbade the holding of accounts with other institutions.[466] Abs seems here to have been not far removed from engaging in person in murky dealings of a very Kurzmeyerian kind.

Deutsche Bank and the New Order

Especially in the period between the defeat of France in May 1940 and the launching of Operation Barbarossa in June 1941, business saw and enthused about the dramatic reordering of Europe to Germany's advantage. Businessmen and bankers envisaged a speedy shift into a postwar world that would learn the lessons from the interwar years, from the failure of internationalism, and from the 1930s restriction and bilateralization of trade. The new postwar period would in their view be centered around the fact of German economic power.

Economics Minister Walther Funk developed the familiar National Socialist idea of a Co-Prosperity Sphere or "Grossraumwirtschaft" into a future European trading and currency bloc in which fixed exchange rates and free convertibility would replicate some of the certainties of the gold standard world but in the context of integration of the European continent. Funk maintained his position long after it seemed to most others unrealizable and bizarrely unrealistic. As late as 1944, when German clearing balances had built up to staggering amounts, when repressed inflation led to misallocations and the development of a black market, and of course when Germany was very obviously losing the war, he was explaining that "one of our basic principles for the recasting of the economy in the new Europe is the stability of exchange rates and price stability."[467]

These were themes that Hermann Abs had raised in a speech of July 17, 1941, to the Trade Policy Committee of the Reich Economic Chamber on the theme "Europe and the United States from an Economic Viewpoint." The main message of his presentation was that the clearing system created in the 1930s had damaged the development of trade and the spread of prosperity, and that payments should be made in convertible currencies through an international banking system; but that because of the differences in economic performance between Europe and the U.S., the liberalization should first be attempted on a continental basis. Looked at in one way, it was a version of the European Payments Union of the 1950s; looked at through the political lens of 1941, however, it was a defense of German imperialism. "The perspectives for the German economy at the end of the war, which suggest a closer integration of the European economies, in regard to the external economy justify a consideration which counterpoises continental Europe with the American continent."[468]

The vision of a reordered Europe that formed an economic community controlled by German interests appeared most compelling in the wake of the easy military victories of 1940. But long after the euphoria had passed, the mechanism of international payments remained acutely problematic. The difficulties were frequently debated in the Reichsbank, as well as in a Working Group on External Economic Relations created in 1944, which was composed of bureaucrats from the Reich Economics Ministry and businessmen, including Abs.

Already in December 1939 Abs had criticized the clearing mechanism as inefficient, ineffective, and restrictive of trade, and he appealed for a return to multilateral trade.[469] This theme remained quite consistent in Abs's statements on trade policy, whether they were made when Germany appeared to be winning the war or when she was losing.

In the course of 1943, Abs became involved in a rather intriguing international discussion of the likely shape of the postwar order. In May 1943, the Economic Adviser of the Basel-based Bank for International Settlements, the Swede Per Jacobsson, spoke with Abs as well as with Emil Puhl of the Reichsbank and Carl Goetz of the Dresdner Bank. In the setting of the Zurich Hotel Baur en Ville, the bankers discussed the currency plans developed by John Maynard

Keynes and Harry Dexter White (in part conceived as a response to Funk's New Order). The Germans expressed a strong preference for the British version: "Puhl seems to think that the American plan was too much US hegemony. Abs said unitas [the unit of account in the U.S. Treasury Plan as developed by White] was a fig-leave [*sic*] for the dollar." But quite surprisingly, the German bankers also criticized the German practice of clearings, and they described the German currency regime as simply an emergency solution [*Notlösung*]. The discussion resumed one month later in Berlin, when Jacobsson arrived to set out the details of the White and Keynes plans to a broader financial circle, again including Abs.[470] Germany should – Abs believed – develop a more satisfactory response than that laid out in the speeches of Economics Minister Funk.

In 1943 in the Reichsbank's Council [*Beirat*], Abs urged that Germany should sell more to the countries of continental Europe and in this way avoid the building up of large clearing balances. "The publication of the Keynes plan and the White plan have provided an interesting vision of the differences in opinion between the English and the Americans. Germany hardly has the possibility of putting forward any similar plan. But we could show what advantages would be brought by a generous trading policy."[471] In the defense of a liberal trade policy, Abs was speaking against one of the most important and characteristic elements of National Socialist economic foreign policy; but it was impossible to discuss in a similar way the much broader complex of National Socialist economic thought and the extension of state control.

6

The Expansion of State and Party
during the War

In dealing with the foreign activity of the Deutsche Bank, the gradual expansion of German state influence was everywhere evident: in directing the armaments economy of occupied Europe, in the extension of direct ownership of public sector corporations, and in dividing banking activity into geographic spheres of influence. Only occasionally was this momentum interrupted, usually when one of the figures at the top of the public sector enterprises suffered a personal reverse in the complex and dangerous faction politics of National Socialist Germany. The same tendency – an increase in state and party authority mitigated only by the effects of political factionalism – characterized the development of the German economy on the home front. Wars create considerable opportunities for private business, but they also create a very powerful countervailing demand for the limitation of illegitimate private gains and for the extension of state control over the economy. In the case of National Socialism at war, there was no doubt that the latter took the upper hand and that the party wanted to take over the positions of control held (in its view illegitimately) by the private sector.

The Expansion of the State

In the early years of the war, the bank's business included not only the purchase of assets in occupied Europe but also a continuation of privatizations in Germany. A unique investment climate combined increasing inflationary pressure (as a result of government deficits financed through the printing press) with imposed ceilings on stock prices. This made real assets especially attractive to those with speculative natures who remembered the inflationary experiences of Germany's first twentieth-century war, and the profits to be made from rapid industrial expansion and the acquisition of real assets [Sachwerte] with paper money. Some important debit accounts with the Deutsche Bank suddenly expanded, mainly that of the tobacco empire of Reemtsma, and the Accumulatorenfabrik AG of Günther Quandt. Both used bank borrowing to expand their industrial holdings. Reemtsma, a major shareholder of the bank, had drawn 46 m. RM credit by October 1944 and was the bank's largest debit account.[472]

Hapag was privatized in as inconspicuous a fashion as possible in 1941 by a syndicate led by Philipp Reemtsma and financed by the Deutsche Bank. Reemtsma purchased 4 m. RM shares, with an option on another 4 m., without any consultations whatsoever with the supervisory board (which merely recorded its "regret [. . .] that the supervisory board only discovered this fact and the further details through the press").[473]

Also in 1941, the Deutsche Bank carried out a privatization of 120 m. RM shares of Vereinigte Stahlwerke (the leading German steel concern). Göring, now a much less significant figure in the power hierarchy of the Third Reich, and who had previously fought bitterly with the management of Vereinigte Stahlwerke when he had been setting up the state Reichswerke, agreed rather meekly. He gave his consent, the Deutsche Bank believed, "since at present the higher authorities are leaning towards the private side."[474] But this observation was made just at the moment when the course of the war, and with it the nature of economic policy, began to change in a newly radicalized direction.

After the failure of Operation Barbarossa to achieve an immediate victory over the Soviet Union, a complete reordering of the war economy took place. On December 3, 1941 a Führer command restricted the output of consumer goods and ordered the concentration of war-related production in the most efficient and economical plants. In mid-January 1942 Germany started to restructure the economy to meet the demands of a long conflict. Rationalization initiatives later produced a Central Planning administration, created in April 1942 under Albert Speer, which allocated raw materials centrally and worked with the industrial committees already established by Speer's predecessor as Minister of Armaments, Fritz Todt.[475]

At the same time as Speer's ministry built up its position, the party's influence expanded through the institution of control at a regional level by Gau Economic Chambers [*Gauwirtschaftskammer*], which replaced the old system of chambers of commerce, and the appointment of Gau Economic Leaders [*Gauwirtschaftsführer*].

Industrial reorganization also brought a much more powerful involvement of the state in the financing of war production. The major armaments producers expanded their capacity by means of consortia put together out of several commercial banks but with a leading role taken by public sector institutions. For instance, the newly established German Aero-Bank [*Bank der deutschen Luftfahrt*] took this role in the highly capital-intensive aircraft manufacturing industry. Commercial credit played a significant but fundamentally subordinate role in the increase of munitions output. The companies historically connected with the Deutsche Bank were no exception when it came to the financing of expanded munitions production. In 1944, the aero-engine works of Daimler–Benz Motoren GmbH Gemshagen, which had originally been 95 percent owned by the Luftfahrtkontor, the predecessor of the Aero-Bank, had liabilities of 17,750,000 RM, of which 7,000,000 RM was an operating loan of the Aero-Bank and 3,125,000 RM was a government-provided mobilization credit ("Mob-Kredit"). BMW's Eisenach works were similarly in part state-owned,[476] and the state's share of credits increased during the war. In July 1939, out of a total of 43.5 m RM credits, 19.5 m. came from the bank syndicate (in which the Deutsche Bank participated with two-thirds, the Dresdner Bank with one-third), and 17.0 m. came from the Luftfahrtkontor, with another 7.0 m. from another public sector bank, the bank for Industrial Bonds. By 1941, credits had risen to 77 m. RM, of which the two commercial banks between them could account for only 13.5 m. RM.[477] In 1942, the Aero-Bank demanded to participate in operating credit as well as "Mob-Kredit."[478] Another example is the Junkers aero-works, where out of an investment credit of 65 m. RM in 1941, the Aero-Bank provided 29 m. RM and the Deutsche Bank 11 m. RM; and of its operating credit, the Aero-Bank had 40 m. RM and the Deutsche Bank 12 m. RM.[479] The public sector banks – the Aero-Bank and the Bank for Industrial Bonds – had the advantage over the commercial banks that their credits could automatically be rediscounted at the Reichsbank, whereas other credits needed to be discussed by the Reichsbank's Credit Committee.[480]

Criticism of Banks

If industry were to be rationalized and commercial banks were to be squeezed out by government-controlled lending institutions, then there might also be an opportunity for those in the party hostile to finance capitalism to reassert the original radical elements of the National Socialist program. The old ideological slogans reappeared. "The credit industry is not an end in itself, but is only justified in as far as the economy requires it." The consequence was that "simplification measures" would be needed.[481] Proposals for a regionalization of the German banking structure emerged once more.[482]

There were complaints about interest rates; that there were too many branches in the major cities; that banks had abused their right to vote the shares of their customers at shareholders' meetings [Depotstimmrecht]; that banks exercised an unhealthy influence through their supervisory board presence. The National Socialist party newspaper *Völkischer Beobachter* believed that the bank provision of industrial credit had led to a distorted economy: "If the banks and in particular the investment banks had not mixed themselves up in financing in the course of the second half of the nineteenth century, economic development would have been much smoother and simpler, and less crisis prone [...] All financing through credit is speculative."[483] The SS Security Service used public opinion surveys to justify its call for action against finance capitalism: "There is an overwhelming rejection of the idea of Great Banks, but many emphasize the usefulness of credit institutes that would serve a wider regional base."[484] By the beginning of 1944 the SS had begun a general attack on the principles of the private economy, claiming "in the last analysis it is a matter of indifference, whether in [the] future economic investment is carried out by the private economy or by the public sector."[485]

The bank supervision system built up in 1931–4, in the late Weimar Republic and at the beginning of the Nazi dictatorship, was attacked as ineffective, and progressively dismantled. In 1942, control of local bank branches was transferred from the Reich Supervisory Office for Credit to the Reichsbank, which thus took over the day-to-day invigilation of banking activity. In 1944 the Supervisory Office was dissolved altogether.[486] The abolition was justified primarily in terms of a wartime economy drive. But it also formed part of a general attack on the position of banks. Because their position had become essentially administrative, in dealing with payment transactions and in channeling private savings into the state's coffers, banks might well be pruned back in the same way as the public fiscal administration had been.[487]

The offensive began with a letter of Hitler's Secretary Martin Bormann to Reich Economics Minister Walther Funk on the subject of credit costs and excessive bank profits in wartime: the Deutsche Bank, it was claimed, had managed to quadruple its profits from 1939 to 1940.[488] The Party Chancellery responded by demanding a limitation of supervisory board seats for bankers, and the replacement of bankers by technicians.[489] Rationalization, the major slogan of the winter of 1941–2 applied across all areas of

administration and the economy, could be used by the party to produce a reordering of German finance and a reduction of its power.

In May 1942 all banks were instructed to close ten percent of
their branches. The party did not think this sufficiently radical.
The Reich Economics Ministry official responsible for the banking section, Ministerial Director Joachim Riehle, noted that "with
the Reich Administrators and the Gauleiters the impression has
been created that the Berlin authorities are not pursuing rationalization measures with appropriate emphasis." Later in the year,
he told journalists that banks had become too concentrated: "The
fact that <u>one single Great Bank</u> [original emphasis] had collected
roughly one third of all credit bank deposits was a political issue. 'The fate and attitude' of a Great Bank must be treated as a
political affair."[490] One immediate result was a list of additional
branches to be closed.[491] In 1942 the Deutsche Bank closed twenty-
one branches and twenty-four city deposit offices; in 1943 it closed
sixty-one branches and thirty offices.

In October 1943, the government ordered a simplification of
supervisory boards, in which the number of bankers on the board
would be reduced and the majority of its business delegated to
a five-man committee. The Deutsche Bank responded by trying
to reduce the number of bank representatives on supervisory
boards of associated companies to one-third of the total board
membership.[492]

Banks and their political allies tried to mount some defense.
Banks may have looked superfluous to the requirements of a
wartime economy – but what about peace? Only by looking to the
future could the banks hope to justify their position. In a speech
of December 1942, Wilhelm Zangen of Mannesmann, the leader
of the interest association Reich Group Industry, pointed out that
banks would play a vital part in the conversion of military production facilities to peaceful use.[493] By early 1944, even a politically
prominent banker such as Otto Christian Fischer, Führer of the
Reich Group Banks, was circulating a memorandum on "reconstruction of the peacetime economy," in which he called for the
restoration of "pure economy [...] which operates on the basis of

supply and demand on the basis of competition and the calculation of cost."[494]

The Deutsche Bank was especially vulnerable to the new attack because of Stauss's death in December 1942: the bank no longer had a prominently situated political protector. He needed to be replaced, urgently. An initial consequence was greater party involvement in the supervisory board. In March 1943, while the supervisory board's Working Committee discussed the issue of bank rationalization, Albert Pietzsch, President of the Reich Economic Chamber and a member of the Deutsche Bank supervisory board since 1939, was invited to present the views of the party. Pietzsch was a longstanding member of the NSDAP, a so-called "Old Fighter" [*Alter Kämpfer*], and a personal friend of Hitler's. The minutes record only "a lively discussion."[495] In April 1943, the Gau Economic Leader of Middle Silesia, Otto Fitzner, was added to the Deutsche Bank's supervisory board.

Modifying the supervisory board alone would not be enough to forestall political pressure. Should the management board not also include a committed and active National Socialist, and not merely the ineffective and inoffensive Ritter von Halt? The political balance of the board had already been disturbed in 1940 by the addition of an outsider to the bank (coming from the board of Rudolph Karstadt AG) who was a practicing Catholic, Clemens Plassmann. Because there were already three Catholic members of the management board, Abs, Rösler, and Bechtolf (the latter, however, was a non-practicing Catholic), critics in the party, such as Rudolf Lencer of the DAF, began to call the Deutsche Bank the "Catholic bank." In November 1942, von Halt was summoned to a meeting at which the representative of the Gau Economic Adviser explained that "it was the wish of the party and the Economics Minister that soldiers coming home from a victorious war would find an economy fully managed on National Socialist lines. Thus the question should be examined whether all members of the management board of Deutsche Bank corresponded to the legitimate expectations of such key positions." Abs in particular was singled out for criticism.[496] In May 1943, an additional party member besides Halt was taken on after the party started to attack the presence of two Catholics, Plassmann and Abs. The new man was Robert Frowein, head of the Frankfurt branch since 1938 and a member of the NSDAP since 1936.[497] But Frowein also remained in his Frankfurt position and was rarely in Berlin, only moving there in February 1945.[498] He was hardly an effective National Socialist presence.

An initial suggestion that came from the party was that Landrat Hellmut Boernicke, Director-General of the public sector Girozentrale Brandenburg and a militant party member, should be the new commanding figure in the Deutsche Bank. But this proposal for a more intimate involvement of the party in the affairs of the bank was vetoed by the Party Chancellery. Hitler and Bormann made it clear that they agreed with the general aim of a "pushing back of bank influence," but for this reason they should not allow the party or its representatives to take direct responsibility for running the nerve centers of finance capitalism. "He [Hitler] believed that these plans [of the Deutsche Bank] could not be carried out, because there could not be any question of the party taking responsibility for banks." The banks should certainly appoint and promote Party Comrades, but this should not be interpreted as the state supporting private capitalism. "If the Deutsche Bank had itself suggested Herr Boernicke for the management board, there would on the other hand have been no objections."[499]

Eventually, the Deutsche Bank chose as the party man on the board Professor Heinrich Hunke, the editor of the journal *Die deutsche Volkswirtschaft* (The German Economy), a civil servant [*Ministerialdirektor*] in the Propaganda Ministry of Joseph Goebbels, and in the late 1930s the most influential of National Socialist economic theorists. Hunke had been educated as a primary school teacher and only later entered the university and eventually obtained a doctorate with a dissertation on "The Acoustic Measurement of Intensity." He was in the odd position of only completing the university matriculation requirements in 1929, after finishing his doctorate. In 1935 he was awarded the title of honorary Professor at the Berlin Technische Hochschule. From 1927 to 1933 he worked in the Army Ministry. He joined the NSDAP in 1928,[500] and in 1932 he became a Reichstag deputy. In 1933 he became Vice-President of the *Werberat der deutschen Wirtschaft* (Advertising Council), an institution created in 1933 as part of the new autarkic stance and intended to use advertising in order to influence consumer behavior. In 1934 he wrote an article advocating the nationalization of the Great Berlin Banks.[501] In the Propaganda Ministry after 1940 he was responsible for the Foreign Department, and he propagated Funkian schemes for a new European economic order and economic community.[502] Abs and Rösler had initially asked Hunke to join the board of Deutsche Bank in the course of an overnight train journey to Vienna, but at first he declined. He apparently later changed his mind as his relations with the Propaganda Ministry deteriorated.[503]

The Deutsche Bank Working Committee, when discussing Hunke, explicitly discussed the dangers of a political appointment and the implications for the functioning of the management board. "In particular the management board has always maintained the principle of collegiality, which is the only system possible for a private bank, and in particular our bank, rather than the *Führerprinzip*." Hunke had been informed about the duties and obligations of a Speaker ("Even the office of Speaker brings no privileges, but is only a matter of confidence, in order to make easier the process of forming an opinion on the management board, and representing it to the outside"); and he had declared himself "in solidarity with the views of the Board."[504] The Deutsche Bank's press representative, Morgenstern, explained Hunke's move in private in the following way: Hunke had wanted to establish himself as a major figure in economic life by becoming President of the Gau Economic Chamber of Berlin, and a "precondition for this was a corresponding position in the private economy."[505] In subsequent Allied intelligence reports, Hunke was sometimes evaluated dismissively ("a rabid Nazi and an utter fool" was the verdict of one British report); but other officials remarked on his mental ability.[506]

What about the rest of the bank? Party membership figures have often been used by historians as measures of the extent of political commitment and the politicization of business. They may also be used to indicate the extent to which businesses were able to disengage from politics. For a bank such as the Deutsche Bank to have had no managing directors or leading managers who were members of the NSDAP would clearly have been impossible, as the debates about the appointments of Halt and Hunke revealed. It is equally clear that most of the bank's directors preferred to avoid direct political commitment.

Below the board level, among the leading managers, the extent of party membership was much greater. A list prepared towards the end of the war gives details of 84 branch directors. Of these 44 were party members. None of them had joined before 1933. Most branches at this time had two directors, but there seems to have been no attempt to create a balance. In a few branches, such as Danzig (Gdansk), both directors were party members; in others, such as Kattowitz (Katowice), neither was.[507] This statistic seems not untypical of German business life in general. It certainly makes it clear that neither party membership nor non-party membership was a prerequisite for a successful career in banking. Apart from the three party managing directors, Halt, Frowein, and Hunke, I have been unable to find a case of anyone promoted because of party membership who otherwise would not have been. Neither did party membership offer bankers any kind of protection from attacks by party militants. It is difficult to avoid the conclusion that those of the Deutsche Bank's managers who joined the party wanted to be members.

The party in fact was quite suspicious of business converts, and even of the new managing directors. The Reich Labor Trustee [*Reichstreuhänder der Arbeit*], whose approval was required for the contract, spent several months attempting, in the end unsuccessfully, to limit their income from supervisory board positions.[508]

Party membership gave only one particular advantage. Party officials could take part in department meetings where staff and department managers decided salary questions. A captured bank official stated in a wartime interrogation by British officials:

"They actually had the power to prevent the granting of increases in salary to an efficient colleague, even if he was sponsored by a Direktor, if they did not consider him sufficiently Nazi. This was much resented, according to PW [Prisoner of War], by the majority of staff and it resulted in distrust and suspicion between employees and those of their colleagues who were Party officials."[509]

Hunke's appointment established a link between business and the party's new economic organizations. Hunke had just set out his economic philosophy in an address to the Berlin Society of Friends of the German Academy (an institution, incidentally, created by von Stauss). It appeared at least to leave a limited role to private enterprise and to reject complete socialization. "We support the principle of the politically directed economy [...] A guided economy however is not a planned economy, steered in every detail according to a central will." An international orientation was required, but this – for the foreseeable future – meant state control. "Even after the War, Germany will not buy on the principles of a liberal trading policy, but rather according to the demands of the European economic community."[510]

Such discussions about the future and about the relationship of the German economy to the rest of the European economy were inevitable in a bank that wanted to think in long-term strategies. But they were deeply problematic, for the very obvious reason that by 1943 it looked unlikely that the world war would be won by National Socialist Germany. The extent of political criticism of banking, and the existence of a terror regime, made it almost impossible for the bank to function in the traditional way, as a network of economic intelligence.

Relationships with Firms

Traditionally, bankers on the supervisory board of companies had been called to play the role of a wise uncle, who might arbitrate internal disputes and bring a fresh and impartial eye to the personal divisions inevitably arising in business life. During the war, such an arbitrating role necessarily brought political ramifications and imbroglios.

Stauss had been a master of intrigues involving the party. In 1939, as deputy chairman of the supervisory board of the major brewery Schultheiss–Patzenhofer, he had to deal with the case of a "Workers' Steward" who built up a patronage and bribery system within the firm and the German Labor Front. The management upheaval that followed resulted in the reappointment of Stauss to his old position from the Weimar Republic as supervisory board chairman.[511]

Other cases of companies in political difficulties rapidly involved not just one executive of the bank, but the whole management board. Two examples: in 1942, the party and the Munitions Ministry attacked the director of a family-managed firm with strong connections with the Deutsche Bank, the United West German Wagon Works, Vereinigte Westdeutsche Waggonfabriken AG Köln-Deutz, which was usually known simply as Westwaggon. Director Jackowski's failure to meet supply schedules was interpreted as sabotage. But it soon appeared that behind the accusations lurked an intrigue. The Gau Economic Adviser of Cologne, the politically active and energetically National Socialist banker Kurt von Schröder, accompanied the party's attack with a raid to purchase Westwaggon shares. The party began to say that it was the Deutsche Bank, and its Cologne manager Jean Baptist Rath (incidentally, a party member), who were responsible for the inadequacies of Westwaggon. Westwaggon had been highly indebted in the later 1920s, and its wartime failure to supply sufficient rolling stock was attributed to bank credit policies, because "Westwaggon was very heavily influenced by banks." Westwaggon required an active defense, and Abs, the managing director responsible for the Cologne area, circulated a note to the rest of the board asking for nominations for a new managing director.[512]

The most difficult case for the bank as a holder of the chairmanship of a supervisory board arose in the Bayerische Motoren Werke

AG. It had been founded as the Rapp-Motorenwerke in 1913, and in the First World War developed rapidly, primarily as a manufacturer of aero-engines, a line of production to which it returned in the 1930s. Since 1917, the firm had been managed in high autocratic style by an Austrian engineer, Franz Josef Popp. It had been rescued in 1928 by a major cash infusion of the Deutsche Bank,[513] and Stauss played a leading role in pushing it to closer cooperation with Daimler–Benz. In the Depression, Popp had tried to keep BMW alive by moving to the production of cheaper automobiles.

After 1933, the firm initially derived major gains from motorization as well as from the expansion of Lufthansa,[514] although Popp pointed out that the Entente countries had already moved far ahead technically in aero-engines. The problem from his viewpoint was that producing for the state meant accepting the imposition of external control. Already in January 1934 a State Commissar (Dr. Höfeld) was appointed by the Reich Air Ministry to invigilate BMW, with the result that Popp was "not especially happy about it."[515] In 1936 a major expansion began, substantially financed by the Deutsche Bank, with a credit of 8 m. RM and a purchase of 1 m. RM shares.[516] But the major part of the expansion was paid for by the state through the provision of Mefo-bills and through participations of the Luftfahrtkontor in two new works. The Aero-Engine Factory at Allach and the Aero-Engine Factory at Eisenach existed as non-public limited liability companies to disguise the extent of military production.[517] BMW's historical expertise had been in lighter air-cooled motors, which initially were regarded as less powerful and hence less important to Germany's air rearmament than water-cooled motors. Later, when combat height became a more important consideration in air war, air cooling suddenly became crucial as water-cooling systems were in danger of freezing at high altitudes. The intention of the Reich Air Ministry in 1936 was to rationalize production of types, "so that BMW and Siemens will be the two factories in Germany for air-cooled motors, while Junkers and Daimler-Benz will continue to concentrate exclusively on water or liquid cooling systems."[518]

The other air-cooled engine producer was another limited liability company, a subsidiary of Siemens, the Siemens-Apparate-und-Maschinenbau GmbH in Berlin–Spandau. As part of the reorganization of production in 1936, Siemens gave up control of this factory, because it required excessively high investments and meant a "technology that is foreign to our own real specialty in electro-technical matters."[519] The works continued as the Brandenburgische Motorenwerk Gesellschaft mbH, and the Deutsche Bank worked intensively to secure its sale to BMW. The transaction was completed in 1939, again with a majority of the financing coming from public institutions (*Luftfahrtkontor* and Bank for Industrial Bonds). As a result BMW had three aero-engine works, in Spandau, Eisenach, and Munich–Allach, and a German monopoly on air-cooled engines. Its performance became critical for the conduct of the German air war. The firm's turnover increased from 32.5 m. RM in 1933 to 280.0 m. RM in 1939 (of which 190.0 m. RM came from aero-engines).[520] As in 1933, Popp viewed the dramatic expansion with some skepticism: he later noted that though he had not wanted "expansionary policy involving the purchase of other firms [...] we were more or less forced by purely external circumstances."[521] At the time of the deal, Popp claimed that he had been pushed into the deal by his deputy Fritz Hille: "Since over 25 years, it has been his principle to keep BMW from expanding. It was really a great strain to have one development plant in Munich and another in Spandau."[522]

Such a dogmatic statement about the limitation of the size of an ideal business already appeared dated to BMW's supervisory board, and to the two Deutsche Bank members, Stauss and Hans Rummel, the deputy chairman of the supervisory board. It was even more hopelessly antiquated in the circumstances of the world war, during which the demand for state control, intervention, and large-scale enterprise appeared as an overriding military necessity. During the war, BMW expanded its production to plants in Alsace, in occupied France, in Denmark, and in the Generalgouvernement. At the same time, output in the German works was increased through "systematic personnel planning [...] in particular the quick supplementation of the Allach work force with foreign workers," as well as the use of concentration camp labor in Allach and Eisenach.[523]

Coordination of the activities of the three German motor plants never worked well. The Munich research and development plant worked painfully slowly, and it did not have sufficient resources for the star-piston motor project on which Germany's fortunes in the air now depended. The fundamental technical problem was that funds were divided between two projects, the 800 motor in Spandau (a one-star piston arrangement) and the 801 double-star arrangement in Munich. The 800 was initially stopped, and then – at a time of desperate shortage of motors – made out of 801 parts. By the middle of 1940, the output of motors had become the major constraint on aircraft production and on the fighting of the air war.[524] Göring personally insisted on the stepping up of output, addressing a fierce personal letter to Popp: "Once again I wish to entreat you how urgently necessary the new two star motor is for us, and how no hour must be lost in bringing this motor into action on the front."[525] BMW predictably blamed shortages of labor and machine tools, but also the procurement policies of the Reich Air Ministry: "The 800 was down-graded in urgency at the beginning of the War, because this motor was not intended for use in [what was planned to be a short] war. This motor was to be used after the war as a basis for developing the 132 Model."[526] But then the Reich Air Ministry demanded production of the 800 at the rate of 200 a month in Eisenach and 170 in the French factories. Popp continued to complain: "We had the bad luck, that because of the war situation, our motor suddenly appears as the most urgent priority, although only half a year ago the Air Ministry spoke in very different tones."[527] The ministry replied by attacking Popp's record ("a disturbing lack of knowledge of the real technical conditions and an irresponsible carelessness"),[528] and eventually, at the beginning of 1942 by replacing Popp by his deputy Hille.

The removal of Popp, who had long exercised a kind of personal dictatorship over the firm, did not help either BMW or the Luftwaffe. Instead increasingly politicized conflicts within the senior management multiplied. Then Stauss died, the man who always ensured that the firm greased the right party wheels[529] and who might have been able to deal with the politics of wartime Germany. His successor as chairman of the BMW supervisory board, Hans Rummel, a far less political figure, was completely out of his depth in the politically charged struggles over engine output.

To recapitalize the firm without incurring a total dependence on the state, in May 1942 Vereinigte Stahlwerke was invited to take a substantial minority stake in BMW. Vereinigte Stahlwerke tried to pay off the government credits and to provide a long-term credit of 50–70 m. RM in the hope of building a basis for automobile and tractor production in the postwar period.[530] Hille felt that his position might become vulnerable, and he demanded a firm five-year contract as managing director; when Stauss refused, Hille unsuccessfully encouraged Vereinigte Stahlwerke to take a majority of BMW and exclude the Deutsche Bank from intervening in its management.

By the end of 1943, BMW's failure to supply the agreed quantity of aero-engines to the Luftwaffe again became critical, and it made the management vulnerable to a political attack. Eventually, at the end of May 1944, the head of the Luftwaffe, Field Marshal Erhard Milch, demanded the restructuring of BMW's management within forty-eight hours and the removal of Hille from any technical responsibility within BMW. The new direction of the firm was entrusted by Milch to the technical manager of the Eisenach works, Schaaf, a man who had originally been appointed at the suggestion of Albert Speer's Munitions Ministry. But the problems of the firm in maintaining production levels remained acute, and by November 1944 Hille was predicting a further shortfall of 1,500–1,800 motors for the period October–December.[531] Not content with pessimistic forecasts, Hille turned to the Berlin Party Chancellery to denounce Schaaf for sabotage and high treason. Faced with a crisis, Rummel on December 11 raced to Munich despite the physical difficulties of travelling at this stage in the war; he found a letter dated December 9 from Hille to Schaaf, which denied Schaaf's authority and attempted to reassert control over the firm's management. Hille said that he would carry out "all measures [. . .] necessary in order to deal with the unrest, disorder and redundant organization arising out of your behavior and from the failure of the supervisory board Chairman, as well as with the direct and indirect rumors which undermine the exercise of any authority."[532] Rummel placed Hille on immediate leave. Hille replied that the government had placed a wartime ban on taking holidays. Rummel then dismissed him. Hille tore up the letter, and he accused Rummel and the Deutsche Bank of high treason.

In dealing with BMW's management, Rummel initially thought he could look for allies in the Munich party leadership. It was an unsuccessful maneuver. The Munich Gauleiter Paul Giesler refused to receive Rummel, and Hille shouted "Only my Gauleiter can give me directions. Please take note, Herr Rummel, that I am a National Socialist." Giesler saw an opportunity, less to support Hille (whose claim that Giesler was his "Paladin" embarrassed him) than to turn BMW back into being a Bavarian firm and thus part of his political fiefdom. Giesler suggested that either the Bavarian State Bank or the Flick concern should finance the Bavarianization and reorganization of BMW.

Rummel's seriously threatened situation was rescued in Berlin by the intervention of the Deutsche Bank's political contact man.[533] Heinrich Hunke worked at the highest level, with the party official Reich Leader Philipp Bouhler, and urged Rummel to prepare a memorandum in self-defense. "In our opinion you should begin as soon as possible to draw up a comprehensive memorandum, which will also be useful for your verbal presentation. On the other hand, we do not believe that, as the situation lies, the composition of the supervisory board and in particular your own position as Chairman will be exempt from discussion."[534] But despite this pessimistic and stern warning, Rummel and the Deutsche Bank seem to have won at least a technical victory: on February 2, 1945, the supervisory board of BMW appointed Schaaf as chairman of the management board.[535]

The episode showed how inexorably tangled industrial politics had become as a result of National Socialist ideology and the waging of total war. It is also quite typical of the bank's conception of how it should respond to the challenges of the political situation and the offensive of a new and radical vision of state-run capitalism. In the light of the virulence of the attack, and the fanaticism of its perpetrators, it is perhaps regrettable but by no means surprising that the bank's major policy makers thought only of defensive, damage-limiting responses.

The Deutsche Bank and Forced Labor

The Deutsche Bank was not an industrial enterprise and obviously did not consequently employ forced industrial labor in the sense usually understood (although its directors sat on the supervisory boards of companies that did use forced and slave labor on a large scale: BMW, Daimler–Benz, and above all IG Farben).

It did, however, have a large office, with some 200 employees, which was concerned with the administration of payment transfers on behalf of foreign workers. The sums concerned were savings, which could be transferred home, and the Deutsche Bank's advantage lay in its strength as an international bank. In the world of exchange control established in the early 1930s, such payments had to be made through the clearing agreements. The first such operation took place in regard to Italian migrant workers in 1937. From 1939, Belgians and Hungarians could make payments in a similar way. These workers were volunteer migrants, not conscripted labor. From 1940, there were Belgian, Danish, and French workers, many of whom were conscripted; and from 1941, Norwegians, Serbs, and Slovaks.[536] The largest number of transfers (about a third of the total: see Figure 24) were for Italian workers; the second largest national group was French.[537] For the Italians, there existed special arrangements whereby Deutsche Bank officials worked on the train between Freiburg and the Swiss frontier Basel to make the transfer arrangements for workers returning to Italy.

On these transfers, Deutsche Bank deducted 60 Pfg from each transaction as an administrative cost, and it also received a

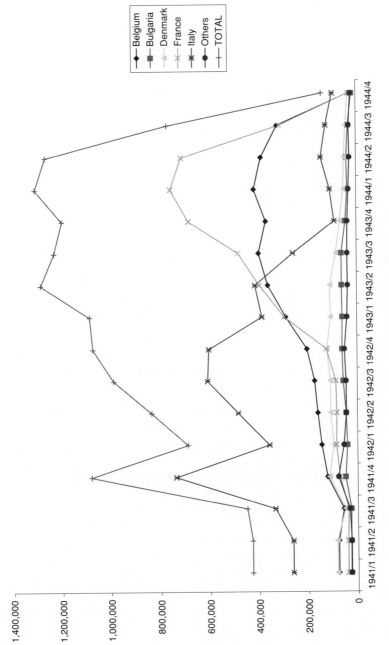

Figure 24. Payments to Foreign Workers by Quarter, 1941–44.

subsidy [*Zuschuss*] of 15 Pfg from the Four-Year Plan's currency authorities.

There is no record of any such payments being made in 1945, and it is possible and indeed likely that because of the political and military circumstances this operation ceased. At the end of the war, there were substantial amounts on collective accounts [*Sammelkonten*] for foreign workers: 14.1 m. RM for Belgian workers, 14.5 m. RM for French workers, and 3.4 m. RM for Italians.[538]

Some of the Deutsche Bank employees who dealt with the payments were themselves foreign, doubtless because some linguistic competence was required. Between 150 and 200 French workers, who had spent their days working in Berlin factories, worked between seven and ten in the evening at the Deutsche Bank's foreign wage payments department, for which they were paid at the usual German overtime rates, and in addition received soup and a transport allowance. There were workers of other nationalities: one example recorded in the Deutsche Bank's personnel records concerns a Dutchman who had previously worked in a Dutch bank and was conscripted in 1943 for compulsory labor service in Germany. He was to be sent to an industrial plant in Kassel, but he used some contacts in the Netherlands and wrote a letter of application to Deutsche Bank. A Deutsche Bank courier then collected him from the transit camp for forced workers at Rehbrücke, and he worked in the Berlin office until he was eventually sent to work in an armaments factory. His file includes some complaints about his behavior: that he made "unsuitable remarks," and that in the course of an air raid he had said that "it would be no harm if all of Germany were damaged by bombs." These remarks, however, perhaps surprisingly, did not lead to any punishment, and his managers, who were clearly pleased with his work, protected him from any consequences.[539] His file also indicates that he was paid at the standard rate for German bank employees.

The bank also used political and other prisoners for unskilled manual work. In at least one branch, prisoners of the Gestapo were employed in clearing and making emergency repairs after bombing raids. After the air raids of December 4, 1943, and February 20, 1944, on Leipzig, 2,844 hours of such labor (for which the Deutsche Bank paid the Gestapo at a rate of 60 Pfg an hour) were bought by the bank; and another 3,410 hours were bought from April to August 1944, and 395 hours between September 1944 and March 1945. From the payments records, it appears that around 20 prisoners worked at a time. They arrived from a "substitute prison" under the supervision of the city police or the Gestapo, who were paid separately for guard duties, but while they worked they were also supervised by two Deutsche Bank employees, one who had a weapons permit issued in connection with "police services" that he performed for the party, and one who was a heating engineer, "who as a former soldier was experienced with guns." The prisoners are variously described in the invoices and payments records as "civil internees," "penal internees," and "political prisoners." The Gestapo instructions specified that "the prisoners provided for work are political prisoners and may not come into contact with the civilan population. They are prohibited from writing or speaking."[540]

The employment of forced foreign workers and political prisoners, while clearly not a major part of the bank's activity, demonstrates a feature of the German wartime economy that has only become fully apparent in the course of research in the later 1990s: the extent to which the employment of involuntary labor went well beyond classical industrial employment and indeed permeated all of the German society and economy.

Political Dangers

If slave and forced labor was ubiquitous in the German wartime economy, so too was politics, especially now that economic decisions were being made in the context of a command economy. Debate over business strategies, particularly long-term plans that depended on a view of the likely shape of the postwar order, could easily be interpreted by party and state activists as sabotage. In addition, of course, bankers might be involved in discussions that went beyond the technicalities of banking and touched on the wide terrain of political issues.

It is striking that the operation of the Advisory Councils [Beiräte], in the past a key part of economic intelligence gathering and distribution, became practically impossible. Many economic subjects – including notably the prospects for the postwar order – became taboo. When, for instance, Hermann Abs presented the bank's view to the Rhineland–Westphalia Advisory Council in Cologne, he avoided the kind of criticism of state actions that had been characteristic of Kimmich's addresses. Instead he confined himself to the details of the driest, most unrevealing, and most technical sides of the bank's activities.

In the course of 1943 the political dangers associated with banking became frighteningly clear. In November 1943, the Working Committee heard without comment a report by Ritter von Halt, still responsible for the bank's personnel, that the directors of the Deutsche Bank's branches in Hindenburg (Zabrze, Upper Silesia) and Stuttgart had been sentenced to death for "defeatist remarks."[541]

The Stuttgart manager, Hermann Koehler (Figure 25), then aged 67, had been the Deutsche Bank's most senior branch director. On a rail journey from Munich to Stuttgart after a business meeting, shortly after the collapse of Mussolini's regime, he had told some of his colleagues travelling with him that: "Fascism had disappeared without a murmur; the same would happen with us; National Socialism was in any case nothing more than a fart." These remarks were reported by a passenger in the same compartment. Koehler was arrested and tried in Berlin before the People's Court [Volksgerichtshof]. His defense that he had drunk too much beer because of the hot weather and that he could not remember the words he had used in the train was rejected; on October 8 the court pronounced the death sentence (as well as a 100,000 RM fine). Relatives of Koehler later reported that von Halt had made considerable efforts to save him, but he was not successful. One

Figure 25. Hermann Koehler, director of Stuttgart branch of Deutsche Bank 1924–43.

Source: Courtesy of Deutsche Bank AG.

month after the verdict, on November 8, 1943, Koehler was executed in Brandenburg prison.

Only three weeks before Koehler's conviction, director Georg Miethe (Figure 26) from Hindenburg (Upper Silesia) had similarly been condemned, as a result of accusations brought by employees of his own bank branch. Miethe had been in a little difficulty with the party before the war, when he had refused to join the Labor Front organization with an apparently frivolous explanation (that as the director of the branch, he was not paid enough). On August 10, 1943, he had been arrested at 9:30 a.m. in his office by the Gestapo. The nearby Katowice branch office of Deutsche Bank reported that Miethe had been denounced by his secretary, Fräulein S., "who sat immediately next to the entry door to the Director's office and claims to have heard through the closed door that Herr Miethe made dismissive comments about the Führer, the state, the party and the army." One day after the arrest, the director of the Katowice office, Richard Gdynia, approached the party director [*Kreisleiter*] of Hindenburg, whom he had known for twenty years, as well as the Gestapo chief, whom he also knew, in an attempt to play down the incident. But it seemed that this was all the bank could do to save its director. A member of the management board, Johannes Kiehl, wrote to an acquaintance of Miethe who had asked for more help from the bank, that: "We hope that the investigation will absolve Herr Miethe. But unfortunately we are not in the position to intervene with the Gestapo or the SS headquarters, even just to get more information." All Kiehl could do was recommend an attorney, Dr. Rudolf Dix.[542]

The trial before the People's Court later heard that two bank clerks had complained about Miethe's "whining"; he had allegedly called Goebbels an "ape" and a "shit," Göring a "stuffed belly," and Hitler a "swindler." In the *Volksgerichtshof*'s judgment these reported remarks are followed by the comment, in the authentically demagogic and chilling language of the court's President Roland Freisler, "This was said by a man in a high position of authority, by an educated man." Miethe's social position clearly played a part in the court's sentence. But the court also heard about Miethe's views on the progress of the war in Russia and of the air war, and that he had asked the question: "Well, and when will the end come with us?"[543] Miethe was executed on September 21. The Nazi newspaper, *Der Völkische Beobachter*, reported one month later that "Miethe's criminal behavior had to be punished especially severely because he misused his leadership position, instead of offereing his staff an example and a model."[544] The tragic affair had a postwar epilogue. The secretary who had denounced Miethe moved to West Germany and lived under an assumed name until she was tried before a Munich court in 1957, and sentenced to four years' imprisonment. She tried to explain that she had lost her brother and fiancé during the war, and that she had been psychically undermined by Herr Miethe's continual abuse. But the court also heard that even as a schoolgirl she had been an active denouncer.[545] Dissatisfied employees in the dictatorship – and especially during the

Figure 26. Georg Miethe, director of Hindenburg branch of Deutsche Bank 1935–43.

Source: Courtesy of Deutsche Bank AG.

war – had quite remarkable possibilities for exacting revenge on their bosses.

There were some other cases of political "crimes": Reinhold Meissner, who worked in the foreign workers department of the bank, was denounced by the works council boss (*Betriebsobmann*), arrested by the Gestapo, and accused of high treason. He admitted having written slogans on the walls of the bank, such as "Hitler is our deadly enemy" and "Kill Hitler." His wife committed suicide, and Meissner himself died during the last days of the war.[546]

There can be no doubt that the senior managers of the bank knew about their environment, about the course and conduct of the war, and also about some of the criminal aspects of the regime. They were aware of the network of concentration camps across Germany: this was no secret. On the other hand, the regime kept a veil of mystery and euphemism around its genocide directed against racially defined minorities: Jews, Slavs, gypsies. At least one of the purposes of this semi-secrecy was to bind the perpetrators of crimes, and those who acquiesced in them, more closely to the regime. Documents that survive from this period as a result often give the historian little direct evidence about the extent of knowledge about the holocaust. In the case of the Deutsche Bank, for instance, there are numerous files relating to the accounts and property of ethnic Germans [*Volksdeutsche*] resettled in Łódź (known as Litzmannstadt under the Germans), but there are no written indications whatsoever about the fate of the previous owners of the property transferred, or of the fate of the inhabitants of the Łódź ghetto. Did no one at the time give any thought to this?

We also know that Hermann Abs sat on the supervisory board of IG Farben, a company deeply implicated in the realization of the racist and annihilationist projects of the Nazi state. Abs's involvement in IG Farben is the war crime of which he has most frequently been accused by critics such as Eberhard Czichon and Tom Bower.[547] Abs joined the supervisory board of IG Farben in 1940, at the suggestion of the company, as a successor to the deceased Eduard Mosler of Deutsche Bank. This body did not meet frequently, and it exercised no systematic control over the company. Did it ever discuss the Farben plant in Auschwitz? There is no way to tell from the written record. IG Farben had in 1940 begun to plan a large plant for the production of synthetic rubber in the east. It was originally to have been located at Rattwitz, near Breslau, but eventually the site chosen was near Auschwitz. In part this was for strategic reasons, but the availability of labor from the nearby camp (which in 1940 still contained mostly Polish political and military prisoners) may also have been a consideration. The plant eventually developed on the basis of a murderously brutal exploitation of largely Jewish forced labor. IG Farben made the decision to build at Auschwitz on February 6, 1941. The next day, February 7, was the first supervisory board meeting attended by Abs. It was a short meeting, lasting just an hour and a half, and it is likely that Auschwitz was not discussed. On July 11, 1941 the supervisory board of IG Farben discussed the employment of foreign workers and prisoners of war, as a response to the labor shortage, according to the written record, without referring directly to the new plant in Auschwitz.[548]

Deutsche Bank supplied a substantial credit to IG Farben for the Auschwitz plant (eventually the sum was 500,000 RM), of which Abs was certainly aware. In July 1943, he attended another supervisory board meeting, at which the extraordinary depreciation allowed to IG Farben on the very large new plant investments were discussed. The Auschwitz factory cost some 400 m. RM. Abs recorded the financial conclusion for the benefit of his colleagues: "the plant, which is valued at 617 m. RM included additional plant worth 400 m. RM; this new plant has been fully depreciated."[549] This is the only written evidence that IG Farben's Auschwitz factory was discussed at the level of the Deutsche Bank's management board.

Might Abs have discussed what was going on more fully with his colleagues on the board of IG Farben and in Deutsche Bank? The public culture of Germany under the dictatorship required an avoidance of discussion (which continued after 1945), and as a result partial acquiescence and complicity. It is very characteristic of that culture that IG Farben attached a covering letter when it sent its 1942 annual report to the Deutsche Bank's Katowice branch: "We specifically draw to your attention that the report is intended only for your personal and confidential use. Publication, commentary, or transmission to third persons is not permitted."[550]

Undoubtedly many by 1942 were profoundly disenchanted with the regime. Some of the Deutsche Bank's directors, such as Abs and Clemens Plassmann possessed as a result of their Catholicism a world view fundamentally at variance with that of National Socialism, and in the course of the discussions on bank reform of 1943 the party unsuccessfully demanded their removal. Abs had some contacts with the resistance, and he reports that he was asked by Adam von Trott zu Solz to join the conspiracy but refused, because, as he later said in interviews, of his commitment to the bank and to his family. He also once attended a meeting of the Goerdeler circle, but – as he later claimed – saw Goerdeler taking notes and resolved never to court danger in this way. Leaving a paper trail of conspiracy seemed a sure path to the cells of the Gestapo. In fact the paper trail did reach wartime Washington, though not apparently the Gestapo center in the Prinz-Albrecht-Strasse of Berlin. The U.S. Treasury Foreign Funds Control noted in its reports on banks in occupied Europe that Abs was

> "one of the most prominent lay Catholic leaders in Germany and rumors persist that he is a potential leader of the Catholic opposition in the country. However, no reference to his political activities is available and it may be concluded that his preoccupation arising from affiliation with forty banks and commercial enterprises had prevented any appreciable contribution to the work of the opposition."[551]

This seems a not inappropriate verdict on Abs. Abs worked very closely with the publisher Peter Suhrkamp, who had taken over the famous house of S. Fischer, and who was arrested in April 1944 after being denounced by a Gestapo spy. The Kiel banker Wilhelm Ahlmann, an anti-Nazi who later killed himself in order to avoid the Gestapo, visited Abs immediately after Suhrkamp's arrest, and the two bankers clearly tried to help Suhrkamp, who was indeed eventually released.[552]

There are, perhaps surprisingly, buried in the Deutsche Bank's archives, some records of Abs's contacts with the German resistance. In June 1940, Abs's secretary noted that Trott had called ("on the basis of your arrangement with him") and "regretted very much, that you were so pressed for time, and hoped that you might have a quarter of an hour for him."[553] Trott, a member of the German Foreign Office, had recently returned from a trip to the U.S., where he had visited prominent German émigrés and also tried to persuade the U.S. administration that a substantial anti-Nazi contingent existed within Germany that might be encouraged by a conciliatory foreign policy. Once back in Germany, he tried to find men of reputation whom he could present to American and British contacts as representatives of an anti-Hitler opposition. He contacted Hjalmar Schacht and Hans von Dohnanyi as well as Abs.[554]

From 1940, Abs repeatedly met the lawyer Helmuth James von Moltke in Berlin, almost always in the company of Peter Count Yorck von Wartenburg. Moltke liked Abs and wanted to draw him closer to the conspiracy, inviting him to meetings in Kreisau. He wrote to his wife: "Abs has improved. He has arrived to such an extent that he no longer needs to be vain and ambitious. He is simply now the primus inter pares of German bankers." The meetings became much more frequent after June 1941, when Moltke was quick to recognize the difficulty of defeating the USSR. In May 1943, Abs was invited to visit Kreisau, but for one reason or another he could not go.[555]

In October 1943, the Deutsche Bank was providing funds for the support of Frau von Moltke (Davida née Yorck, the widow of Ambassador Hans Adolf von Moltke, Helmuth James's uncle); and York von Wartenburg was the intermediary in making the financial arrangement.[556] In a postwar affidavit, the widow of York, Gräfin Marion Yorck von Wartenburg, stated that: "Shortly before July 20, 1944, when my husband already knew the date of the attempt, he had a conversation with Abs, in which my husband asked Abs to be part of the delegation which would negotiate with England after the 'event', and Abs agreed."[557]

But there are no wartime records of any closer contacts in 1944, and the July bomb plot did not involve any directors or employees of the Deutsche Bank. In the proposed government under the Chancellorship of Carl Goerdeler, the German opposition in 1944 envisaged as Economics Minister and Reichsbank President not Abs but Karl Blessing of Kontinentale Oel (another friend of Peter Yorck's).[558] One managing director of the Deutsche Bank, Oswald Rösler, was tried before the *Volksgerichtshof* because one of Goerdeler's acquaintances claimed he had told him about the plot, but there was no clear evidence of any involvement of Rösler, and he was acquitted.[559] The case made it clear that bankers' contacts, of which there were bound to be many, could lead to the suspicion of the security authorities.

Abs had already excited the attention of the SS because of the wide range of his foreign contacts. After Deutsche Bank had launched an official complaint about the activities of an Amsterdam bank that was close to the SS, Rebholz Bankierkantoor, an SS report complained that Abs had written to Reichsbank Vice-President Emil Puhl. The SS report mentions that "Abs has, as is well known, strong Catholic links," and it concluded: "Because the Reichssicherheitshauptamt [SS headquarters] has a great interest in Abs, RSH III D will be informed of the contents of Abs' letter to Pohl [sic: Puhl]."[560]

Abs, although he never sympathized with Nazi ideology and was close to some of the central leaders of the German resistance, was not a part of that resistance, and he self-consciously chose not to be a hero. He believed that in doing this, he was following the interests of his family (to whom he had a primary responsibility) and also of the bank (to which he also felt responsible); he did not believe himself obliged to make a useless sacrifice. It is quite possible that he explored the moral dilemmas of his position in the Catholic Church's sacrament of confession and even raised such issues on his numerous trips to the Vatican, before and during the war. In a new century, today many people may wish he had acted otherwise, but it is hard to blame him for his inaction.

7

The End of Dictatorship

The course of the war profoundly affected the bank's day to day operations. In 1939 there had been 17,805 employees. At the beginning of 1941, 5,900 had been called up for military service, by February 1942, 7,300, and by October 1944, 9,705 (out of a total of 19,343 regular personnel and 1,400 auxiliaries).[561] The proportion of women in the workforce rose to 27.6 percent in 1941 and 33.0 percent in 1943. At the same time, the opening of large numbers of new accounts increased the strain on the functioning of the bank.[562]

By 1943 the physical environment had deteriorated. Air raids damaged and destroyed records and buildings, and killed employees. By the summer of 1943, the bank's branch offices in Lübeck, Mainz, Barmen, and Cologne had been completely destroyed, as well as eight Stadtdepositenkassen (subsidiary offices).[563] On November 22 and 23, 1943, the central Berlin office was almost completely destroyed (Figure 27), and 3,000 employees had to be moved to alternate quarters. The simple maintenance of normal business began to require an extensive decentralization. Already in late 1942, the Deutsche Bank's Cologne director, Jean Baptist Rath, suggested, partly in response to party criticism, that the bank's regions should be run independently as separate regional banks.[564] In September 1943, as part of the push toward increased regionalization, ten major branch managers were appointed as "Directors of the Bank with Power of Attorney for All Branches."[565]

In the first ten months of 1944 another 26 branches were completely destroyed by bombing, and 19 more were seriously damaged. In Berlin, in spring 1944 the bank's emergency quarters [*Ausweichstelle*] on the Hausvogteiplatz was also destroyed. Nevertheless by July, the bank's operations were shown off to the Berlin press as an example of how reconstruction after severe bombing damage was possible.[566] Only in the last days of the war did discipline break down, and large-scale bomb damage, as in the extensive raid on Würzburg in March 1945, was followed by looting.

In 1943, three-fifths of the staff were simply engaged in "maintaining payments."[567] As the bank's center disintegrated, the leeway possessed by branches in making new credits also fell, and investment credits were restricted by policy to the construction of new raw materials industries (especially cellulose and hydrogenation) and to the financing of inventories. The drop in credit business already evident in the 1930s continued at a more rapid rate during the war. By 1942, credits and advances on goods represented only 18.7 percent of the balance sheet; by the end of 1944, this ratio had fallen to 13.4 percent.

Even ordinary business began to collapse. Eventually in the summer of 1944 the physical movement of money became difficult as gasoline allowances were cut.[568] Then came the invasion of Germany and the evacuation of branches.[569] In areas close to the fighting, there were runs on the banks as customers tried to close their accounts before being evacuated.[570] Three regional evacuation centers [*Verbindungsstellen*] were established in Hamburg, Wiesbaden, and Erfurt, which continued to operate after the military defeat.

In October 1944 the bank modified its operating rules to allow 1,000 RM to be paid out to the private customers of "the cut off branches"; in February 1945 further payments were authorized. But the regulations for dealing with the occupation of parts of

Figure 27. Central offices of Deutsche Bank after a bombing raid in November 1943.

Source: Courtesy of Deutsche Bank AG.

Germany and the breakdown of communication brought tensions with industrial customers. Wilhelm Zangen of Mannesmann, the Leader of the Reich Group Industry, demanded that the bank in Berlin pay out the account of Mannesmann's Katowice account. Rösler refused completely: he noted angrily that "The gentlemen are in short demanding that all the accounts that they have with the Deutsche Bank should, for instance, be paid out in Miesbach

[in Bavaria] if industry thinks fit in current circumstances to evac-
uate to there."571

On March 16, 1945, Reich Economics Minister Funk presided
over a meeting to discuss the evacuation of banks and their management boards from Berlin in the "Ivan case" – if the Soviet army
rather than the western allies took Berlin. The suggestion was that
the bank's main office with six or seven managing directors and
about 25–30 others should be moved to Hamburg.572

On April 9, 1945 the bank celebrated its seventy-fifth anniversary. The board sent a congratulatory circular to those branches
still in contact with Berlin: "Events do not permit us to look back
on this important anniversary with a quiet feeling of pride in our
successes and a secure possession of that for which we and our
predecessors have worked." Employees received a bonus of a half
month's pay, although the result made little difference because of
gathering inflation.573

One week later, on April 16, the battle for Berlin began. The last
wartime meeting of the management board took place on April 18,
1945, with four directors present and von Halt excused to command the reserve militia [*Volkssturm*] in its defense of Berlin. By
the 21st, Soviet troops were fighting in the streets of the German
capital. On the 23rd, Hunke left Berlin, frightened by the reac-
tion of Joseph Goebbels to Hunke's persistent arguments on the
senselessness of a military defense of Berlin.574 But bank business
went on with a quite astonishing attempt to make believe that circumstances were normal. Customers were still trying to withdraw
deposits, but the chaos and dislocation, and the impossibility of
travelling in the city, meant that many of the safe keys were missing.
Rösler managed to obtain 500,000 RM from the Reichsbank.
When on May 2 Russian troops occupied the bank's buildings in
the Mauerstrasse, they confiscated the 498,130 RM still remaining
in the emergency cash reserve [*Notkasse*]. The bank's Berlin activities only stopped on May 11 when Soviet soldiers temporarily
arrested Rösler and other leading employees for questioning, and
used explosives to open the bank's vaults.575

A day before the final Soviet attack on Berlin began, Hermann
Abs left for Hamburg at the request of the rest of the Berlin

board;[576] from Hamburg a directing office composed of Abs, Bechtolf, and Plassmann (for the time being in Erfurt) attempted to continue the activities of the Deutsche Bank in the circumstances of a
military defeat they had long foreseen but had not dared publicly to
contemplate. Stauss and Hunke may have believed in the triumphs
of National Socialism; but by 1945 Stauss was dead and Hunke
was cold-shouldered by the senior managers of the Deutsche Bank.
Bankers, it has already been pointed out, adjust to realities – that
is their mission. The reality of 1945 was that National Socialism,
and National Socialist economics, was militarily as well as morally
bankrupt.

8

Conclusion

The fundamental dilemma of the bank under the National Socialist dictatorship had involved the extent to which it should fit in and adapt to the new spirit of the times. To a considerable extent the bank was driven by forces it could not control. Bankers did not after all – despite the fantasies held by conspiracy theorists of the National Socialist party regarding the power of finance capitalism – make German politics. In some cases, however, some individual bankers made the consequences and repercussions of German political decisions more damaging and pernicious for the victims than they would otherwise have been: this was especially true when relatively junior bank officials operated in occupied Europe, seizing goods and assets whose loss made their legitimate possessors even more vulnerable. The bank, especially after September 1938, became part of the machine of German imperialism, and its employees the agents of a brutal political process. The older managers of the bank regarded such behavior with considerable suspicion. Even during the Nazi dictatorship, one member of the Deutsche Bank's management board had noted about the most destructively energetic of Deutsche Bank's "new men":

"He undoubtedly possesses a great deal of vigor, appetite for work, and eagerness to assume responsibility, but in addition an unbridled ambition from which his management style suffers. We were able in the 'Creditanstalt' case to gain some idea of the stupidities into which his ambition leads him astray and of how, even in a hopeless situation, he cannot muster the insight to admit his mistake. He is temporarily lacking in the self-discipline required for the development of personal maturity, being very much inclined to see things only from the standpoint of commercial success, never mind how that success has been achieved."[577]

In other cases, particularly within the territory of pre-1937 Germany, the actions of the Deutsche Bank may have assisted some of the victims of the regime. In particular, in helping to carry out the official policy target of "Aryanization," there are cases both of the bank taking the initiative (especially on the local level) and of the bank and their officials quite actively and positively assisting old business partners.

In conscious or unconscious calculations of how their adaptation to the New Germany would affect the financial and social standing of bankers, most financiers could only come to the conclusion that whatever happened, they were bound to lose as representatives of a world and a style of business that the new regime had declared to be obsolete and discredited. German banking had traditionally depended on large networks of contacts, both formal and informal, both national and international, in which commitments were made on the basis of trust and honor. This social and cosmopolitan environment corresponded to one of the primary economic functions of banks, as collectors and transmitters of large quantities of information. To the National Socialists this appeared simply as a discredited old-boy network; but this new ideology (which had a substantially egalitarian dimension) was not just something that came from the outside, from the state or the party organization. The new doctrine was convincing to many of the bank's employees, and at least a substantial part of the National Socialist revolution in this financial corporation was driven by a dynamic internal to the bank as a bureaucratic structure.

Faced by this change of intellectual climate, bankers became more and more passive. The bank's leading figures did not participate in the resistance or in plots against Hitler. It is interesting that of Germany's old elites, soldiers, diplomats, civil servants, and to some extent churchmen, were involved in the resistance; but there were almost no businessmen and no bankers. It seems to me too easy to say that this was because bankers simply kept their heads down and wanted to make money. Unlike generals and diplomats, who still felt valued and important under the dictatorship, bankers were fundamentally regarded as parasitical. To the extent to which they internalized this criticism, it constituted a brake on effective political action. Soldiers and generals occupied a more prominent position. Correspondingly, many committed greater crimes than any banker sitting at a desk dealing with the balance of debit and credit could possibly undertake; but their moral possibilities and choices were greater too. They were more likely than bankers to be villains, but they were also more likely to have the historic chance of being heroes. Their moral spectrum was longer: it encompassed the ruthless brutality and atrocities of the Eastern Front but also the heroism of July 20, 1944. The two Deutsche Bank managers who were condemned by the People's Court, on the other hand, were not heroes: they were simply very unlucky. Hermann Abs, without doubt the most dynamic and imaginative of the Deutsche Bank's managing directors during the war was happy to attack, in only slightly veiled form, the entire trading policy of National Socialist Germany. But when he had contacts with the men of the resistance, he self-consciously decided not to be a hero. Should it be the historian's role to condemn him for this?

In the course of their progressive marginalization, many bankers retreated into that world with which they were most familiar: the comfortable certainties of a rational economic world. They went on behaving in a traditional way in a world that had become strange and irrational. It may seem to many subsequent observers extraordinary that what bankers, businessmen, and civil servants criticized most vehemently about the regime in the 1930s were relatively mundane characteristics – such as its tendency to run large budget deficits – and not its spectacular inhumanity. There can be no doubt that this vision was the product of an extreme moral shortsightedness. The banking world was in this view trapped by the regime, and by the way it presented itself to Germans. National Socialism claimed insistently and militantly that it was the embodiment of the common good and that others represented merely narrow self-interest. Told repeatedly that they had nothing to say about the social and political ordering of society, that the social vision of the business community was nothing more than rampant egoism, bankers tried ever harder not to look beyond the ends of their own noses. The result was that bankers too played their part in Germany's moral catastrophe.

Notes

1. From October 1929 to October 1937 the official name of the corporation was "Deutsche Bank and Disconto–Gesellschaft." It will be referred to herein simply as "Deutsche Bank."

2. See Lothar Gall, "The Deutsche Bank from Its Founding to the Great War," in: Lothar Gall/Gerald D. Feldman/Harold James/Carl-Ludwig Holtfrerich/Hans E. Büschgen (eds.), *The Deutsche Bank 1870–1995*, London: Weidenfeld & Nicolson, 1995, pp. 1–127.

3. Boris Barth, *Die deutsche Hochfinanz und die Imperialismen: Banken und Aussenpolitik vor 1914*, Stuttgart: Franz Steiner, 1995, pp. 15–42.

4. See Harold James, *Monetary and Fiscal Unification in Nineteenth-Century Germany: What Can Kohl Learn from Bismarck?* (Essays in International Finance, No. 202), Princeton, 1997.

5. See Manfred Pohl/Angelika Raab-Rebentisch, *Von Stambul nach Bagdad: Die Geschichte einer berühmten Eisenbahn*, Munich: Piper, 1999; Gall, "Deutsche Bank from Its Founding," pp. 67–77.

6. Manfred Pohl, *Entstehung und Entwicklung des Universalbankensystems: Konzentration und Krise als wichtige Faktoren*, Frankfurt: Fritz Knapp, 1986, p. 67.

7. Enquête-Ausschuss, (Ausschuss zur Untersuchung der Erzeugungs- und Absatzbedingungen der deutschen Volkswirtschaft), *Der Bankkredit*, Berlin: E. S. Mittler & Sohn, 1930.

8. See Caroline Fohlin, "The Rise of Interlocking Directorates in Imperial Germany," in: *Economic History Review* 52/2, Oxford: Blackwell, 1999, pp. 307–33.

9. On the issue of the geographic distribution of Jewish-owned businesses, see Werner E. Mosse, *Jews in the German Economy: The German-Jewish Business Elite*, Oxford: Oxford University Press, 1987.

10. Peter Hüttenberger, "Nationalsozialistische Polykratie," in: *Geschichte und Gesellschaft* 2, Göttingen: Vandenhoeck & Ruprecht, 1976, pp. 417–42; Dieter Rebentisch, *Führerstaat und Verwaltung im Zweiten Weltkrieg: Verfassungsentwicklung und Verwaltungspolitik*, Stuttgart: Franz Steiner, 1989; Ian Kershaw, *The Nazi Dictatorship: Problems and Perspectives of Interpretation*, London: Edward Arnold, 1989, pp. 42–81.

11. Graciela L. Kaminsky and Carmen M. Reinhart, "The Twin Crises: The Causes of Banking and Balance-of-Payments Problems," Board of Governors of the Federal Reserve System, International Finance Discussion Papers no. 544, March 1996.

12. Rudolf Morsey, *Zur Entstehung, Authentizität und Kritik von Brünings "Memoiren 1918–1934*," Opladen: Westdeutscher Verlag, 1975; Stephen A. Schuker, "Ambivalent Exile: Heinrich Brüning and America's Good War," in: Christoph Buchheim, Harold James, and Michael Hutter, *Zerrissene Zwischenkriegszeit: Wirtschaftshistorische Beiträge. Knut Borchardt zum 65. Geburtstag*, Baden-Baden: Nomos Verlagsgesellschaft, 1994, pp. 329–56.

13. Gerald D. Feldman, "The Deutsche Bank from World War to World Economic Crisis 1914–1933," in: Lothar Gall/Gerald D. Feldman/Harold James/Carl-Ludwig Holtfrerich/Hans E. Büschgen (eds.), *The Deutsche Bank 1870–1995*, London: Weidenfeld & Nicolson, 1995, pp. 264–7.

14. See on this Harold James, *The German Slump: Politics and Economics 1924–1936*, Oxford: Oxford University Press, 1986, pp. 303–7.

15. Lord d'Abernon, *Ambassador of Peace*, London, 1929.

16. E. W. Schmidt to Müller-Jabusch, December 28, 1953, Deutsche Bank Historical Archive (HADB), RWB, 27.

17. Thomas Balogh, *Studies in Financial Organization*, Cambridge: Cambridge University Press, 1947, p. 78: "a secular tendency for the demand for bank loans to decline." See also *Frankfurter Zeitung*, June 3, 1934: The state had financed new credit through work creation programs, but: "The credit created in this way did not stay in the economy, because important sectors still preferred to liquidate inventories in order to repay credit."

18. From Gewinn-Übersicht und Kalkulationen für das Jahr 1933, Deutsche Bank Historical Archive (HADB) B305.

19. August 22, 1933 Circular to Branch Managers, Bundesarchiv Berlin (BA), R 8119 F, P24000.

20. Meetings of October 6, 1936 and August 30, 1938, HADB, SG8/5.

21. Deutsche Bank Special Circulars, S62/33, August 16, 1933, HADB, F63/1053.

22. Cited in Rainer Zitelmann, *Hitler. Selbstverständnis eines Revolutionärs*, Stuttgart: Klett-Cotta, 1991 (2nd ed.), p. 260–1. In general, on Hitler's economic views, see in particular also: Henry A. Turner, "Hitlers Einstellung zu Wirtschaft und Gesellschaft vor 1933," in: *Geschichte und Gesellschaft* 2, Göttingen: Vandenhoeck & Ruprecht, 1976, pp. 89–117; and Avraham Barkai, "Sozialdarwinismus und Antiliberalismus in Hitlers Wirtschaftskonzept. Zu Henry A. Turner Jr. 'Hitlers Einstellung zu Wirtschaft und Gesellschaft vor 1933,'" in: *Geschichte und Gesellschaft* 3, Vandenhoeck & Ruprecht, 1977, pp. 406–17. For more extensive, discussion, see Avraham Barkai, *Das Wirtschaftssystem des Nationalsozialismus*, Frankfurt: Fischer, 1988, pp. 27ff.

23. Cited in Klaus Kreimeier, *Die Ufa-Story. Geschichte eines Filmkonzerns*, Munich: Hanser, 1992, p. 306.

24. Eduard Rosenbaum/A. J. Sherman, *M. M. Warburg & Co. 1798–1938. Merchant Bankers of Hamburg*, London: East and West Library, 1979, p. xi.

25. This is a point made by Gerald Feldman in his study of Allianz: Gerald D. Feldman, *Allianz and the German Insurance Business 1933–1945*, Cambridge and New York: Cambridge University Press, 2001.

26. For examples, see Eberhard Czichon, *Der Bankier und die Macht: Hermann Josef Abs in der deutschen Politik*, Cologne: Pahl-Rugenstein, 1970; Kurt Gossweiler, *Grossbanken, Industriemonopole, Staat, Ökonomie und Politik des staatsmonopolistischen Kapitalismus in Deutschland 1914–1932*, Berlin: Deutscher Verlag der Wissenschaften, 1971; Karl Heinz Roth, "Bankenkrise, Faschismus und Macht," in: Kritische Aktionäre der Deutschen Bank (eds.), *Macht ohne Kontrolle: Berichte über die Geschäfte der Deutschen Bank*, Stuttgart: Schmetterling, 1990, pp. 13–23; *OMGUS. Ermittlungen gegen die Deutsche Bank*, Hans Magnus Enzensberger (ed.), Nördlingen: Greno, 1985.

27. Wilhelm Keppler in Bank Inquiry Meeting, September 6, 1933, Bundesarchiv (BA), R2/13682, fol. 15–21.

28. Gottfried Feder in Bank Inquiry Meeting, September 6, 1933, BA, R2/13682, fol. 23; Feder in Bank Inquiry on November 23, 1933, BA, R2/13683, fol. 69–70.

29. Mosler, November 23 and 24, 1933, BA, R2/13683, fol. 65, 66, 76.

30. G. H. Pinsent notes on an interview with Schacht, October 6, 1933, Bank of England Archive, OV34/5.

31. Reich Deputy in Braunschweig and Anhalt Leeper to Deputy of Führer Rudolf Hess, March 13, 1934, BA, R43II/243, fol. 74–5.

32. Mosler note for management board of December 5, 1934, BA, R 8119 F, P24004.

33. Reich Finance Ministry Note of May 25, 1939, BA, R2/13685, fol. 64.

34. Mosler and Kimmich note (only for the management board) of February 21, 1934, HADB, B228.

35. "The Development of Banking Since the Seizure of Power," May 1938, Bundesbank Archive Reichsbank file 6520.

36. Prospectus: Conversion of Daimler–Benz Bonds, BA, R 8119 F, P3191, fol. 260ff.

37. See Manfred Pohl, *Die Finanzierung der Russengeschäfte zwischen den beiden Weltkriegen. Die Entwicklung der 12 grossen Russlandkonsortien*, Frankfurt: Fritz Knapp, 1975, pp. 44–8.

38. Note of February 10, 1938, BA, R2/3847. In general, see Rudolf Stucken, *Deutsche Geld- und Kreditpolitik 1914–1953*, Tübingen: Mohr, 1953, p. 143.

39. Figures from BA, R 8119 F, P294.

40. Reichsbank to Reich Finance Minister, December 29, 1938, BA, R2/3847. See Heinz Pentzlin, *Hjalmar Schacht. Leben und Wirken einer umstrittenen Persönlichkeit*, Berlin et al.: Ullstein, 1980, p. 250. Wilhelm Vocke, *Memoiren*, Stuttgart: Deutsche Verlags-Anstalt, 1973, p. 110.

41. Meeting of Reich Bond Syndicate on January 10, 1939, BA, R 8119 F, P296, fol. 68ff.

42. Reichsbank to Reich Finance Minister, December 29, 1938, BA, R2/3847.

43. Kimmich note of July 19, 1939, BA, R 8119 F, P3359, fol. 198.

44. Peter Hayes, *Industry and Ideology. IG Farben in the Nazi Era*, Cambridge: Cambridge University Press, 1987, pp. 176, 184.

45. Mosler memorandum of January 27, 1938, BA, R 8119 F, P1775, fol. 423ff.

46. Mosler memorandum of May 25, 1939, BA, R 8119 F, P1767 fol. 106ff.

47. Deutsche Bank to Deutsche Bank supervisory board, November 24, 1933, BA, NL Silverberg 83, fol. 169–70. See Manfred Pohl, *Konzentration im deutschen Bankwesen 1848–1980*, Frankfurt: Fritz Knapp, 1980, p. 353.

48. Kimmich at the Rhineland–Westphalia Advisory Council meeting on November 27, 1935, BA, R 8119 F, P41, fol. 31.

49. Advisory Council meeting on May 5, 1936 BA, R 8119 F, P41, fol. 43f.

50. Meeting of the Rhineland–Westphalia Advisory Council on November 11, 1936, BA, R 8119 F, P41, fol. 62; Meeting of the Advisory Council on October 28, 1937, BA, R 8119 F, P41, fol. 98.

51. Meeting of the Rhineland–Westphalia Advisory Council on April 30, 1940, BA, R 8119 F, P41, fol. 137.

52. Eckard Wandel/Hans Schäffer, *Steuermann in wirtschaftlichen und politischen Krisen*, Stuttgart: Deutsche Verlags-Anstalt, 1974,

pp. 160–1; Institut für Zeitgeschichte, Munich, Schäffer diary, ED93/16, December 4, 1931 diary entry.

53. *Frankfurter Zeitung*, December 9, 1932.

54. Deutsche Bank (signed Solmssen and Schlitter) to Silverberg, March 19, 1932, BA, NL Silverberg 83, fol. 72–3.

55. Silverberg to Urbig, March 22, 1932, BA, NL Silverberg 83, fol. 78–80.

56. Urbig cable to Silverberg, May 28, 1933, BA, NL Silverberg 83, fol. 151.

57. Report of Urbig of July 1933, BA, R 8119 F, P55, fol. 18–19.

58. Report of Urbig of July 1933, BA, R 8119 F, P55. See also Christopher Kopper, *Zwischen Marktwirtschaft und Dirigismus. Staat, Banken und Bankenpolitik im "Dritten Reich" von 1933 bis 1939*, Bonn: Bouvier, 1995, pp. 132ff.

59. *Frankfurter Zeitung*, No. 398–400, May 31, 1933.

60. Urbig to Russell, January 18, 1934, HADB, P1/14.

61. HADB, B198, October 29, 1930, Solmssen to von Batocki; October 17, 1930, Solmssen to Harms.

62. BA NL Luther 340, Club von Berlin, February 4, 1932.

63. Solmssen to Urbig, April 9, 1933, HADB, P1/14.

64. Martin H. Sommerfeldt, *Ich war dabei: Die Verschwörung der Dämonen 1933–1939*, Darmstadt: Drei Quellen Verlag, 1949, p. 41. I owe this reference to Professor Gerhard Schulz.

65. Kiehl to Philipp Reemtsma, April 19, 1934, BA, R 8119 F, P4746.

66. Notice on Meeting with Schlieper of May 3, 1935, HADB, RWB, 54.

67. Kimmich to Schlegelberger, January 4, 1939, BA, R 8119 F, P24008 fol. 13.

68. Monatshefte für die Beamten der Deutschen Bank und Disconto–Gesellschaft, November–December 1933, p. 88, speech of Pg. Hertel.

69. ibid., pp. 84–5.

70. Kranefuss (office of Wilhelm Keppler) to Sippell, July 7, 1934, HADB, RWB, 54; note of Sippell of December 19, 1933 HADB,

RWB, 54. On the case of Dresdner Bank, which was influenced by the state ownership of the bank, see Dieter Ziegler, "Die Verdrängung der Juden aus der Dresdner Bank," *Vierteljahrshefte für Zeitgeschichte* 47, Munich: Oldenbourg, 1999, pp. 187–216.

71. Deutsche Bank Frankfurt to Zentrale Personalabteilung, June 2, 1933, HABD P3/A144.

72. Reichsbank Directorate to Reich Economics Ministry, March 23, 1933, BA, R43II/244, fol. 7–8.

73. Kaiser notice of March 14, 1933, BA, R 8119 F, P24001; Berndts (Hirschberg) to May, June 28, 1935, BA, R 8119 F, P24001.

74. HADB, P5/74, September 21, 1935, Stück (Kreiswalter der DAF) to Vetrauensrat of Görlitz Deutsche Bank; January 3, 1936, Deutsche Bank Görlitz to S. D.

75. Letter to Chief of Special Service, SS Gruppenführer Heydrich (with membership list), Berlin Document Center (BDC), August 22, 1934, Society of Friends Special File; Reichsführer SS, Head of Chief Reich Security Office to Supreme Party Court of NSDAP, October 2, 1934, BDC, Society of Friends Special File.

76. Aktennotiz v. Briese v. 20.8.1946 betr. Verhalten gegenüber jüdischen Angestellten, HADB B0381.

77. List (December 1936) marked von Halt, HADB 381. On Goldenberg, see also Jonathan Steinberg, *The Deutsche Bank and Its Gold Transactions During the Second World War*, Munich: Beck, 1999, pp. 46–8.

78. Von Halt note, October 30, 1939, HADB B381.

79. Memorandum of July 1, 1940, in HADB B377.

80. Deutsche Bank circular, December 3, 1941, in HADB B377.

81. Stand der jüdischen Pensionäre und Witwen, May 26, 1944, HADB B381.

82. Russell to Glum (Danzig), December 1, 1921; December 8, 1928, Aktenvermerk, in HADB P2/H364.

83. Sippell note for Kimmich, September 29, 1934, HADB, RWB 54.

84. See in general Robert Gellately, *The Gestapo and German Society. Enforcing Racial Policy 1933–1945*, Oxford: Oxford University Press, 1990, especially pp. 130–58.

85. Winkelmann to management board, September 3, 1934, HADB, RWB 54; Winkelmann to Sippell, September 9, 1934, HADB, RWB, 54.

86. Sippell memorandum of December 6, 1935, HADB, RWB 54; also Rösler letter to Maximilian Müller-Jabusch, March 1, 1951, HADB, RWB 54.

87. Von Halt had joined the NSDAP in May 1933: party membership number 3204950 (BDC).

88. Hermann Hess, *Ritter von Halt: Der Sportler und Soldat*, Berlin: Batschari, 1936, pp. 126–9.

89. BDC, von Halt file.

90. Tregaskes to Dougherty, February 1, 1945, NA, RG 260/2/148/16, OMGUS.

91. Dohmen interview with Frau von Halt (August 25, 1982, HADB, interviews) gives an extreme version: "The board of management asked my husband who was after all quite fit and slim to give them classes in gymnastics. My husband said yes."

92. HADB, *Schwibbogen* 7/2, February 1937, p. 22.

93. Deutsche Bank submission, August 1, 1947, HADB, P2/H2; Süddeutsche Zeitung, November 2, 1964.

94. Rösler Declaration under Oath of March 20, 1950, HADB, RWB, 31.

95. HADB, *Schwibbogen* 7/11, November 1937, pp. 250–1.

96. HADB, Mitteilungen für die NSBO Deutsche Bank und Disconto–Gesellschaft 12 (1934), p. 12.

97. *Deutsche Juristenzeitung*, 23 (1929), Column 1597.

98. BA, R 8119 F, P41, fol. 93.

99. Pfeiffer (Deutsche Bank Kassel) to Deutsche Bank Head Office, July 13, 1933, BA, R 8119 F, P24001.

100. Hutschenreuther AG to Urbig, December 1, 1933, BA, R 8119 F, P4295, fol. 106.

101. Eugen Schweisheimer to Urbig, November 15, 1933, BA R 8119 F, P4295, fol. 96.

102. Rudolf Sies memorandum on negotiations in Braunes Haus, Selb, November 5, 1934, BA, R 8119 F, P4295, fol. 223.

103. Joh. Jeserich AG to Benz (Deutsche Bank), April 3, 1933, BA, R 8119 F, P2372, fol. 2–4.

104. Benz note of April 20, 1933, BA, R 8119 F, P2372, fol. 94.

105. Benz memorandum of May 29, 1933, BA, R 8119 F, P2372, fol. 139; Feuchtmann to Benz, July 10, 1933, BA, R 8119 F, P2372, fol. 177–8; Feuchtmann to Benz, July 24, 1933, BA, R 8119 F, P2372, fol. 187–8.

106. Hertie-Kaufhaus-Beteiligungs GmbH to Advisory Council, August 30, 1933, BA, R 8119 F, P5218, fol. 9–10.

107. Avraham Barkai, *From Boycott to Annihilation*, Hanover: University Press of New England, 1989, pp. 69–72.

108. Avraham Barkai, "Die deutschen Unternehmer und die Judenpolitik im Dritten Reich," in: *Geschichte und Gesellschaft* 15, Göttingen: Vandenhoeck und Ruprecht, 1989, pp. 227–47.

109. Robert M. W. Kempner, "Hitler und die Zerstörung des Hauses Ullstein," in: *Hundert Jahre Ullstein 1877–1977*, Vol. 3, Berlin: Ullstein, 1977, p. 285.

110. Kempner, "Hitler," pp. 273–5.

111. Kempner, "Hitler," p. 278.

112. Mosler note of June 9, 1934, HADB, B200.

113. Helmut Engel/Steffi Jersch-Wenzel/Wilhelm Treue (eds.), *Geschichtslandschaft Berlin: Orte und Ereignisse: Charlottenburg: Die historische Stadt* (Vol. I), Berlin: Nicolai, 1986, pp. 189–91.

114. Rhineland–Westphalia Advisory Council meeting, November 11, 1936, BA, R 8119 F, P41, fol. 63.

115. See Peter Hayes, "State Policy and Corporate Involvement in the Holocaust," in: US Holocaust Museum (ed.), *The Holocaust: The Known, the Unknown, the Disputed and the Reexamined*, Washington, DC 1994.

116. Reich Economic Chamber to Reich Economic Groups, January 7, 1938, BA, R 8119 F, P2947, fol. 114–15.

117. Memorandum on visit of Dr. Schacht, September 25, 1935, BA, R 8119 F, P24002.

118. Deutsche Bank to Branch Managers, January 14, 1938, BA, R 8119 F, P10562, fol. 112–13.

119. Memorandum on Meeting of Branch Managers in Nuremberg, June 21, 1938, BA, R 8119 F, P24330.

120. Letter to Berlin Head Office, Branch Department, December 29, 1938, Saxon State Archive, (StAL) Deutsche Bank files 623.

121. Rhineland–Westphalia Advisory Council meeting, November 2, 1938, BA, R 8119 F, P41, fol. 126.

122. Note of November 21, 1938, BA R8119 F, P24235.

123. Copy of May 30, 1938 Vermerk in Hauptstaatsarchiv Wiesbaden (HHStA), 520 F 649 (Spruchkammerakten Carl Luer: Dresdner Bank).

124. Memorandum of Rodolfo Löb (previously a partner of Mendelssohn & Co.), December 20, 1947, HADB, RWB, 31.

125. See Kopper, *Zwischen Marktwirtschaft und Dirigismus*, pp. 290–3.

126. See Julius H. Schoeps, "Wie die Deutsche Bank Mendelssohn & Co. Schluckte," in: *Frankfurter Rundschau*, November 27, 1998.

127. Abs's account of the meetings and the transaction is reproduced in Treue, "Bankhaus Mendelssohn als Beispeil einer Privatbank im 19. und 20. Jahrhundert," in Mendelssohn–Studien, Vol. 1, Berlin: Duncker & Humblot, 1972, pp. 76–80.

128. *Die Bank*, 1938, p. 1593.

129. *Bank-Archiv*, XXXVII/XXXVIII, 1938, p. 756.

130. Mendelsohn i.L. to Wirtschaftsgruppe Privates Bankgewerbe, January 14, 1943 and February 13, 1945, BDB.

131. Dr. Kremer memorandum of April 2, 1946: "Bericht über die Entwicklung der Firma Mendelssohn," OMGUS-FINAD 2/169/11 and 2/181/2.

132. Reich Security Chief Office report, BA, R58/717, fol. 165.

133. BA, R7/1010 and 1011 for negotiations. The critical meeting was on June 28, 1939 in the Reich Economics Ministry, R7/1011, fol. 323–8.

134. Note of October 18, 1948, Rheinbraun Archive, 210/328. Supreme Finance President Hanover: Security Decree under Paragraph 37a of Law on Foreign Exchange, October 19, 1938, Rheinbraun Archive, 374/328.

135. Hubertus Braunkohlen AG to Reich Economics Ministry, March 11, 1939, BA, R 8119 F, P964, fol. 101–4. The valuation is set out in Dr. Josef Abs to H. J. Abs, March 30, 1939, BA, R 8119 F, P964, fol. 108–17.

136. Verdict 2077, Bad Godesberg, December 30, 1950, Rheinbraun Archive, 378/328.

137. Deutsche Bank Special Circulars, S25/38, Strictly Confidential: To Branch Managers, May 19, 1938, HADB, F50/1001.

138. Deutsche Bank Frankfurt/Main to Head Office Personnel Department, December 10, 1938, BA, R 8119 F, 24151.

139. December 7, 1938: "Betr.: Nichtarier-Engagements per November 1938," HADB B310.

140. Deutsche Bank Hildesheim to Deutsche Bank Hanover, March 30, 1938, HADB, F88/580.

141. HADB, F167/95.

142. HADB, Abs notecards, Steinbeck, June 16, 1938.

143. The former banking house Sal. Oppenheim jr. & Cie. The firm was registered under the name Pferdmenges on May 20, 1938. The name was changed again into Sal. Oppenheim jr. & Cie. in July 1947. See Michael Stürmer/Gabriele Teichmann/Wilhelm Treue, *Wägen und Wagen: Sal. Oppenheim jr. & Cie: Geschichte einer Bank und einer Familie*, Munich and Zurich: Piper, 1989, pp. 379 and 422f.

144. E.g. Sekretariat to Paul Oppenheimer, London, December 29, 1939, HADB, B32.

145. Abs note of November 30, 1938, HADB, B31.

146. Abs note of November 30, 1938, HADB, B31.

147. HADB, Abs notecards, Steinbeck September 23, 1938.

148. Pollems note of February 27, 1939, HADB, B31.

149. "Niederschrift über die am 12. Juli 1939 zwischen Herrn Abs und den Herren Hendriks und Rykens getroffenen Absprachen betreffend Adler & Oppenheimer-Aktien," HADB, B31.

150. "Aktenvermerk über die am 12. Juli 1939 geführte Unterredung im Reichswirtschaftsministerium," HADB, B31.

151. Note of July 12, 1939, SAM, 1458-1-454.

152. HADB, B31, April 8, 1940 note.

153. Hermann Koehler (Stuttgart) to Abs, June 18, 1940, HADB, B31.

154. Abs to Friedrich Herbst, May 30, 1940, HADB, B31.

155. HADB, Abs notecards, Steinbeck, October 2, 1940 (acquisition of 3 million shares).

156. Elkmann note of October 14, 1940, HADB, B32.

157. Note of November 11, 1940, HADB, B32.

158. HADB, Abs notecards, Steinbeck, February 3, 1941.

159. Abs to August Neuerburg, November 23, 1940, HADB, B31.

160. "Mitwirkung der Deutschen Bank bei den Übernahmen," no date (pencil 3/7), HADB, B32.

161. HADB, Abs notecards, Schaefer (Reichs-Kredit-Gesellschaft), August 9, 1938, July 16, 1941.

162. Deutsche Bank to Reich Economics Ministry, March 1, 1943, HADB, B32.

163. "Teilbericht der Deutschen Revisions- und Treuhandgesellschaft," Anlage 3, HADB, V1/4919.

164. See Ron Chernow, *The Warburgs: The Twentieth Century Odyssey of a Remarkable Jewish Family*, New York: Vintage Books, 1994.

165. Depositenkasse A to Kreditbüro Dresden, November 22, 1935, Deutsche Bank Dresden to Zentrale-Filialbüro, November 28, 1935, BA/ZE [Zwischenlager Hoppegarten] (Box 39283, Regal 2197). The original Rundschreiben was 72/35, November 12, 1935.

166. Commerz- und Privatbank, Enstehung und Verwendungsmöglichkeiten der verschiedenen Arten von Reichsmarkguthaben für Ausländer.

167. RGBl 1938 I, p. 414.

168. Herbert Wolf, "Zur Kontrolle und Enteignung jüdischen Vermögens in der NS-Zeit," in: *Bankhistorisches Archiv* 16/1, Frankfurt: Fritz Knapp, 1990, pp. 55–62; p. 56.

169. Barkai, *Boycott*, p. 171.

170. "Verfügungen nichtarischer Kunden," November 14, 1938, BA/ZE [Zwischenlager Hoppegarten] (Box 39283, Regal 2197).

171. Note, November 15, 1938, BA/ZE [Zwischenlager Hoppegarten] (Box 39283, Regal 2197).

172. Wirtschaftsgrupe Privates Bankgewerbe – Centralverband des Deutschen Bank- und Bankiergewerbes to Deutsche Bank, January 6, 1939. Mosler note, January 13, 1939, HADB, B214.

173. Oberfinanzpräsident Karlsruhe: Genehmigungsbescheid 57903, February 21, 1939, HADB, F28/204. The rest of the information in this paragraph comes from the account file in HADB, F28/204.

174. Barkai, *Boycott*, pp. 179–80.

175. Bekanntmachung (Baden Interior Ministry), April 4, 1941, SAM,1458-1-1044.

176. RGBl 1941 I, p. 303.

177. There is, however, no evidence that any bank refused to make the transfer to the Reich on the grounds that the account holder had been deported to Auschwitz.

178. Cited in Wolf, *Kontrolle*, p. 60.

179. Bundesverband deutscher Banken (BDB), Rundschreiben 180/1941.

180. Deutsche Bank to Wirtschaftsgruppe Privates Bankgewerbe, March 19, 1942, BA, R13 VIII/6.

181. Roer note, April 13, 1942, BA, R13 VIII/7.

182. Wirtschaftsgruppe Privates Bankgewerbe note (Roer), March 11, 1942, BA, R13 VIII/6.

183. Deutsche Bank to Wirtschaftsgruppe Privates Bankgewerbe, May 8, 1942, BA, R13 VIII/6.

184. For example, Deutsche Bank to Oberfinanzpräsident Hamburg, May 6, 1942, Staatsarchiv Hamburg 314–15 Oberfinanzpräsident Nr. 36, UA 2. This document, in which the Hamburg branch points out that one person named on the list had not been "evacuated" but had been seen in the bank, was published and has been erroneously interpreted by Karl Heinz Roth as a "Denunzieren" and "Beihilfe zum Judenmord" ("denouncing" "acting as an accessory to the murder of the Jews"). The bank was clearly stating that this particular account could not be subject to asset confiscation

("Vermögensbeschlagnahme"). See Karl Heinz Roth, "Hehler des Holocaust: Degussa und Deutsche Bank," in: *1999. Zeitschrift für Sozialgeschichte des 20. und 21. Jahrhunderts* 13, Köln: Janus, 1998, pp. 137–44. In fact the account holder concerned emigrated to Cuba in 1942.

185. Emma K. was deported to Theresienstadt on August 19, 1942. She died there only two weeks later on September 2, 1942. *Theresienstädter Gedenkbuch. Die Opfer der Judentransporte aus Deutschland nach Theresienstadt 1942–1945*, Institut Theresienstädter Initiative (ed.), [Prague]: Academia, 2000, p. 599.

186. Wirtschaftsgruppe Privates Bankgewerbe, Rundschreiben 141,- October 9, 1942.

187. HADB, F28/7.

188. Dingeldey to Dieckmann, April 27, 1933, BA, NL Dingeldey. Larry E. Jones, *German Liberalism and the Dissolution of the Weimar Party System*, Chapel Hill: University of North Carolina Press, 1988, p. 474. (I owe this reference to Professor Henry Turner.)

189. Telegram of Deputy of Führer to NSDAP Reich Treasurer, Munich, May 19, 1938, BDC, Papen file. Tiessler (Propaganda Ministry) to Schmidt-Römer, Party Chancellery Munich, October 2, 1942, BA, NS 18/579. The OMGUS report is clearly mistaken in claiming that von Stauss had joined the party already before the National Socialist seizure of power (Report on the Investigation of the Deutsche Bank, November 1946, p. 35, National Archives, Washington DC, RG 360, OMGUS, BICO, Box 71). Chistopher Kopper repeated this mistake (*Zwischen Marktwirtschaft und Dirigismus*, p. 28).

190. Stauss note of March 11, 1933, BA, R 8119 F, P24404.

191. Securities Office: Universum-Film Aktiengesellschaft, November 24, 1933, BA, R 8119 F, P6014, fol. 378.

192. Kreimeier, *Ufa-Story*, pp. 244, 248.

193. Kreimeier, *Ufa-Story*, p. 265.

194. Attachment to April 6, 1934 letter of Klitzsch to Stauss, BA, R 8119 F, P6015, fol. 82.

195. UfA AG to Stauss, May 14, 1934, BA, R 8119 F, P6015, fol. 138/2.

196. Development of Star Remuneration, November 16, 1936, BA, R 8119 F, P6016, fol. 236ff.; Contract with Hans Albers of April 8, 1933, BA, R 8119 F, P6014, fol. 332; Contract with Zarah Leander of November 5, 1936, BA, R 8119 F, P6016, fol. 227.

197. Meeting of supervisory board of Filmkredit-Bank GmbH, July 16, 1936, BA, R 8119 F, P5360, fol. 159.

198. Kiehl memorandum: Filmkredit-Bank GmbH, August 14, 1936, BA, R 8119 F, P5359, fol. 93. David Welch, *Propaganda and the German Cinema 1933–1945*, Oxford: Clarendon, 1983, p. 32.

199. Kiehl note of July 28, 1938: Ufa, July 28, 1938, BA, R 8119 F, P6017, fol. 308–10; Decision of May 14, 1942, BA, R 8119 F, P6020, fol. 32ff.

200. Stauss to Klitzsch (Ufa), 1936, BA, R 8119 F, P6016, fol. 165.

201. Riedel to Stauss, May 9, 1939, BA, R 8119 F, P6018, fol. 194; Ernst H. Correll to Stauss, August 5, 1938, BA, R 8119 F, P6017, fol. 316.

202. Siebert to Stauss, August 25, 1940, BA, R 8119 F, P5953, fol. 142.

203. Siebert to Stauss, August 13, 1940, BA, R 8119 F, P5953, fol. 135; Siebert to Lammers, July 22, 1941, BA, R 8119 F, P5953, fol. 522–6.

204. Siebert to Stauss, August 25, 1940, BA, R 8119 F, P5953, fol. 142.

205. Meeting of Small Council, February 22, 1939, BA, R 8119 F, P5956, fol. 70.

206. Siebert to Stauss, July 6, 1939, BA, R 8119 F, P2952, fol. 251; Siebert memorandum, May 7, 1940, BA, R 8119 F, P5953, fol. 53–4.

207. Siebert memorandum, November 4, 1940, BA, R 8119 F, P5953, fol. 208.

208. Supervisory board meeting, June 9, 1933, BA, R 8119 F, P5052, fol. 95.

209. Hans Pohl/Stephanie Habeth/Beate Brüninghaus, *Die Daimler-Benz AG in den Jahren 1933 bis 1944*, Wiesbaden: Franz Steiner, 1986, p. 44.

210. Werlin: Confidental Information, November 29, 1933, BA, R 8119 F, P3297, fol. 151.

211. Werlin to Kissel, March 5, 1935, BA, R 8119 F, P3297, fol. 173.

212. Lewinski (Secretariate of Stauss) to Werlin, May 12, 1934, BA, R 8119 F, P3297, fol. 165.

213. BMW to Stauss, February 15, 1938, BA, R 8119 F, P3075, fol. 321–3.

214. Statement of Hermann Kaiser, March 19, 1946, NA, OMGUS, Exhibit 12: "The other members of the Kreditausschuss were not in favor of these credits but could not intervene as von Stauss was obviously collaborating with the Reich government in these matters." (Interrogation by Charles E. Bancroft.)

215. Stauss to Daimler–Benz management board, November 23, 1934, BA, R 8119 F, P3228, fol. 434.

216. Benrath to Stauss, January 12, 1934, BA, R 8119 F, P7276, fol. 134.

217. Decision of Wuppertal Court, September 14, 1933, BA, R 8119 F, P7276, fol. 123–4.

218. AKU supervisory board, May 17, 1933, BA, R 8119 F, P7284, fol. 73ff.

219. *Berliner Börsen Zeitung*, December 13, 1934. AKU to L.J.A. Trip (President of Nederlandsche Bank), February 6, 1935, BA, R 8119 F, P7277.

220. Oberst Löb to Stauss, March 11, 1937, BA, R 8119 F, P7278, fol. 106; Stauss to Löb, March 19, 1937, BA, R 8119 F, P7278, fol. 107–8.

221. Delegates' Committee, where these arguments were repeated again, March 17, 1939, BA, R 8119 F, P7278, fol. 374.

222. Meeting with State Secretary Körner, May 5, 1939, BA, R 8119 F, P7329, fol. 57ff.

223. Kiehl to Philipp Reemtsma, May 30, 1939, BA, R 8119 F, P7329, fol. 102–3.

224. Lothar Gall, "Hermann Josef Abs and the Third Reich: 'A Man for All Seasons,'" in: *Financial History Review* 6, Cambridge: Cambridge University Press, 1999, pp. 147–202.

225. Halt to Himmler, January 20, 1941, BA, NS19/1043.

226. NA, RG260, OMGUS, Economics Division, Records held by HICOG, Decartelization branch HICOG, Schröder file, Box 160.

227. Fritz Kranefuss to Himmler, April 21, 1943, BA, NS19/2219, fol. 36–8.

228. NSDAP membership number 4245867 (BDC).

229. Speech to Reich Chamber of Labor, November 24, 1936, BA, R 8119 F, 24534, fol. 190ff.

230. Klaus Hildebrand, *Vom Reich zum Weltreich. Hitler, NSDAP und koloniale Frage 1919–1945*, Munich: W. Fink, 1969, pp. 189–200.

231. Weigelt note for Schlieper, January 16, 1936, BA, R 8119 F, 24526, fol. 277.

232. See recently Harald Wixforth, *Auftakt zur Ostexpansion: Die Dresdner Bank und die Umgestaltung des Bankwesens im Sudetenland 1938/39*, Dresden: Hannah-Arendt-Institut für Totalitarismusforschung, 2001.

233. Hans-Erich Volkmann, "Die NS-Wirtschaft in Vorbereitung des Krieges," in: Militärgeschichtliches Forschungsamt Freiburg (ed.), *Das Deutsche Reich und der Zweite Weltkrieg*, Vol. I, Stuttgart: Deutsche Verlags-Anstalt, 1979, pp. 177–368; p. 329.

234. Federal Reserve System, Board of Governors, Preliminary Draft (September 1944), German Banking Penetration of Continental Europe, p. iv.

235. Reichsbank Bourse Committee, September 25, 1941, BA, R 8119 F, P5182.

236. Alan S. Milward, "The Reichsmark Bloc and the International Economy," in: Gerhard Hirschfeld/Lothar Kettenacker (eds.), *The "Führer State": Myth and Reality: Studies on the Structure and Politics of the Third Reich*, Stuttgart: Klett-Cotta, 1981, p. 387.

237. Note of March 24, 1938, SAM, 1458-2-77.

238. Memorandum, n.d., probably end of March or beginning of April 1938, SAM, 1458-2-305, fol. 9.

239. See "Rechnungshof: Strafverfahren und Haftungsansprüche gegen ehemalige Vorstandsmitglieder der Credit-Anstalt," September 15, 1938, ÖStA, 4/2-92/2165/2/8.

240. Memorandum: "Auf welche Weise liesse sich eine deutschösterreichische Währungsunion durchführen?," February 26, 1938, BA, R 2501, 6673.

241. Minutes of meeting of April 4, 1938, April 5, 1938, SAM, 1458-2-77.

242. Mosler note, March 14, 1938, HADB, B203.

243. Note, March 31, 1938, HADB, B51.

244. Abs note, April 13, 1938, HADB, B51.

245. Note, March 31, 1938, HADB, B51.

246. Deutsche Bank Cologne, BA, R8119 F, P6507.

247. Note on negotiation, April 15, 1938, Mosler note, May 7, 1938, HADB, B51. Note, May 16, 1938, ÖStA, 4/2-92/2165/0 vol. I.

248. See Manfred Pohl/Andrea Schneider, *VIAG 1923–1998: Vom Staatskonzern zum internationalen Konzern*, Munich: Piper, 1998, pp. 134ff.

249. Pollems note, April 14, 1938, HADB, B51.

250. Minutes of meeting of May 20, 1938, May 21, 1938, HADB, B51.

251. Deutsche Bank memorandum, May 31, 1938, ÖStA, 4/2-92/2165/0 vol. I.

252. Note (IV Kred. 4), August 31, 1938, SAM, 1458-2-84.

253. Note, November 1, 1938, HADB, B51.

254. Bürckel to Ernst, February 10, 1939, Bürckel to Ernst, September 21, 1939, ÖStA, 4/2-92/2165/0 vol. I.

255. Bunzl & Biach AG was in part owned by a Swiss holding company, "Bunzl Konzern Holding AG, Zug," and had a large and diversified industrial portofolio. It was partly "Aryanized" in 1938 through the Kontrolbank. In 1941 its name was changed to Kontinentale Rohstoff und Papier AG. In attempting to take it over, the Dresdner Bank and its affiliate in Vienna, the Länderbank, tried to ward off initiatives of the Creditanstalt, but in 1942 the Länderbank and the Creditanstalt each took 36 percent of the shares. See Gerald D. Feldman, "The Länderbank Wien AG in the National Socialist Period," 2003 preliminary report available on www.histcom.at. Also Hans Witek, "'Arisierungen' in Wien: Aspekte nationalsozialialistischer Enteignungspolitik 1938–1940," in: Emmerich Talos/Ernst Hanisch/Wolfgang Neugebauer (eds.), *NS-Herrschaft in Österreich*, Vienna: Verlag für Gesellschaftskritik, 1988, p. 209.

256. Creditanstalt to Reich Economics Ministry (Riehle), May 24, 1939, SAM, 1458-2-91.

257. 1938 report of the Deutsche Revisions- und Treuhandgesellschaft, Brüder Eisert, SAM, 1458-2-153.

258. Note (Viag), March 3, 1942, HADB, B53. Abs note, March 2, 1942, B56.

259. Riehle (Reich Economics Ministry) to Auswärtiges Amt, April 11, 1940, SAM, 1458-10-81: "These transfers, performed without the assistance, indeed without the knowledge of the Reich Economics Ministry, were reported to me over the telephone only when completed."

260. Minutes of the Arbeitsausschuss, August 12, 1941, BA, R8119 F, P6510.

261. E.g. Note, November 9, 1940, SAM, 1458-9-158.

262. Abs to Joham, May 24, 1939, BA, R 8119 F, P6503, fol. 39.

263. Hasslacher to Abs, July 7, 1939, BA, R 8119 F, P6503, fol. 77–8; Abs to Hasslacher, July 11, 1939, BA, R 8119 F, P6503, fol. 80–2.

264. Abs note, June 10, 1941, BA, R 8119 F, P24158.

265. Creditanstalt Working Committee, September 3, 1940, BA, R 8119 F, P6504, fol. 20–5; Joham to Abs, October 27, 1941, BA, R 8119 F, P6504, fol. 311; Creditanstalt to Reich Economics Ministry, September 26, 1940, BA, R 8119 F, P6504, fol. 59–60.

266. The name was changed in October 1938, to Czecho-Slovakia.

267. František Vencovský et al. (eds.), *Dejiny Bankovnictví Českých Zemích*, Prague: Bankovní Institut, 1999, pp. 242–5.

268. Stauss to Regierungspräsident Fritz Krebs, March 7, 1939, BA, R8119 F, P24419.

269. Deutsche Bank, Böhmen und Mähren im deutschen Wirtschaftsraum, April 1939.

270. Christopher Kopper, "Die 'Arisierung' der deutsch-böhmischen Aktienbanken," in: Boris Barth/Josef Faltus/Jan Kren/Eduard Kubu (eds.), *Konkurrenzpartnerschaft: Die deutsche und die tschechoslowakische Wirtschaft in der Zwischenkriegszeit*, Essen: Klartext Verlag, 1998, pp. 236–45; p. 237. Also Wixforth, *Auftakt zur Ostexpansion.*

271. Klaus Hildebrand, *Das vergangene Reich: Deutsche Aussenpolitik von Bismarck bis Hitler*, Stuttgart: Deutsche Verlags-Anstalt, 1995, p. 606.

272. Miroslav Karny/Jaroslava Milotova/Margita Karna (eds.), *Deutsche Politik im "Protektorat Böhmen und Mähren" unter Reinhard Heydrich 1941–1942: Eine Dokumentation*, Berlin: Metropol, 1997, p. 45.

273. Abs note, October 8, 1938, OMGUS FINAD 2/47/2; Abs statement, October 10, 1945, Exhibit 195; see also Kopper, *Zwischen Marktwirtschaft und Dirigismus*, pp. 345–8.

274. SAM, 1458-10-228.

275. Note, November 24, 1938, ÖStA, 4/2-92/2165/0 vol. I.

276. HADB, Abs notecards, Victor Ulbrich, October 15, 1938 conversation.

277. Letter of Dr. Ernst, October 14, 1938, HADB, B138.

278. Elizabeth Wiskemann, *Czechs and Germans: A Study of the Struggle in the Historic Provinces of Bohemia and Moravia*, London: Oxford University Press and Royal Institute of International Affairs, 1938, pp. 166–7.

279. Mosler note, October 27, 1938, HADB, B163.

280. Memorandum of "Důvěrnický sbor 'Sdružení,'" December 14, 1938, Czech National Archives, Ministry of Finance 944/1939, box 1956.

281. Hans-Erich Volkmann, "Die NS-Wirtschaft in Vorbereitung des Krieges," p. 331.

282. Note on November 22, 1938 meeting, November 28, 1938, SAM, 1458-10-228.

283. Deutsche Bank and Dresdner Bank to Reich Economics Ministry, March 14, 1939, HADB, B153.

284. Deutsche Bank to Reich Economics Ministry, March 16, 1939, HADB, B153.

285. Minutes of the Aufsichtsrat of March 16, 1939 and April 12, 1939, CFM, 67/1830. Dr. F. Kavan, affidavit, November 28, 1950, CFM, Finance Ministry, CUB (reference files).

286. Minutes of the Aufsichtsrat of June 27, 1939 and September 29, 1939, CFM, 67/1830; minutes of the Engerer Ausschuss, January 26, 1940.

287. Handschriftliche Abschrift betr. Entnazifizierungsverfahren, January 4, 1947, HADB, NL38/3.

288. Deutsche Bank to BUB (Pohle), May 19, 1939, HADB, B167.

289. Deutsche Bank Zentrale to BUB (Pohle), April 27, 1939, HADB, B167.

290. Pohle to Reich Economics Ministry and attachment, March 23, 1939, SAM, 1458-10-84. Dr. F. Kavan, affidavit, November 28, 1950, CFM, Finance Ministry, CUB (reference files).

291. Minutes of the Arbeitsausschuss, July 13, 1939, CFM, 67/1831.

292. "Stand der BUB Aktien per 28.3.39," HADB, B167.

293. Abs note, October 13, 1938, HADB, B163; BUB to Reich Economics Ministry, August 12, 1939, HADB, B162. Dr. F. Kavan, affidavit, November 28, 1950, CFM, Finance Ministry, CUB (reference files).

294. Annex to Pohle letter to Deutsche Bank, May 22, 1939, HADB, B167.

295. Correspondence with British Overseas Bank and Société Générale, August and September 1939, HADB, B167.

296. BUB to Deutsche Bank, December 13, 1939, HADB, B169; Abs note, February 13, 1940, HADB, B176.

297. "Gedächtnisprotokoll" of December 12, 1939, HADB, B161.

298. Pohle speech, December 12, 1939, HADB, B169.

299. Pohle speech, December 12, 1939, HADB, B169.

300. Dr. F. Kavan, affidavit, November 28, 1950, CFM, Finance Ministry, CUB (reference files).

301. Deutsche Bank to Reich Economics Ministry, November 14, 1939, BA, R2, 13533, fol. 136.

302. Deutsche Bank to Emil Kreibich, August 7, 1939, HADB, B162.

303. Minutes of the Arbeitsausschuss, July 13, 1939, CFM, 67/1831.

304. Minutes of the Exekutiv-Komitee of April 30, 1942 and October 21, 1942, CFM, 67/1831.

305. Minutes of the Engerer Ausschuss, November 27, 1940, CFM, 67/1831.

306. HADB, B165.

307. *OMGUS Ermittlungen*, p. 415 (OMGUS Annex to the Report on the Investigation of Deutsche Bank, March 1947, p. 29), Exhibit 372; note, May 10, 1940, HADB, B162.

308. OMGUS Exhibit 194; statement of Hermann Abs, October 10, 1945, Exhibit 195.

309. Reich Economics Ministry to Deutsche Bank, April 18, 1940, HADB, B162.

310. July 10, 1934; January 21, January 22, and January 27, 1937 memoranda, BA ZE/14060.

311. HADB, B189.

312. Josef Krebs, Walter Pohle, Dr. Max Ludwig Rohde, Dr. Max Selige (until 1939), Viktor Ulbrich.

313. Deutsche Bank to Reich Economics Ministry, June 2, 1939, requesting the use of the £ 80,000 transaction not required for the DAIB transaction to be transferred for the purpose of acquiring BUB, HADB, B143.

314. Memorandum, March 30, 1939, p. 20, BA, R2, 13532.

315. Deutsche Bank to Reich Economics Ministry, November 13, 1939, BA, R2, 13533, fol. 119–20.

316. Kimmich memorandum, June 28, 1939, BA, R8119 F, P5351, fol. 147–8.

317. Note on conversation, January 24, 1941, HADB, B175.

318. Note on conversation, January 24, 1941, HADB, B175.

319. Letter of Reich Finance Ministry, February 5, 1942, HADB, B175.

320. Devisenprüfungsbericht, April 19, 1941, HADB, B166.

321. BA, R2, 14087; Deutsche Bank to Reich Economics Ministry, November 14, 1939, BA, R2, 13533, fol. 141; Reich Finance Ministry memorandum, January 1942, BA, R2, 13535 fol. 300–03; Deutsche Bank to Reich Finance Ministry, May 3, 1940, BA, R2, 13536, fol. 124–5.

322. *Die Wirtschaft*, April 21, 1945.

323. Minutes of the Aufsichtsrat, February 11, 1943, CFM, 67/1830.

324. Reich Economics Ministry (Generalreferat Kehrl) to Reich Finance Ministry, May 15, 1940, BA, R2, 13536, fol. 136–7. Reich Finance Ministry memorandum, April 28, 1939, BA, R2, 13532, fol. 43–4.

325. BUB to Deutsche Bank, October 19, 1939, HADB, P2/G1.

326. Minutes of the Engerer Ausschuss, March 5, 1940, CFM, 67/1830.

327. Minutes of the Engerer Ausschuss, March 11, 1941, CFM, 67/1830.

328. Deutsche Bank to Reich Economics Ministry, January 20, 1940, SAM, 1458-10-396. Hayes claims that this was a "lucrative" transaction, in that the Deutsche Bank sold claims of over 600,000 RM against the Bohemia Ceramics Works for 750,000 RM (Peter Hayes, "The Deutsche Bank and the Holocaust," in: Peter Hayes (ed.), *Lessons and Legacies III: Memory, Memorialization and Denial*, Evanston Ill.: Northwestern University Press, 1999, pp. 71–98; p. 88). In fact, the Deutsche Bank and the Prague bank Petschek in liquidation each owned over 600,000 RM in claims, and each were paid 325,000 RM by the SS, with the result that each took a loss. See also Gabriele Huber, *Die Porzellan-Manufaktur Allach-München GmbH: Eine "Wirtschaftsunternehmung" der SS Zum Schutz der "deutschen Seele,"* Marburg: Jonas, 1992, pp. 35–6.

329. Reich Economics Ministry note, March 28, 1940, SAM, 1458-10-396.

330. Walter Naasner, *SS-Wirtschaft und SS-Verwaltung: "Das SS-Wirtschafts-Verwaltungshauptamt und die unter seiner Dienstaufsicht stehenden wirtschaftlichen Vertretungen und Weitere Dokumente"* (Schriften des Bundesarchivs Bd. 45a), Düsseldorf: Droste, 1998, pp. 143–6.

331. Reich Economics Ministry to Devisenstelle Berlin, April 18, 1940, BA, R2, 13536 fol. 96–7; Pohle to Benz, August 25, 1939, BA, R2, 14894, fol. 6; Benz memorandum, August 31, 1939, fol. 8–9. See also Huber: *Die Porzellan-Manufaktur Allach-München GmbH*, pp. 35–48.

332. BUB to BUB Budweis, May 14, 1943, CFM, 69/1948.

333. E.g. Auswanderungsfonds für Böhmen und Mähren to BUB, September 23, 1942, CFM, 69/1948.

334. BUB Budweis to Zentralamt für die Regelung der Judenfrage, case of M. Neubauer Budweis, March 22, 1943, CFM, 69/1948.

335. Vencovský, Dějiný Bankovnictví v Českých Zemích, pp. 328–9.

336. BUB to Gestapo (Dr. Arthur Czeczowiczka), January 15, 1943, CFM, Finance Ministry, CUB (reference files). Dr. Arthur C. was the owner of the 3 bills for 5000 CKr which the Gestapo ordered to be transferred to Lebensborn e.V.

337. November 30, 1942 accounts, BA, R8119 F, P11013, fol. 4. See also Hans Günther Adler, *Theresienstadt 1941–1945: Das Antlitz einer Zwangsgemeinschaft*, Tübingen: Mohr 1960.

338. Minutes of the Exekutiv Komitee, November 24, 1944, CFM, 67/1831.

339. February 28, 1945 accounts, BA, R8119 F, P11013, fol. 136.

340. See in general Gerhard Mollin, *Montankonzerne und "Drittes Reich": Der Gegensatz zwischen Monopolindustrie und Befehlswirtschaft in der deutschen Rüstung und Expansion 1936–1944* (Kritische Studien zur Geschichtswissenschaft, Bd. 78), Göttingen: Vandenhoeck & Ruprecht, 1988, pp. 187–8.

341. Kiehl note on conversation with Rasche and Rinn (Dresdner Bank), October 18, 1937, BA, R8119 F, P1418, fol. 36–7.

342. Kimmich note, July 28, 1937, BA, R8119 F, P1416, fol. 11–13.

343. Kimmich note, June 28, 1939, BA, R8119 F, P1416, fol. 91–2; Reich Economics Ministry Generalreferat Kehrl, BA R7, 2268, fol. 7–9.

344. Minutes of the Engerer Ausschuss, May 30, 1940, CFM, 67/1831.

345. Minutes of the Engerer Ausschuss, January 26, 1940, CFM, 67/1831.

346. Dr. Müller memorandum, June 12, 1943, BA, R2, 17830.

347. Jonathan Steinberg, *All or Nothing: The Axis and the Holocaust*, London: Routledge, 1990, p. 171.

348. Kimmich to Pohle, June 26, 1940, BA, R8119 F, P1416, fol. 116.

349. Kiehl to BUB, June 23, 1939, BA, R8119 F, P1417, fol. 84.

350. Willy A. Boelcke, *Die Deutsche Wirtschaft 1930–1945: Interna des Reichswirtschaftsministeriums*, Düsseldorf: Droste 1983, p. 265. Hans Umbreit, "Auf dem Weg zur Kontinentalherrschaft," in: Militärgeschichtliches Forschungsamt Freiburg (ed.), *Das Deutsche Reich und der Zweite Weltkrieg*, V/1, Stuttgart: Deutsche Verlags-Anstalt, 1988, pp. 3–345; pp. 213–15.

351. Veltjens (Oberst der Luftwaffe): "Zusammengefasster Bericht über die Kapitalverflechtung mit Holland und Belgien seit der Besatzung," 1941, BA, R7, 3158, fol. 4–5. Also *OMGUS Ermittlungen*, pp. 202ff., 221ff. (OMGUS Report on the Investigation of Deutsche Bank, November 1946, pp. 184ff., 202ff.)

352. Note, April 1, 1941, HADB, B129.

353. BA, R8119 F, P6875 in general; see also BA, R8119 F, P6854, fol. 349.

354. Pohle to Rösler, October 16, 1940, BA, R8119 F, P6854.

355. Pohle to Kimmich, November 18, 1940; Pohle to Kehrl, February 10, 1941, BA, R8119 F, P6942. Hayes in his essay incorrectly calculates the commission on the purchase of the Jewish sales as almost six times the actual level, and on this basis he concludes that this was "perhaps the most profitable of the BUB's services." Hayes, "Deutsche Bank," p. 88.

356. Minutes of the Engerer Ausschuss of November 27, 1940 and December 16, 1941 CFM, 67/1831.

357. Minutes of the Engerer Ausschuss, February 23, 1942, CFM, 67/1831.

358. Minutes of the Engerer Ausschuss, June 11, 1941, CFM, 67/1831.

359. Lippmann & Rosenthal to Deutsche Bank, April 20, 1944, BA, R8119 F, P6876, fol. 321; Deutsche Bank to BUB, August 9, 1944, fol. 528.

360. Note, July 27, 1943, BA, R8119 F, P6875.

361. Minutes of the Exekutiv-Komitee, March 1, 1944, CFM, 67/1831.

362. Pohle to Bechtolf, June 11, 1942, BA, R8119 F, P6931, fol. 28–30.

363. BUB to Sicherheitsdienst RF SS SD Leitabschnitt Prag July 19, 1940, HADB, B191.

364. "Geschäftsverteilung für den Vorstand," May 22, 1941, HADB, B191.

365. Rösler to Rohde, April 25, 1941 and May 23, 1941, HADB, B191.

366. Pohle to Rösler, June 9, 1942, BA, R8119 F, P6876, fol. 571–2.

367. Note, June 6, 1942, BA, R8119 F, P6931, fol. 1–15.

368. Beate Ruhm von Oppen (ed.), *Helmuth James von Moltke: Briefe an Freya 1939–1945*, Munich: Beck, 1988, p. 369.

369. Bechtolf letter, April 26, 1943, BA, R8119 F, P6932; Rolf-Dieter Müller, "Von der Wirtschaftsallianz zum kolonialen Ausbeutungskrieg," in: Militärgeschichtliches Forschungsamt Freiburg (ed.), *Das Deutsche Reich und der Zweite Weltkrieg*, IV, Stuttgart:

Deutsche Verlags-Anstalt, 1983, pp. 98–189; p. 140. Franz Neumann saw the supervisory board of Kontinentale Oel as "the model
of a new ruling class, composed of the party, the army, the bureaucracy, and industry" and resting on "the oppression and exploitation
of foreign countries and of the German people alike." Franz Neumann, *Behemoth: The Structure and Practice of National Socialism*,
New York: Oxford University Press, 1944 (2nd edition), p. 396.

370. Pott to Kiehl, October 30, 1940, BA, R8119 F, P7236, fol. 33; Kiehl
note, January 29, 1941, fol. 43–8.

371. Bechtolf to Pohle, May 5, 1943, BA, R8119 F, P6932; Rohde and
Pohle to Bechtolf, March 3, 1942, BA, R8119 F, P6931, fol. 315–16.

372. Deutsche Bank Vorstand to Dresdner Bank, October 19, 1944, BA,
R8119 F, P1416, fol. 141.

373. BA, R8119 F, P6854, fol. 123, fol. 204; BA, R8119 F, P6855, fol.
188–93.

374. Rösler note, July 20, 1943, BA, R8119 F, P6855, fol. 179.

375. Denazification, October 10, 1945, copy in HADB V01/4852.

376. Memorandum, February 13, 1939, SAM, 1458-10-234. Exekutiv-
Ausschuss of the Creditanstalt, March 21, 1939, ÖStA, Ministerium
für Wirtschaft und Arbeit (1939), No. 32577.

377. Note, September 6, 1941, SAM, 1458-10-66; Report of Finance
Ministry Bratislava, April 26, 1940, SAM, 1458-10-233.

378. Letter of BUB, August 22, 1940, HADB, B174.

379. Dr. Fritscher speech, October 29, 1940, SAM, 1458-10-66.

380. Minutes of the Verwaltungsrat, August 20, 1941, NBS, UB353/1.

381. Minutes of the Verwaltungsrat, November 3, 1941, NBS, UB353/1.
See in general Livia Rothkirchen, "The Situation of Jews in Slovakia
between 1939 and 1945," in: *Jahrbuch für Antisemitismusforschung*
7, Frankfurt: Campus, 1998, pp. 46–70.

382. The Geneva agreement of May 15, 1922, which dealt with the future
constitutional and legal conditions of Upper Silesia was signed by
the German and Polish representatives on June 11, 1922. Concerning the German banks' branches in East Upper Silesia (which had
become Polish territory after the referendum of 1921) – the bank
für Handel und Industrie, Deutsche Bank, and Dresdner Bank – the

Geneva agreement stated that these banks were entitled for the following fifteen years to go about their business as before. The same applied to the Polish banks in the German part of Upper Silesia – the bank Przemyslowców and the Polski Bank Handlowy. See RGBl 1922 II, p. 375.

383. Note, May 3, 1937 and April 8, 1938, SAM, 1458-15-167.

384. Pollems note, February 11, 1936, HADB, P416.

385. Deutsche Bank to Reichsaufsichtsamt für das Kreditwesen, December 12, 1939, SAM, 1458-15-124.

386. Devisenfahndungsamt Teschen, September 8, 1939, Beauftragter des Devisenfahndungsamts, Krakau, September 23, 1939, ANN, GG 1291, 17.

387. Report of Reichsbankstelle Litzmannstadt, April 30, 1940, SAM, 1585-15-124.

388. "Betr. Bankeinflüsse und Behörden," May 29, 1941, SAM, 1458-15-129.

389. Deutsche Bank to Reich Economics Ministry, September 24, 1940, SAM, 1458-15-81.

390. HADB, F122/001.

391. Note, September 3, 1943, HADB, F119/85.

392. HADB, F119/0064, F119/0068.

393. HADB, F119/848, F119/32.

394. Note, April 2, 1943, HADB, F119/848.

395. Note of Reichsaufsichtsamt für das Kreditwesen, April 26, 1940, SAM, 1458-15-125.

396. Ulrich to Abs referring to the minutes of the Arbeitsausschuss of Creditanstalt-Bankverein of October 12, 1939, August 27, 1943, HADB, B54.

397. Note of Reichsaufsichtsamt für das Kreditwesen, October 21, 1940, SAM, 1458-15-125.

398. Deutsche Bank to Reich Economics Ministry, November 2, 1940, HADB, B52.

399. Minutes of the Arbeitsausschuss of Creditanstalt-Bankverein, September 3, 1940, BA, R8119 F, P6510.

400. Deutsche Bank to Creditanstalt, January 24, 1941, HADB, B52.

401. Letter to Kommissar für die Behandlung feindlichen Vermögens, June 27, 1942, ANN, Kom. Rzadu Mienie Nieprzyjec, 20/318.

402. ANN, Kom. Rzadu Mienie Nieprzyjec, 10, fol. 27.

403. Kiehl to Generalkonsul Winkelmann (Danzig), April 10, 1942, HADB, B53.

404. August 7, 1945 account of Dr. Wachowiak, ANN, Bank Handlowy 331.

405. Note of Aufsichtsstelle on visit of Glathe August 21, 1943, August 24, 1943, ANN, GG 1388.

406. Abs note, October 22, 1942, HADB, B54.

407. Krakauer Zeitung 1942, No. 240, ANN, GG 1265, 141–42.

408. I owe this information to Bertrand Perz. See *"Profil"* September 14, 1998: "Das grauenvolle Geheimnis der CA" and interview with Perz.

409. Arbeitsausschuss, July 28, 1943, BA, R8119 F, P6511.

410. Bankaufsichtsstelle (visit of Tron, October 12/13, 1942), October 20, 1942, ANN, GG 1401.

411. Bankaufsichtsstelle (visit of Tron, August 25, 1943), August 30, 1943, ANN, GG 1401.

412. Arbeitsausschuss, April 26 and 27, 1944, BA, R8119 F, P6511.

413. Arbeitsausschuss, June 13, 1944, BA, R8119 F, P6511.

414. See Walter Naasner, *Neue Machtzentren in der deutschen Kriegswirtschaft 1942–1945*, Boppard: Boldt, 1994, pp. 412–13.

415. Bankdirigent der Emissionsbank to Staatssekretär Generalgouvernement, July 31, 1944, ANN, GG 1388.

416. Reich Economics Ministry note, February 3, 1941, SAM, 1458-19-75.

417. Kimmich note of July 24, 1940, HADB, B129.

418. Kimmich note of August 29, 1940, HADB, B129.

419. Mojert: Links of Dutch and German Economy, October 15, 1941, HADB, B129.

420. Ulrich memorandum: On Foreign Business, August 14, 1941, BA, R 8119 F, P24151.

421. Kimmich memorandum, August 13, 1940, HADB, B128.

422. See Etienne Verhoeyen, "Les grands industriels belges entre collaboration et résistance: le moindre mal," in: *Centre de Recherches et d'études historiques de la seconde guerre mondiale, Cahier* 10, Brussels, 1986, pp. 57-114.

423. Verhoeyen, "Les grands industriels," p. 67.

424. Kurzmeyer: Notice on Events in Brussels August 26-29, 1940, August 29, 1940, HADB, B128.

425. Kimmich notice of October 17, 1940, HADB, B128; Schacht to Reich Economics Minister, October 17, 1940, HADB, B128.

426. Verhoeyen, "Les grands industriels," p. 69; John Gillingham, "The Baron de Launoit. A Case Study in the 'Politics of Production' of Belgian Industry during Nazi Occupation," *Revue belge d'histoire contemporaine* V, Gent, 1974, pp. 1-59.

427. Verhoeyen, "Les grands industriels," p. 71.

428. Pollems note of March 3, 1941, HADB, B128.

429. Abs note of November 14, 1940, BA, R 8119 F, P6504, fol. 110-11; Joham: Memorandum on Meeting with Abs and Rummel, December 4, 1941, BA R 8119 F, P6504, fol. 359.

430. Pilder to Abs, June 5, 1941, BA, R 8119 F, P24158; Pilder to Abs, July 22, 1941, BA, R 8119 F, P24158.

431. Meeting in Badgastein, August 10, 1940, BA, R 8119 F, P24158.

432. Weigelt memorandum, May 3, 1935, BA, R 8119 F, P6968, fol. 268-9.

433. Weigelt memorandum, May 7, 1935, BA, R 8119 F, P6968, fol. 270-1; Supervisory Office for Petroleum to Deutsche Bank, April 24, 1936, BA, R 8119 F, P6968, fol. 290.

434. David E. Kaiser, *Economic Diplomacy and the Origins of the Second World War. Germany, Britain, France and Eastern Europe 1930-1939*, Princeton: Princeton University Press, 1980, p. 144; Andreas Hillgruber, *Hitler, König Carol und Marschall Antonescu: Die deutsch-rumänischen Beziehungen 1938-1944*, Wiesbaden: Franz Steiner, 1954, pp. 28-34.

435. German-Rumanian Society, May 11, 1939, BA, R 8119 F, P24527, fol. 44.

436. Schmidt memorandum: Banks in German–Rumanian Economic Relations, January 26, 1943, BA, R 8119 F, P10880, fol. 419.

437. Ilgner to Abs: Draft: Recommendations on an Intensification of German–Rumanian Economic Relations, February 17, 1942, BA, R 8119 F, P6974, fol. 25ff.

438. Ulrich memorandum: On Foreign Business, August 14, 1941, BA, R 8119 F, P24151. In general: Philippe Marguerat, *Le IIIe Reich et le pétrole roumain, 1938–1940: contribution à l'étude de la pénétration économique allemande dans les Balkans à la veille et au début de la Seconde Guerre mondiale*, Leiden: A. W. Sijthoff, 1977.

439. Sippell minute: Meeting with Director Schroeder, November 11, 1941, BA, R 8119 F, P8586, fol. 263–6; Note of November 22, 1942, BA, R 8119 F, P8586, fol. 338–9; Sippell to Schroeder, November 23, 1942, BA, R 8119 F, P8586, fol. 340.

440. December 11, 1942, BA, R 8119 F, P8586, fol. 342.

441. Morgenstern memorandum of March 19, 1941, HADB, B204, Nr. 177.

442. November 16, 1940; March 3, 1942; April 11, 1942 memoranda [Vermerke], BA/ZE 14404.

443. OMGUS, Exhibit 274: September 13, 1939, Deutsche Bank to Reich Economics Ministry. See also Barbara Bonhage/Hanspeter Lussy/Marc Perrenoud, *Nachrichtenlose Vermögen bei Schweizer Banken: Depots, Konten und Safes von Opfern des nationalsozialistischen Regimes und Restitutionsprobleme in der Nachkriegszeit*, Zurich: Chronos, 2001, p. 135.

444. Memorandum, no title, no date, HADB, P24004.

445. Speech in Rome on October 20, 1941, cited in: Unabhängige Expertenkommission Switzerland (UEK) – Second World War (ed.), *Switzerland and its Gold Transactions in the Second World War*, Bern, 1998, p. 25.

446. UEK, *Switzerland*, p. 39.

447. Johannes Bähr, *Der Goldhandel der Dresdner Bank im Zweiten Weltkrieg*, Leipzig: Kiepenheuer & Witsch, 1999, p. 29.

448. Bähr, *Goldhandel*, pp. 49–51. Jonathan Steinberg, *The Deutsche Bank and Its Gold Transactions During the Second World War*, Munich: Beck, 1999, p. 38.

449. Steinberg, *Deutsche Bank*, p. 56.

450. Interrogation of Kurt Haussmann (manager of Deutsche Bank Istanbul), October 4, 1946, OMGUS, Exhibit 338.

451. Bähr (*Goldhandel*) is completely convincing on this point (pp. 84–5). See U.S. State Department, U.S. and Allied Wartime and Postwar Relations and Negotiations with Argentina, Portugal, Spain, Sweden and Turkey on Looted Gold and German External Assets, Washington D.C., 1998.

452. Steinberg, *Deutsche Bank*, pp. 31–2, 38.

453. Bähr, *Goldhandel*, p. 59.

454. Steinberg, *Deutsche Bank*, pp. 59–66.

455. See Christiane Uhlig et al., *Tarnung, Transfer, Transit: Die Schweiz als Drehscheibe verdeckter deutscher Operationen (1938–1952)*, Zurich: Chronos, 2001, pp. 156, 169.

456. See Gall, *"Man for All Seasons,"* pp. 149–53.

457. DUB to Kurzmeyer, February 20, 1941, HADB, P24546.

458. Abs to Kurzmeyer, January 4, 1946, HADB, RWB, 31.

459. DUB to Reichsbank, April 7, 1941, HADB, K8/18.

460. DUB to Reichsbank (Werner), June 25, 1941, HADB, K8/18.

461. Note, October 18, 1944, K8/18.

462. DUB to Reichsbank (Streng vertraulich), November 16, 1944, K8/18.

463. DUB to Kurzmeyer, December 13, 1944, DUB to Auswärtiges Amt, January 23, 1945, HADB, K8/18.

464. James H. Mann note, August 29, 1947, Bundesarchiv Bern, E2801 1968/84, Band 66, Az 140.129 (Handakten Walter Stucki).

465. UBS archive, SBV/SBC (Bankverein) documents D2269, September 30, 1944 letter of SBV to Hermann Abs. Cited in Marc Perrenoud et al., *La place financière et les banques suisses à l'époque du national-socialisme: Les relations des grandes banques avec l'Allemagne (1931–1946)*, Unabhängige Experten kommission Schweiz–Zweiter Weltkrieg; Bd. 13, Lausanne: Payot, 2002, p. 420.

466. Marc Perrenoud et al., *La place financière et les banques suisses à l'époque du national-socialisme*, Lausanne: Payot, 2002. The 1935 supplement to the conditions of employment of Deutsche Bank

(paragraph 8) stated that: Employees are not permitted to have an account, depot account, or safe at another bank.

467. Walther Funk, Die Länder des Südostens und die Europäische Wirtschaftsgemeinschaft. Rede, gehalten vor der Südosteuropa-Gesellschaft in Wien am 10. März 1944, p. 15, BA, R63/281.

468. BA, R11/271, fol. 84ff. For examples of how widely differing interpretations can be made of the same speech, see Dietrich Eichholtz, *Geschichte der deutschen Kriegswirtschaft 1939–1945*, vol. I, Berlin: Akademie-Verlag, 1971, pp. 176–8; and Ludolf Herbst, *Der Totale Krieg und die Ordnung der Wirtschaft*, Stuttgart: Deutsche Verlags-Anstalt, 1982, pp. 142–4. The DDR printed this speech selectively in a collection: Di Eichholtz/W. Schumann (eds.), *Anatomie des Krieges: Neue Dokumente zur Rolle des deutschen Monopolkapitals bei der Vorbereitung und Durchführung des zweiten Weltkrieges*, Berlin: Deutscher Verlag der Wissenschaffen, 1969, Document No. 173.

469. Reichsbank Advisory Council Foreign Trade Sub-Committee, December 19, 1939, BA, R 8119 F, P349, fol. 126ff.

470. Per Jacobsson diary, 45, entries of May 14–15, and June 2, 1943, University of Basel. The Dresdner Bank representative is called Görg in the diary: it is almost certain that this man was Carl Goetz and that Jacobsson misheard or misremembered the name. See also: Erin E. Jacobsson, *A Life for Sound Money: Per Jacobsson, His Biography*, Oxford: Clarendon, 1979, pp. 178–9.

471. Reichsbank Advisory Council, June 24, 1943, BA, R 8119 F, P349, fol. 27.

472. List of debtors, HADB, NL1/5.

473. Bechtolf memorandum, February 11, 1942, BA, R 8119 F, P4969, fol. 2–3; Bechtolf note: Strictly Confidential, October 20, 1941, BA, R 8119 F, P4968. The acrimonious correspondence between Philipp Reemtsma and Emil Helfferich, the chairman of the HAPAG AR, is reproduced in: Emil Helfferich, *Tatsachen 1932–1946. Ein Beitrag zur Wahrheitsfindung*, Oldenburg: Mettcker, 1968, pp. 245–55.

474. Kimmich memorandum, September 1, 1941, BA, R 8119 F, P1563.

475. See Alan S. Milward, *The German Economy at War*, University of London: Athlone Press, 1965, pp. 59–85, and Ludolf Herbst, *Der Totale Krieg*, pp. 171–241.

476. To the dismay of BMW's management, which complained about "conditions which [...] always give the Reich the occasion to intervene in the affairs of BMW": Hille to Rummel, February 27, 1940, BA, R 8119 F, P3076, fol. 430.

477. BMW: Development of Credits (n.d.), BA, R 8119 F, P3167; Financial Report, November 18, 1941, BA, R 8119 F, P3078.

478. Rummel note of August 12, 1942, BA, R 8119 F, P3078, fol. 336.

479. Junkers Flugzeug- und Motorenwerke AG Dessau, Credit Report January 7, 1941, BA, R 8119 F, P3336.

480. See the discussion of Reichsbank Advisory Council Credit Sub-Committee of November 28, 1939, BA, R 8119 F, P350, in which the commercial banks complained about their disadvantaged position.

481. Reich Supervisory Office for Credit, June 3, 1941, BA, R2/13551, fol. 16. *Frankfurter Zeitung* No.463/4, September 12, 1941.

482. *Deutsche Allgemeine Zeitung* No.384, August 12, 1942, Wirtschaftsblatt.

483. "Gehören die Banken in die Aufsichtsräte?," *Völkischer Beobachter*, No. 9, January 9, 1943.

484. Security Service Reports, August 5, 1943, BA, R58/187, fol. 106.

485. E. W. Schmidt memorandum: "News Reports for the Works Leader," January 12, 1944, BA, R 8119 F, P10882, fol. 630–1.

486. Schmidt memorandum, October 26, 1944, BA, R 8119 F, P10883, fol. 121–2. The Supervisory Office had tried to argue for simplification, but ineffectively. In 1941 it had stated: "Since the state reorganization of the credit apparatus, in other words since 1935, credit has been extended more widely, and in part also the administrative machinery has been simplified; but fundamentally the organization of credit still depends on the economic ideas of a past age." (Memorandum of June 3, 1941, BA, R2/13551.)

487. Jens van Scherpenberg, *Öffentliche Finanzwirtschaft in Westdeutschland 1944–1948* (Munich Univ. Diss.), Frankfurt: Fischer, 1984, pp. 51ff.

488. Meeting of February 19, 1942, BA, R2/13686, fol. 241–2.

489. Reich Finance Ministry note of December 1942, BA, R2/13530, fol. 269–70.

490. Note (meeting in Reich Supervisory Office for Credit), June 12, 1942, BA, R2/13551, fol. 62; Meeting with Press, October 15, 1942, BA, R 8119 F, P10879, fol. 280–2.

491. Circular of Reich Economics Ministry for Reich Defense Commissars, February 16, 1943, BA, R2/13551, fol. 210–11.

492. Deutsche Bank Special Circulars, S31/43, November 17, 1943, HADB, F63/1050.

493. Wilhelm Zangen: "Industry and Banks," December 1942, BA, R 8119 F, P10879, fol. 67–77.

494. Schmidt memorandum, January 10, 1944, BA, R 8119 F, P10882, fol. 640.

495. Working Committee minutes, March 11, 1943, BA, R 8119 F, P31, fol. 8.

496. Rösler declaration under oath, March 20, 1950, HADB, RWB, 31. Also von Halt memorandum, Unterredung im Fürstenhof November 17, 1942, in V1/4852 (this memorandum is undated and may well originate after the war).

497. NSDAP membership number 6927011 (BDC).

498. Deutsche Bank to Gau Economic Chamber Berlin, February 15, 1945, HADB, P1/4.

499. Berlin: Meeting with Reich Minister Walther Funk, February 18, 1943, BA, R43II/245 b, fol. 1.

500. NSDAP membership number 91273 (BDC).

501. Heinrich Hunke, "Verstaatlichung der Grossbanken," *Die Deutsche Volkswirtschaft* 3, 1934, 1, p. 3–6.

502. NA, OMGUS, Deutsche Bank, p. 61; and information collected by Carl-Ludwig Holtfrerich.

503. See Carl-Ludwig Holtfrerich, "The Deutsche Bank 1945–1957: War, Military Rule and Reconstruction," in: Lothar Gall/Gerald D. Feldman/Harold James/Carl-Ludwig Holtfrerich/Hans E. Büschgen, London: Weidenfeld & Nicolson 1995, pp. 357–521.

504. Working Committee, September 16, 1943, BA, R 8119 F, P31, fol. 27–32.

505. Dr. Hanel memorandum of October 6, 1943, BA, R63/198, fol. 12.

506. Tregaskes to Dougherty, February 1, 1945, NA, RG260/2/148/16, OMGUS.

507. This list is contained in the HADB, NL1/6: it is undated but must be from 1944 or later. It may even have been prepared as part of a denazification exercise, although I have not seen a copy of this document in the extensive material collected by OMGUS.

508. Rösler to Frowein, February 14, 1944, HADB, P1/4.

509. NA, RG 1165, Box 642/folder 7, PWP 67, April 1945, CSDIC (UK), "The Reichsbank and its Relations with Other Institutions."

510. Hunke, "Zehn Thesen zur Wirtschaftspolitik," published in *Der neue Tag*, No. 257, September 17, 1943.

511. In general BA, R 8119 F, P4653; Memorandum, March 27, 1941, BA, R 8119 F, P4654, fol. 28–30.

512. Rath (Deutsche Bank Köln) to Kurt von Schroeder, September 19, 1942, BA, R 8119 F, P24133; Abs note of September 24, 1942, BA, R 8119 F, P24133.

513. See also Gerald D. Feldman, "The Deutsche Bank from World War to World Economic Crisis 1914–1933," in: *The Deutsche Bank 1870–1995*, pp. 218–20.

514. Supervisory board meeting, December 21, 1933, BA, R 8119 F, P3073, fol. 304–7.

515. Note of February 5, 1934, BA, R 8119 F, P3073, fol. 343.

516. Stauss to Rummel, June 11, 1936, BA, R 8119 F, P3075, fol. 25.

517. Secret: Bayerische Motoren Werke, May 7, 1942, BA, R 8119 F, P3146, fol. 462.

518. Popp to Stauss, November 11, 1936, BA, R 8119 F, P3075, fol. 90–1.

519. Siemens & Halske to Reich Air Ministry, March 31, 1936, BA, R 8119 F, P3167, fol. 10.

520. "The BMW Concern: Organizational Questions," April 12, 1940, BA, R 8119 F, P3076, fol. 465.

521. Popp to Lucht (Reich Air Ministry), February 8, 1941, BA, R 8119 F, P3146, fol. 252.

522. Memorandum for Stauss and Rummel, May 17, 1939, BA, R 8119 F, P3167, fol. 107–8.

523. Meeting of management board, November 11, 1941, BA, R 8119 F, P3078, fol. 96ff.

524. Popp to Admiral Lahs, April 19, 1940, BA, R 8119 F, P3136, fol. 302: "In the end, in the case of a long war the new production capacity will determine the size of the air fleet."

525. Göring to Popp, November 25, 1940, BA, R 8119 F, P3077, fol. 199.

526. Popp to Lucht, February 6, 1941, BA, R 8119 F, P3146, fol. 235.

527. Popp to Stauss, March 22, 1941, BA, R 8119 F, P3146, fol. 349.

528. Reich Air Ministry (LC3), February 14, 1941, BA, R 8119 F, P3146, fol. 285.

529. E.g. Stauss to Frau Eva von Schröder, National Socialist Welfare Office (NSV), Berlin, October 11, 1938, BA, R 8119 F, P6132, fol. 128: "In particular, I was very pleased that the automobile and parts industry in the end exceeded 2.5 million Marks, after I convinced BMW to go up by 50,000 Marks, even though Opel had failed to pay."

530. Rummel note of August 12, 1942, BA, R 8119 F, P3078, fol. 336.

531. Hille to Rummel, September 20, 1944, BA, R 8119 F, P3114, fol. 191.

532. Rummel note (Hille's letter of December 9, is appended), December 12, 1944, BA, R 8119 F, P3114, fol. 248–51.

533. Rummel memorandum of December 15, 1944, BA, R 8119 F, P3114, fol. 254–5.

534. Deutsche Bank to Rummel, December 20, 1944, BA, R 8119 F, P3114, fol. 266–7.

535. BMW AG to BMW Flugmotorenwerke Brandenburg, February 2, 1945, BA, R 8119 F, P3114, fol. 319.

536. Lorenz Kleber statement, March 24, 1946, NA, RG242/Roll 2, Exhibits 86, 273.

537. Quarterly statistics, DB (alt)/5930.

538. Deutsche Bank to Bundesminister der Finanzen, March 28, 1951, DB (alt)/52931.

539. HADB, P2/K509.

540. Staatsarchiv Leipzig, Deutsche Bank 630, June 15, 1944, Deutsche Bank Leipzig to Staatspolizeistelle Leipzig; January 15, 1944 note signed by Jütl, Beamter für Strafgefangene der Staatspolizeistelle Leipzig; Deutsche Bank 790, payments records.

541. Working Committee meeting, November 4, 1943, BA, R 8119 F, P31, fol. 38.

542. August 11, 1943 Deutsche Bank Kattowitz to Zentarle Personal Abteilung; August 11, 1943 Gdynia to Halt; September 6, 1943 Kiehl to Palm, HADB P2/11426.

543. People's Court judgment, October 8, 1943, BA, R60I/548; People's Court judgment, September 14, 1943, R60I/369.

544. *Der Völkische Beobachter*, October 29, 1943.

545. December 16, 1957, report of Deutsche Bank Munich, HADB P6/M37.

546. Note on denazification, January 4, 1947, HADB, NL38/3.

547. Eberhard Czichon, *Der Bankier und die Macht*, p. 137ff.; Tom Bower, *Blind Eye to Murder – A Pledge Betrayed*, London: Andre Deutsch, 1981, pp. 17ff.

548. See Peter Hayes, *Industry and Ideology*, pp. 347–51; Lothar Gall, "Man for All Seasons," pp. 166–9. *Trials of War Criminals before the Nuernberg Military Tribunals under Control Council Law No. 10, Nuernberg October 1946–April 1949*, Volume VIII, Washington, D.C.: Government Printing Office, 1952, p. 391.

549. Note, July 10, 1943, HADB, P1773.

550. IG Farben to Deutsche Bank Kattowitz, August 2, 1943, HADB, F119/848.

551. Finance Group, Misc. Reports and Publications: Preliminary Study of the Deutsche Bank, prepared by Program Planning Section, Treasury Department, Foreign Funds Control, NA, RG260, Box 71, Folder 3.

552. Notes, May 2, and June 1, 1944, BA R8119F, P6088.

553. Note of June 27, 1940, BA, R 8119 F, P24130.

554. Giles MacDonogh, *A Good German. Adam von Trott zu Solz*, London and New York: Quartet Books, 1989, p. 164.

555. Beate Ruhm von Oppen (ed.), *Helmuth James von Moltke, Briefe an Freya*, Munich: Beck, 1988, pp. 261, 265, 481.

556. Note of October 15, 1943, BA, R 8119 F, P68, fol. 7–8.

557. December 29, 1947 adffidavit of Dr. Gräfin Maron York von Wartenburg, HADB V1/4852.

558. Hans-Adolf Jacobsen, *"Spiegelbild einer Verschwörung." Die Opposition gegen Hitler und der Staatsstreich vom 20. Juli 1944 in der SD-Berichterstattung*, vol. I, Stuttgart: Seewald, 1984, p. 60.

559. Telegrams, Dr. Lorenzen to Bormann, November 14, 1944, BA, NS6/19, fol. 68–70.

560. Instituut voor Oorlogsdokumentatie, Amsterdam, 77–85 (RSSPF), 65 Aa.

561. HADB, folder "Personal"; Working Committee meeting, April 15, 1942, BA, R 8119 F, P41, fol. 161.

562. Fritz Scholtz (Deutsche Bank Cottbus) to Karl Günkel, Berlin, February 9, 1944, BA, R 8119 F, P10972.

563. Working Committee, July 8, 1943, BA, R 8119 F, P31, fol. 22–3.

564. Meeting of Directors, November 5, 1942, HADB, folder "Direktorensitzungen."

565. Working Committee, September 16, 1943, BA, R 8119 F, P31, fol. 29.

566. Schmidt to Rosentreter, February 26, 1944, BA, R 8119 F, P10882, fol. 459; BA, R 8119 F, P10883; Circular of Deutsche Bank (To Branch Managers), November 29, 1943, P11127, fol. 1–2.

567. Rummel: The German Banking Business in 1943, January 20, 1944, BA, R 8119 F, P10882, fol. 602.

568. Discussion of Reich Group Banking, July 31, 1944, BA, R 8119 F, P10952.

569. To Branch Managers, March 27, 1945, BA, P10914, fol. 53.

570. Minutes of Great Bank Meetings, September 22, 1944, HADB, RWB, 441.

571. Rösler to Wuppermann, March 27, 1945, HADB, RWB, 50.

572. Management board to Gau Economic Chamber Hamburg, March 28, 1945, HADB, RWB, 50.

573. Deutsche Bank to Branch Managers, March 25, 1945, BA, R 8119 F, P10914, fol. 43–4; Deutsche Bank to Branch Managers, March 27, 1945, fol. 52.

574. Holtfrerich, Deutsche Bank, in Gall/Feldman/James. The Deutsche Bank 1870–1995, p. 363.

575. This paragraph is based primarily on the contemporary diary notes of Rosenbrock, Diary notes April/September 1945, HADB, folder "Rosenbrock."

576. Statement of Hermann Abs, April 22, 1950, NA, RG 319-X8001750.

577. Note, June 10, 1942, HADB, B192.

Bibliography

D'Abernon, Edgar Vincent. *Ambassador of Peace*. London: Hodder and Stoughton, 1929.

Adler, Hans Günther. *Theresienstadt 1941–1945: Das Antlitz einer Zwangsgemeinschaft*. Tübingen: Mohr 1960.

Bähr, Johannes. *Der Goldhandel der Dresdner Bank im Zweiten Weltkrieg*. Leipzig: Kiepenheuer & Witsch, 1999.

Balogh, Thomas. *Studies in Financial Organization*. Cambridge: Cambridge University Press, 1947.

Barkai, Avraham. "Die deutschen Unternehmer und die Judenpolitik im Dritten Reich," in: *Geschichte und Gesellschaft 15*. Göttingen: Vandenhoeck und Ruprecht, 1989, 227–47.

Barkai, Avraham. *From Boycott to Annihilation*. Hanover: University Press of New England, 1989.

Barkai, Avraham. "Sozialdarwinismus und Antilberalismus in Hitlers Wirtschaftskonzept. Zu Henry A. Turner Jr. 'Hitlers Einstellung zu Wirtschaft und Gesellschaft vor 1933,'" in: *Geschichte und Gesellschaft 3*. Vandenhoeck & Ruprecht, 1977, 406–17.

Barth, Boris. *Die deutsche Hochfinanz und die Imperialismen: Banken und Aussenpolitik vor 1914* (Beiträge zur Kolonial- und Überseegeschichte, Bd. 61). Stuttgart: Franz Steiner, 1995.

Boelcke, Willy A. *Die deutsche Wirtschaft 1930–1945: Interna des Reichswirtschaftsministeriums.* Düsseldorf: Droste 1983.

Bonhage, Barbara / Lussy. Hanspeter / Perrenoud. Marc. *Nachrichtenlose Vermögen bei Schweizer Banken: Depots, Konten und Safes von Opfern des nationalsozialistischen Regimes und Restitutionsprobleme in der Nachkriegszeit* (Veröffentlichungen der Unabhängigen Expertenkommission Schweiz – Zweiter Weltkrieg, Bd. 15). Zurich: Chronos, 2001.

Bower, Tom. *Blind Eye to Murder – A Pledge Betrayed.* London: Andre Deutsch, 1981.

Chernow, Ron. *The Warburgs: The Twentieth Century Odyssey of a Remarkable Jewish Family.* New York: Vintage Books, 1994.

Czichon, Eberhard. *Der Bankier und die Macht: Hermann Josef Abs in der deutschen Politik.* Cologne: Pahl-Rugenstein, 1970.

Deutsche Bank (ed.). *Böhmen und Mähren im deutschen Wirtschaftsraum.* Berlin, 1939.

Eichholtz, Dietrich. *Geschichte der deutschen Kriegswirtschaft 1939–1945,* vol. I. Berlin: Akademie-Verlag, 1971.

Eichholtz, Dietrich / Schumann. Wolfgang (eds.). *Anatomie des Krieges: Neue Dokumente zur Rolle des deutschen Monopolkapitals bei der Vorbereitung und Durchführung des zweiten Weltkrieges.* Berlin: Deutscher Verlag der Wissenschaften, 1969.

Engel, Helmut / Jersch-Wenzel, Steffi / Treue, Wilhelm (eds.). *Geschichtslandschaft Berlin: Orte und Ereignisse: Charlottenburg: Die historische Stadt* (Vol. I). Berlin: Nicolai, 1986.

Enquête-Ausschuss (Ausschuss zur Untersuchung der Erzeugungs- und Absatzbedingungen der deutschen Volkswirtschaft). *Der Bankkredit.* Berlin: E. S. Mittler & Sohn, 1930.

Enzensberger, Hans Magnus (ed.). *OMGUS. Ermittlungen gegen die Deutsche Bank.* Nördlingen: Greno, 1985.

Feldman, Gerald D. *Allianz and the German Insurance Business 1933–1945.* Cambridge and New York: Cambridge University Press, 2001.

Feldman, Gerald D. "The Länderbank Wien AG in the National Socialist Period," 2003, *www.histcom.at.*

Fohlin, Caroline. "The Rise of Interlocking Directorates in Imperial Germany," in: *Economic History Review* 52/2. Oxford: Blackwell, 1999, 307–33.

Gall, Lothar / Feldman, Gerald D. / James, Harold / Holtfrerich, Carl-Ludwig / Büschgen, Hans E. (eds.). *The Deutsche Bank 1870–1995.* London: Weidenfeld & Nicolson, 1995.

Gall, Lothar. "Hermann Josef Abs and the Third Reich: 'A Man for All Seasons,'" in: *Financial History Review* 6. Cambridge: Cambridge University Press, 1999, 147–202.

Gellately, Robert. *The Gestapo and German Society. Enforcing Racial Policy 1933–1945.* Oxford: Oxford University Press, 1990.

Gillingham, John. "The Baron de Launoit. A Case Study in the 'Politics of Production' of Belgian Industry during Nazi Occupation," *Revue belge d'histoire contemporaine* V. Gent, 1974, 1–59.

Gossweiler, Kurt. *Grossbanken, Industriemonopole, Staat, Ökonomie und Politik des staatsmonopolistischen Kapitalismus in Deutschland 1914–1932.* Berlin: Deutscher Verlag der Wissenschaften, 1971.

Hayes, Peter. "The Deutsche Bank and the Holocaust," in: Peter Hayes (ed.), *Lessons and Legacies III: Memory, Memorialization and Denial.* Evanston Ill.: Northwestern University Press, 1999, 71–98.

Hayes, Peter. *Industry and Ideology. IG Farben in the Nazi Era.* Cambridge: Cambridge University Press, 1987.

Hayes, Peter. "State Policy and Corporate Involvement in the Holocaust," in: US Holocaust Museum (ed.), *The Holocaust: The Known, the Unknown, the Disputed and the Reexamined.* Washington, D.C., 1994.

Helfferich, Emil. *Tatsachen 1932–1946. Ein Beitrag zur Wahrheitsfindung.* Oldenburg: Mettcker, 1968.

Herbst, Ludolf. *Der Totale Krieg und die Ordnung der Wirtschaft.* Stuttgart: Deutsche Verlags-Anstalt, 1982.

Hess, Hermann. *Ritter von Halt: Der Sportler und Soldat.* Berlin: Batschari, 1936.

Hildebrand, Klaus. *Das vergangene Reich: Deutsche Aussenpolitik von Bismarck bis Hitler.* Stuttgart, Deutsche Verlags-Anstalt, 1995.

Hildebrand, Klaus. *Vom Reich zum Weltreich: Hitler, NSDAP und kolo-niale Frage 1919–1945* (Veröffentlichungen des Historischen Instituts der Universität Mannheim, Bd. 1). Munich: W. Fink, 1969.

Hillgruber, Andreas. *Hitler, König Carol und Marschall Antonescu: Die deutsch-rumänischen Beziehungen 1938–1944* (Veröffentlichungen des Instituts für europäische Geschichte Mainz, Bd. 5). Wiesbaden: Franz Steiner, 1954.

Huber, Gabriele. *Die Porzellan-Manufaktur Allach-München GmbH: Eine "Wirtschaftsunternehmung" der SS zum Schutz der "deutschen Seele."* Marburg: Jonas, 1992.

Hüttenberger, Peter. "Nationalsozialistische Polykratie," in: *Geschichte und Gesellschaft* 2. Göttingen: Vandenhoeck & Ruprecht, 1976, 417–42.

Institut Theresienstädter Initiative (ed.). *Theresienstädter Gedenkbuch. Die Opfer der Judentransporte aus Deutschland nach Theresienstadt 1942–1945.* [Prag]: Academia, 2000.

Jacobsson, Erin E. *A Life for Sound Money: Per Jacobsson, His Biography.* Oxford: Clarendon, 1979.

James, Harold. *The German Slump: Politics and Economics 1924–1936.* Oxford: Oxford University Press, 1986.

James, Harold. *Monetary and Fiscal Unification in Nineteenth-Century Germany: What Can Kohl Learn from Bismarck?* (Essays in International Finance, No. 202). Princeton, 1997.

Jones, Larry E. *German Liberalism and the Dissolution of the Weimar Party System.* Chapel Hill: University of North Carolina Press, 1988.

Kaiser, David E. *Economic Diplomacy and the Origins of the Second World War: Germany, Britain, France and Eastern Europe, 1930–1939.* Princeton: Princeton University Press, 1980.

Kaminsky, Graciela L. / Reinhart, Carmen M. "The Twin Crises: The Causes of Banking and Balance-of-Payments Problems," Board of Governors of the Federal Reserve System, International Finance Discussion Papers no. 544, March 1996.

Karny, Miroslav / Milotova, Jaroslava / Karna, Margita (eds.). *Deutsche Politik im "Protektorat Böhmen und Mähren" unter Reinhard Heydrich 1941–1942: Eine Dokumentation* (Nationalsozialistische Besatzungspolitik in Europa 1939–1945, Bd. 2). Berlin: Metropol, 1997.

Kempner, Robert M. W. "Hitler und die Zerstörung des Hauses Ullstein: Dokumente und Vernehmungen," in: *Hundert Jahre Ullstein 1877–1977*, Vol. 3. Berlin: Ullstein, 1977, 267–92.

Kershaw, Ian. *The Nazi Dictatorship: Problems and Perspectives of Interpretation*. London: Edward Arnold, 1989.

Kopper, Christopher. "Die 'Arisierung' der deutsch-böhmischen Aktienbanken," in: Boris Barth / Josef Faltus / Jan Kren / Eduard Kubu (eds.), *Konkurrenzpartnerschaft: Die deutsche und die tschechoslowakische Wirtschaft in der Zwischenkriegszeit* (Veröffentlichungen des Instituts für Kultur und Geschichte der Deutschen im Östlichen Europa, Bd. 14). Essen: Klartext Verlag, 1998, 236–45.

Kopper, Christopher. *Zwischen Marktwirtschaft und Dirigismus. Staat, Banken und Bankenpolitik im "Dritten Reich" von 1933 bis 1939*. Bonn: Bouvier, 1995.

Kreimeier, Klaus. *Die Ufa-Story. Geschichte eines Filmkonzerns*. Munich: Hanser, 1992.

Marguerat, Philippe. *Le IIIe Reich et le Pétrole Roumain, 1938–1940: Contribution à l'Étude de la Pénétration Économique Allemande dans les Balkans à la Veille et au Début de la Seconde Guerre Mondiale*. Leiden: A. W. Sijthoff, 1977.

Milward, Alan S. "The Reichsmark Bloc and the International Economy," in: Gerhard Hirschfeld / Lothar Kettenacker (eds.), *The "Führer State": Myth and Reality: Studies on the Structure and Politics of the Third Reich*. Stuttgart: Klett-Cotta, 1981.

Milward, Alan S. *The German Economy at War*. London: Athlone Press of the University of London, 1965.

Mollin, Gerhard Th. *Montankonzerne und "Drittes Reich": Der Gegensatz zwischen Monopolindustrie und Befehlswirtschaft in der deutschen Rüstung und Expansion 1936–1944* (Kritische Studien zur Geschichtswissenschaft, Bd. 78). Göttingen: Vandenhoeck & Ruprecht, 1988.

Morsey, Rudolf. *Zur Entstehung, Authentizität und Kritik von Brünings "Memoiren 1918–1934."* Opladen: Westdeutscher Verlag, 1975.

Mosse, Werner E. *Jews in the German Economy: The German-Jewish Business Elite*. Oxford: Oxford University Press, 1987.

Müller, Rolf-Dieter. "Von der Wirtschaftsallianz zum kolonialen Ausbeu-tungskrieg," in: Militärgeschichtliches Forschungsamt Freiburg (ed.), *Das Deutsche Reich und der Zweite Weltkrieg*, IV. Stuttgart: Deutsche Verlags-Anstalt, 1983, 98–189.

Naasner, Walter. *Neue Machtzentren in der deutschen Kriegswirtschaft 1942–1945: Die Wirtschaftsorganisation der SS, das Amt des Gen-eralbevollmächtigten für den Arbeitseinsatz und das Reichsminis-terium für Bewaffnung und Munition, Reichsministerium für Rüstung und Kriegsproduktion im Nationalsozialistischen Herrschaftssystem* (Schriften des Bundesarchivs, Bd. 45). Boppard: Boldt, 1994.

Naasner, Walter. *SS-Wirtschaft und SS-Verwaltung: "Das SS-Wirtschafts-Verwaltungshauptamt und die unter seiner Dienstaufsicht stehenden wirtschaftlichen Vertretungen" und weitere Dokumente* (Schriften des Bundesarchivs, Bd. 45a). Düsseldorf: Droste, 1998.

Neumann, Franz. *Behemoth: The Structure and Practice of National So-cialism*. New York: Oxford University Press (2nd edition), 1944.

Pentzlin, Heinz. *Hjalmar Schacht. Leben und Wirken einer umstrittenen Persönlichkeit*. Berlin: Ullstein, 1980.

Perrenoud, Marc et al. *La Place Financière et les Banques Suisses à l'époque du National-Socialisme: Les Relations des Grandes Banques avec l'Allemagne (1931–1946)* (Veröffentlichungen der Unabhängigen Expertenkommission Schweiz – Zweiter Weltkrieg; Bd. 13). Lausanne: Payot, 2002.

Pohl, Hans / Habeth, Stephanie / Brüninghaus, Beate. *Die Daimler-Benz AG in den Jahren 1933 bis 1944* (Zeitschrift für Unternehmens-geschichte, Beiheft 47). Wiesbaden: Franz Steiner, 1986.

Pohl, Manfred. *Entstehung und Entwicklung des Universalbankensys-tems: Konzentration und Krise als wichtige Faktoren* (Schriftenreihe des Instituts für Bankhistorische Forschung, Bd. 7). Frankfurt: Fritz Knapp, 1986.

Pohl, Manfred. *Die Finanzierung der Russengeschäfte zwischen den bei-den Weltkriegen: Die Entwicklung der 12 grossen Russlandkonsortien* (Tradition, Beiheft 9). Frankfurt: Fritz Knapp, 1975.

Pohl, Manfred. *Konzentration im deutschen Bankwesen 1848–1980* (Schriftenreihe des Instituts für Bankhistorische Forschung, Bd. 4). Frankfurt: Fritz Knapp, 1980.

Pohl, Manfred / Raab-Rebentisch, Angelika. *Von Stambul nach Bagdad: Die Geschichte einer berühmten Eisenbahn.* Munich: Piper, 1999.

Pohl, Manfred / Schneider. Andrea. *VIAG 1923–1998: Vom Staatskonzern zum internationalen Konzern.* Munich: Piper, 1998.

Rebentisch, Dieter. *Führerstaat und Verwaltung im Zweiten Weltkrieg: Verfassungsentwicklung und Verwaltungspolitik* (Frankfurter historische Abhandlungen, Bd. 29). Stuttgart: Franz Steiner, 1989.

Rosenbaum, Eduard / Sherman, A. J. M. M. *Warburg & Co. 1798–1938. Merchant Bankers of Hamburg.* London: East and West Library, 1979.

Roth, Karl Heinz. "Bankenkrise, Faschismus und Macht," in: Kritische Aktionäre der Deutschen Bank (eds.). *Macht ohne Kontrolle: Berichte über die Geschäfte der Deutschen Bank.* Stuttgart: Schmetterling, 1990, 13–23.

Roth, Karl Heinz. "Hehler des Holocaust: Degussa und Deutsche Bank," in: *1999. Zeitschrift für Sozialgeschichte des 20. und 21. Jahrhunderts* 13. Köln: Janus, 1998, 137–44.

Rothkirchen, Livia. "The Situation of Jews in Slovakia between 1939 and 1945," in: *Jahrbuch für Antisemitismusforschung* 7. Frankfurt: Campus, 1998, 46–70.

Ruhm von Oppen, Beate (ed.). *Helmuth James von Moltke: Briefe an Freya 1939–1945.* Munich: Beck, 1988.

Scherpenberg, Jens van. *Oeffentliche Finanzwirtschaft in Westdeutschland 1944–1948.* Frankfurt: R. G. Fischer, 1984.

Schoeps, Julius H. "Wie die Deutsche Bank Mendelssohn & Co. Schluckte," in: *Frankfurter Rundschau,* 27 November 1998.

Schuker, Stephen A. "Ambivalent Exile: Heinrich Brüning and America's Good War," in Christoph Buchheim / Harold James / Michael Hutter, *Zerrissene Zwischenkriegszeit: Wirtschaftshistorische Beiträge. Knut Borchardt zum 65. Geburtstag.* Baden-Baden: Nomos Verlagsgesellschaft, 1994, 329–56.

Sommerfeldt, Martin H. *Ich war dabei: Die Verschwörung der Dämonen 1933–1939.* Darmstadt: Drei Quellen Verlag, 1949.

Steinberg, Jonathan. *All or Nothing: The Axis and the Holocaust.* London: Routledge, 1990.

Steinberg, Jonathan. *The Deutsche Bank and Its Gold Transactions During the Second World War.* Munich: Beck, 1999.

Stucken, Rudolf. *Deutsche Geld- und Kreditpolitik 1914–1953,* 2nd edition. Tübingen: Mohr, 1953.

Stürmer, Michael / Teichmann, Gabriele / Treue, Wilhelm. *Wägen und Wagen: Sal. Oppenheim jr. & Cie: Geschichte einer Bank und einer Familie.* Munich and Zurich: Piper, 1989.

Treue, Wilhelm. "Bankhaus Mendelssohn als Beispiel einer Privatbank im 19. und 20. Jahrhundert," in: *Mendelssohn-Studien,* Vol. 1. Berlin: Duncker & Humblot, 1972, 29–80.

Turner, Henry A. "Hitlers Einstellung zu Wirtschaft und Gesellschaft vor 1933," in: *Geschichte und Gesellschaft* 2. Göttingen: Vandenhoeck & Ruprecht, 1976, 89–117.

Uhlig, Christiane et al. *Tarnung, Transfer, Transit: Die Schweiz als Drehscheibe verdeckter deutscher Operationen (1938–1952)* (Veröffentlichungen der Unabhängigen Expertenkommission Schweiz – Zweiter Weltkrieg; Bd. 9). Zurich: Chronos, 2001.

Umbreit, Hans. "Auf dem Weg zur Kontinentalherrschaft," in: Militärgeschichtliches Forschungsamt Freiburg (ed.), *Das Deutsche Reich und der Zweite Weltkrieg,* V/1. Stuttgart: Deutsche Verlags-Anstalt, 1988, 3–345.

Unabhängige Expertenkommission Switzerland – Second World War (ed.), *Switzerland and its Gold Transactions in the Second World War.* Bern, 1998.

Vencovský, František et al. (eds.). *Dejiny Bankovnictví Českých Zemích.* Prague: Bankovní Institut, 1999.

Verhoeyen, Etienne. "Les grands industriels belges entre collaboration et résistance: le moindre mal," in: *Centre de Recherches et d'Études Historiques de la Seconde Guerre Mondiale,* Cahiers 10. Brussels, 1986, 57–114.

Vocke, Wilhelm. *Memoiren.* Stuttgart: Deutsche Verlags-Anstalt, 1973.

Volkmann, Hans-Erich. "Die NS-Wirtschaft in Vorbereitung des Krieges," in: Militärgeschichtliches Forschungsamt Freiburg (ed.), *Das Deutsche Reich und der Zweite Weltkrieg,* Vol. I. Stuttgart: Deutsche Verlags-Anstalt, 1979, 177–368.

Wandel, Eckhard, Hans Schäffer. *Steuermann in Wirtschaftlichen und Politischen Krisen.* Stuttgart: Deutsche Verlags-Anstalt, 1974.

Welch, David. *Propaganda and the German Cinema 1933–1945.* Oxford: Clarendon, 1983.

Wiskemann, Elizabeth. *Czechs and Germans: A Study of the Struggle in the Historic Provinces of Bohemia and Moravia.* London: Oxford University Press and Royal Institute of International Affairs, 1938.

Witek, Hans. "'Arisierungen' in Wien: Aspekte nationalsozialialistischer Enteigungspolitik 1938–1940," in: Emmerich Talos / Ernst Hanisch / Wolfgang Neugebauer (eds.). *NS-Herrschaft in Österreich.* Vienna: Verlag für Gesellschaftskritik, 1988, 199–216.

Wixforth, Harald. *Auftakt zur Ostexpansion: Die Dresdner Bank und die Umgestaltung des Bankwesens im Sudetenland 1938/39.* Dresden: Hannah-Arendt-Institut für Totalitarismusforschung, 2001.

Wolf, Herbert. "Zur Kontrolle und Enteignung jüdischen Vermögens in der NS-Zeit," in: *Bankhistorisches Archiv 16/1.* Frankfurt: Fritz Knapp, 1990, 55–62.

Ziegler, Dieter. "Die Verdrängung der Juden aus der Dresdner Bank," *Vierteljahrshefte für Zeitgeschichte 47.* Munich: Oldenbourg, 1999, 187–216.

Zitelmann, Rainer. *Hitler. Selbstverständnis eines Revolutionärs.* Stuttgart: Klett-Cotta, 1991 (2nd edition).

Index